DATE DUE		

OVERDUE FINE
$0.10 PER DAY

Read It and Eat

A Month-by-Month Guide to Scintillating Book Club Selections and Mouthwatering Menus

Read It and Eat

SARAH GARDNER

HUDSON
STREET
PRESS

HUDSON STREET PRESS
Published by Penguin Group
Penguin Group (USA) Inc., 375 Hudson Street, New York, New York 10014, USA
Penguin Group (Canada), 10 Alcorn Avenue, Toronto, Ontario, Canada M4V 3B2
(a division of Pearson Penguin Canada Inc.)
Penguin Books Ltd, 80 Strand, London WC2R 0RL, England
Penguin Ireland, 25 St Stephen's Green, Dublin 2, Ireland (a division of Penguin Books Ltd)
Penguin Group (Australia), 250 Camberwell Road, Camberwell, Victoria 3124, Australia
(a division of Pearson Australia Group Pty Ltd)
Penguin Books India Pvt Ltd, 11 Community Centre, Panchsheel Park, New Delhi – 110 017, India
Penguin Group (NZ), Cnr Airborne and Rosedale Roads, Albany, Auckland 1310, New Zealand
(a division of Pearson New Zealand Ltd)
Penguin Books (South Africa) (Pty) Ltd, 24 Sturdee Avenue, Rosebank,
Johannesburg 2196, South Africa

Penguin Books Ltd, Registered Offices: 80 Strand, London WC2R 0RL, England

First published by Hudson Street Press, a member of Penguin Group (USA) Inc.

First Printing, May 2005
10 9 8 7 6 5 4 3 2 1

REGISTERED TRADEMARK—MARCA REGISTRADA

HUDSON
STREET
PRESS

LIBRARY OF CONGRESS CATALOGING-IN-PUBLICATION DATA
Gardner, Sarah.
   Read it and eat : a month-by-month guide to scintillating book club selections and mouthwatering
menus / Sarah Gardner.
      p. cm.
Includes index.
ISBN 1-59463-004-6 (alk. paper)
1. Books and reading—United States. 2. Book clubs (Discussion groups)—United States.
   3. Cookery. 4. Menus. I. Title.
Z1003.2.G37 2005
028'.9—dc22   2004023784

Printed in the United States of America
Set in Palatino
Designed by Eve L. Kirch

This book is printed on acid-free paper. ♾

For Jim: my master prep cook, sommelier,
one-man cleanup crew, and love of my life.

Acknowledgments

*I*nnumerable thanks to the following folks; without their support this book would have never come to fruition.

Charlotte Butzin from *Bon Appétit* magazine, for the fantastic little article she wrote in the Starters section that gave me and *The Literary Gathering* a real start.

Laureen Rowland, publisher and founder of Hudson Street Press, for reading the *Bon Appétit* article and blowing me away with the offer to write this book, for the gentle guidance throughout the entire process and much needed positive reinforcement along the way.

Danielle Friedman, for the incredible edits and insight.

Gracias to Becky Metcalf, who generously allowed me to use her quesadilla and guacamole recipes in the biography chapter.

To my coworkers at Sarasota Memorial Hospital, Michelle Perala, Valerie Newman, Wendy Hunter, and boss, Laurie Bennett, I cannot express my gratitude for your tolerance of my constantly distracted mind for the six months it took to write this book.

To my brother Nathan Ogilvie and my sister-in-law Rebecca Ogilvie, for giving me constant support and encouragement.

To my sister, Moriah Ogilvie, my shoulder to cry on, ears to vent to, and closest friend. I would have never made it through the writing of this book had she not offered to read several of the books with me, discuss them endlessly, and take calls at work to answer hundreds of questions pertaining to food and books in general.

My parents, Don and Jane Ogilvie, made it possible for me to start *The*

Literary Gathering not only with a bit of financial support, but also by never doubting for a moment that I was more than capable, despite my wavering confidence. They instilled in me a love of books and culture from very early on in childhood, something that I will be eternally grateful for; but more importantly, they made sure that I had the confidence to use my creativity and encouraged me endlessly. I also forced them to read several books and discuss them with me, despite their unbelievably busy work and travel schedules. I can only hope that I will be able to give so selflessly of myself to my children one day.

Finally, to the love of my life, my husband, Jim, who is the only man alive who is able to tolerate a woman working full time, writing and publishing a newsletter, and writing a book, all while expecting a child. His tolerance for irrational behavior due to hormones, stress, and failed recipe experiments is certainly exemplary, if not divine. He is, by far, the kindest, most caring, patient husband and friend anyone could ever ask for; I'm truly blessed every day with our marriage.

Contents

Introduction

I'm not your typical literature buff.

Don't get me wrong—like any literary fanatic, I love to read books that span genres and time periods, styles and subjects, and I've spent much of my life curled up on the couch with my face hidden behind the pages of a book. It's the way that I like to discuss books that sets me apart.

Although I majored in literature in college, I didn't receive a warm and fuzzy welcome in pursuing my original dream of becoming a literature professor—I simply wasn't "serious" enough for the pretentious and ever-ponderous academic crowd that filled my classes. I endured years of disapproving looks from fellow students and professors when I wanted to compare classic protagonists to television celebrities or movie stars. When we were reading *Jane Eyre*, I wanted to discuss what Oprah would say about Jane's love affair with a married man who kept his crazy wife locked in the basement. (They didn't think that was a very dignified approach.) For one class, we were asked to bring in a newspaper article that had, in some way, changed the life of the person it was written about. While others scoured the archives of the *Washington Post* and the *New York Times*, I simply brought in the latest issue of the *National Enquirer*. Splashed across the cover was one of my favorite celebrities, Bob Barker of *The Price Is Right* fame. He apparently had been dating one of his beauties and was being accused of sexual harassment. Certainly this article changed his life, or at least changed his life for a few months. Throughout my presentation I heard snorts from my peers and witnessed eye rolls coming from my professor. But for me, taking a seemingly dull assignment and making it both fun and applicable to real life was the best part about learning. I was told, by at least two professors, however, that I didn't take literature seriously enough. My confidence was shattered, and I began to feel that everything I had ever thought or felt about reading was incorrect. I hadn't yet realized that my approach wasn't wrong—it was just different.

I was so disillusioned by my college literature experience that I went on a book-reading boycott for the next four years. (I can be a bit melodramatic—and stubborn—at times.) I read only newspapers, magazines, and cookbooks. (I wouldn't even read the stories or introductions in the cookbooks—just the recipes.) My mother and sister, both avid readers, constantly tried to get me to read the latest bestseller or pick up an old favorite. In response, I would often refer to a framed print that my father keeps in his office that reads "Never Stop Learning," and simply say, "Sorry, I've stopped. No more books."

Then one Saturday morning, during my weekly coffee date with my parents at the local bookstore, my father started talking about the Harry Potter phenomenon. The first book—*Harry Potter and the Sorcerer's Stone*—had just come out, and it was all anyone could talk about. At the time, my father was a school superintendent, and he was anticipating questions from parents about the book's appropriateness for the elementary school curriculum. In as sweet a voice as he could muster, my father asked me if I would please read it for him and give him my opinion—he would even buy the book for me right then and there. I was the only one of his children who had (briefly) pursued a career in education, and my father was convinced that, for whatever reason, I was also the only one who could offer crucial insight as to whether or not the book was suitable. Despite misgivings, I reluctantly agreed because, after all, he did spend tens of thousands of dollars so that I could have a degree in literature and, to be honest, the only thing I really needed to break my boycott was the knowledge that someone I respected valued my opinion.

That same week I received a package in the mail from my older sister (and level-headed life advisor) who lives in Lexington, Kentucky, with *The Royals* by Kitty Kelley, a book about the torrid lives and history of England's royal family, enclosed. My sister had attached a note to the book to the tune of, "Just shut up and read it, it's just like the *National Enquirer* in book form." I opened up the books—and devoured them both in forty-eight hours. I had forgotten how much I loved to read, and I began to remember why I had gone into literature in the first place. For the next six weeks, I practically lived at Barnes & Noble, buying every book I could afford, and reading, on average, one book every two or three days; I was on a reading frenzy. I read books that I loved as a child, like *Harriet the Spy* by Louise Fitzhugh, and books that I had read in college and fallen in love with, like *One Hundred Years of Solitude* by Gabriel García Márquez, as well as a few of my all-time favorite beach books by Jackie Collins.

I didn't have to deal with the pretentious pseudo-intellectual blather of my college days. My sister and I could talk about what idiots the characters were, or how we wished we had their wardrobes, thin thighs, bottomless bank accounts, or just their imaginary lives in general, without feeling guilty.

It was during this time that I came up with the idea for my newsletter, *The Literary Gathering*. I wanted to share my love of good books and my love of fun and unpretentious conversation about books with other people.

The natural next step was for me to add recipes. I say "natural" because I am lucky enough to have been raised by a home economics teacher who incorporated cooking lessons not only into everyday living, but also into every birthday party, cast party, marching band party, and cheerleading party I ever had. I think she single-handedly taught every one of my friends how to cook, even though she didn't even teach in our school district!

After completing my first newsletter, I sent it out to a few magazine editors and, with a bit of luck, landed myself an article in the Starters section of *Bon Appétit* magazine. Since then, the newsletter has become quite popular, and I have absolutely loved writing it. I have never spent a penny on advertising, but word of mouth has spread, and so has my subscriber base. This book is simply a natural outgrowth of my newsletter.

How to Use This Book

Now let's get down to business. I want you to know how I chose the books featured in *Read It and Eat*, and how I determined each set of discussion questions and menus.

Reading Selections

I've divided the reading selections into twelve chapters that correspond with the twelve months of the year, and I've also included four bonus chapters, in case your group wants to opt out of a particular month's theme.

I, personally, like to read all genres of books, from classics to contemporary novels, trashy romances to collections of essays. And if your reading group is anything like mine, I can imagine that you would quickly get bored and frustrated reading only one type of book month after month. In my reading group we can only stand to read a long, serious book once every three months, and if we O.D. on chick lit we start to feel a bit shallow. So, I've given you a balanced selection of fiction and nonfiction, serious and funny. I've also tried to include several books that never hit the bestseller lists, but that I discovered or had recommended to me and that turned out to be hidden gems, not only because they are good reads, but also because they offer interesting, thought-provoking discussion options that are well suited to the reading group environment.

Like most of you, I don't have an excessive amount of free time, so if I had to force myself to get through a particular book—even if it had merit—I haven't recommended it to you. And to make sure that I'm not the only person who likes the selections featured within, I have checked the reader reviews for each book on many popular websites, and I've asked my friends and family members to give me a backup read on many of the books as well. I have also included some selections that my newsletter subscribers particularly enjoyed reading and discussing with their individual groups.

Discussion Questions

To keep things interesting, I've tried to vary the types of questions included in each section. And because it's fun to go off on tangents from time to time, I've allowed for this as well—my philosophy is that reading groups aren't just about books, but also about hanging out with people you like and getting into lively conversations. I've also tried to include a few general questions for each book, so that if a member of your group did not read the monthly selection due to a software crisis at work, a cranky child at home, or just plain laziness, she will be able to participate in at least part of the discussion. Remember, this isn't school; there is no "right" or "wrong"—just fun!

Here are some of my suggestions for discussing each book:

- Profanity is acceptable, except if your children are around.

- All comments made about spouses, ex-boyfriends/friends/spouses, in-laws, crazy family members (we all have them), annoying coworkers, idiot bosses, and anyone else you would like to compare to characters in any book *will* be kept secret by the rest of your group members.

- Using references to guests on *Jerry Springer* (we have all seen at least five minutes of an episode just to check it out and perhaps feel better about our current socioeconomic standing), *The Dr. Phil Show*, any celebrity alive or dead, or anyone on the cover of *People* magazine are not only acceptable, but encouraged. (And please feel free to discuss the best and worst dressed list in the aforementioned periodical if everyone forgot to read the book.)

Menus

Okay . . . let's talk food. While many books do, in fact, describe complete menus within the text (think the Cratchet family's Christmas dinner in *A Christmas Carol*), most books do not. In some books the characters are rarely described eating, or are eating things that you and I, with our contemporary palates, just wouldn't find appealing. This is where my creative license kicks in. My hope is that each menu will make your group feel connected, in some way, to the book—to be specific, each menu will be closely related to either the period in which the book takes place, the region in which the book is set, a favorite food item of one of the characters, or a menu or occasion that has been covered in the book. *All menus are scaled to feed eight, unless otherwise noted.* Some generously feed eight, so you can bring your leftovers to work and brag about your fabulous reading group and its fabulous recipes. Some of the menus are quite elaborate (three-course dinners and the like), and some are just snacks and drinks; there are even a few breakfasts, if your group wants to meet on a weekend morning.

I have, possibly, the smallest kitchen than can be visualized. When my husband, Jim, and I are both in it at the same time, I get the claustrophobic crazies. (He's been politely kicked out on several occasions, and when a recipe I'm testing isn't working out the way I want it to, he is sometimes physically thrown out. Don't worry, I married a saint.) The point is, I don't have a lot of room to store complicated gadgetry, so you won't need to buy anything fancy to make the recipes in this book. In terms of who cooks what, I recommend either that (a) the gal who lives at the house at which you're meeting prepares the food, or that (b) you go potluck and assign different recipes to different members for each meeting. For the member of your group who is not a skilled culinary artist—or just wants to freeload off of your good cooking—make her bring the drinks. I have included a few alcoholic beverages in the menus because, well, alcohol is a natural conversation stimulant. If you have members who don't drink, are pregnant, are designated drivers, or are annoying, weepy, or argumentative drunks, just have soft drinks, bottled water, coffee, or tea available for them. In some cases the spiked beverages can be made virgin by simply omitting the alcohol, and I have indicated this in the text.

The purpose of a reading group—and this book—is to help you enjoy the benefits of reading a great book and, most importantly, to help you connect with people you like by sharing a great meal and great conversation. Best of all, when among friends, there is never any need to be anyone but yourself, so bury those old literature class nightmares and be prepared to look at books in a delicious new way.

JANUARY

 Change Your World

If you're like me (and 90 percent of American women, it seems), your New Year's resolutions typically involve going to the gym more often, trying to eat more fruits and veggies, cleaning out the closets, and/or trying to spend less money on clothes. I've rarely kept any of these resolutions until much longer than March, and I usually make the same ones again the following New Year (and the next, and the next . . .).

When I originally planned this chapter, I was going to include books that were in tune with the traditional resolutions we make—i.e., nonfiction books on healthy lifestyles, time management, and the like. I began researching titles and checked out a book from my local library called *The Procrastinator's Handbook: Mastering the Art of Doing It Now* by Rita Emmett to see if it fit the bill. I read the book quickly, and I eagerly tried out the personal growth exercises it provided, such as setting a timer when trying to complete a project and cutting my clutter. But in my typical resolution fashion, I waited so long to return the book to the library—I *procrastinated*, if you will, for three weeks—that I ended up having to pay the library's maximum late fee. And I decided to rethink the selections that I would include in this chapter.

After some serious thought, I realized that what I really need every New Year is fresh inspiration—not necessarily to trim my thighs or rearrange my shoes, but rather to look at the lives of people who truly changed the world in some significant way.

I've chosen the books in this chapter because each demonstrates the power of the human spirit and the ability to create positive change. I'm hoping the selections will give you and your group members some New Year's inspiration for the mind and soul—because giving up chocolate will only make you and those around you miserable and cranky!

The City of Joy by Dominique Lapierre

*A*nonfiction "docu-novel" published in 1985, *The City of Joy* traces the lives of three men living in a slum in Calcutta, India—a priest, a young American doctor from a privileged background, and an Indian man forced to leave his farm due to drought and, with his family in tow, to live on the streets.

The personal sacrifice and poverty in their most extreme forms recounted here touched me deeply, and the human kindness and exuberance of the slum's inhabitants overwhelmed me, to say the least. The vivid images and heartfelt stories are so poignant and memorable that after reading the book for the first time they lingered in my mind for years.

The City of Joy hopefully will make you rethink your daily complaints and aggravations and give you a renewed sense of gratitude about your life. I recommend that you read the foreword and the afterword as well—they will enhance your group's discussion, as well as your understanding of the text. And if you'd like to learn more about the City of Joy organization, check out cityofjoy.org—it's both heartening and sobering to look at the pictures of the children and adults that the this charity serves.

Up for Discussion . . .

- This book is very emotionally intense at times. Describe how reading it made you feel.

- Why does Lapierre tell the story from three points of view?

- Do you think that Lapierre exploited the people of the City of Joy in any way? If so, how? What do you think his motivations were in writing this book?

- Do you think that any of the individuals were glorified in an unrealistic way? If so, how?

- How would you adapt to living in the City of Joy for a year? It's obvious you would have to make practical changes (no comfy bed, limited food, little privacy, no bathroom, etc.), but what changes in your attitude would you have to make?

- What would be the hardest part about living in the City of Joy?

- What would you hope to gain from your experience there?

- How do you think you would feel when you returned home?

- Can you name all of the government agencies in the United States that Hasari and family could have utilized if their plight had taken place here?

- What do you think of Arthur Loeb's idea to simply buy the slum? What do you think that would have accomplished? How would his plans have hurt the inhabitants of the slum?

- Which of the various professions described in this story (rickshaw puller, mobster, priest, doctor, wife and mother, farmer, etc.) would you like to try for a day? A year? What job would you absolutely never do?

- Do you think that poverty to the extent described in the book exists in the United States?

- What role does religion play in the City of Joy? How does it compare to the role that religion plays in your community?

- Why do the inhabitants of the slum riot? Do you think that their motives are similar, in any way, to what we see in the Middle East today?

- Which man's account touched you the most? Why?

An Indian Celebration

There's a lot of celebrating in the City of Joy—despite circumstances that would lead you to assume otherwise—and Lapierre's descriptions of the fragrant and delicious foods served at these celebrations are vivid enough to make your mouth water. Here's a savory Indian menu, complete with chapattis, the flat bread described throughout the novel.

Chapattis

1½ cups unbleached all-purpose
    flour, plus some for rolling out
    the dough
½ cup whole wheat flour

1 teaspoon salt
3 tablespoons butter, melted
About ½ cup water

Mix the all-purpose flour, whole wheat flour, salt, and butter together in a large bowl. Add just enough water to make a firm dough, somewhat like a biscuit dough. Knead for 10 to 15 minutes—the more the dough is kneaded, the lighter the bread will be. Shape the dough into a ball, place into a bowl, cover with a sheet of plastic wrap, and let it rest for at least 1 hour. (If left to rest overnight in the refrigerator, the finished bread will be even lighter.) When ready to bake, take a small piece of dough (about the size of a golf ball) and, on a lightly floured surface, roll each ball into a thin circle, about 5 inches in diameter. Repeat until all the dough is used.

Heat a griddle or heavy-bottomed iron skillet until it is very hot (you will see smoke rising from it). Place the rolled out chapatti on the griddle and let it cook for 2 to 3 minutes, depending on how thin you have rolled it. Using a pair of kitchen tongs, lift the chapatti to see if the underside has turned a golden brown. Flip, and cook the other side about 1 minute. As the chapattis are cooked, store them on a towel in a warm, covered container until ready to serve. Serve as soon as the last chapatti is cooked.

Spinach Dal

1 cup yellow or red split peas
¾ cup water
2 tablespoons olive oil
½ teaspoon black mustard seeds
(or substitute 1 teaspoon yellow
mustard seeds)
1 onion, thinly sliced
2 garlic cloves, crushed
1-inch piece ginger root, grated
1 red chile, finely chopped

1 (10-ounce) package frozen
spinach, thawed
¼ teaspoon cayenne pepper
½ teaspoon ground coriander
½ teaspoon garam masala (a spice
mixture combining Indian spices
such as curry, coriander, and
cardamom—if you can't find it
in your local supermarket just
use regular curry powder)
½ teaspoon salt

Wash the split peas in several changes of cold water. Place in a large bowl, cover with plenty of water, and set aside to soak for 30 to 45 minutes. Drain the split peas and place them in a large saucepan with the water over high heat. Bring to a boil, cover, reduce the heat to a simmer, and cook for 20 to 25 minutes, or until the split peas are soft.

Meanwhile, heat the oil in a large skillet over medium heat, add the mustard seeds, and cook for 2 minutes, or until they begin to sputter. Add the onion, garlic, ginger, and chile, and cook for 5 minutes or until the onion is softened. Add the spinach and cook for 10 minutes, or until the spinach is dry and the liquid has been absorbed. Stir in the cayenne, coriander, garam masala, and salt, and cook for 2 to 3 minutes, or until heated through. Drain the split peas, add them to the spinach mixture, and cook for an additional 5 minutes, or until heated through. Transfer to a serving plate.

Tandoori Chicken

8 skinless chicken breasts
4 tablespoons fresh lemon juice
1 teaspoon salt
2 garlic cloves, roughly chopped
1-inch piece ginger root, roughly
    chopped
2 green chiles, seeded and roughly
    chopped
¾ cup plain yogurt

1 teaspoon salt
1 teaspoon cayenne pepper
1 teaspoon garam masala
1 teaspoon ground cumin
1 teaspoon ground coriander
Red food coloring (optional)
2 tablespoons butter, melted
Mint and Coconut Chutney (recipe
    follows)

Cut deep slashes in the chicken. In a small bowl, mix together the lemon juice and salt. Rub all over the chicken pieces. Let stand for 10 minutes. Place the garlic, ginger, and chiles in a food processor or blender and process until smooth. Combine the garlic mixture, yogurt, salt, cayenne, garam masala, cumin, and coriander in a large bowl. Brush the chicken pieces with the food coloring, if using, and add to the yogurt mixture. Marinate in the refrigerator overnight.

Preheat the oven to 425°F. Place the marinated chicken in a roasting pan and bake for 40 minutes, or until juices run clear, occasionally basting with the butter. Serve with Mint and Coconut Chutney on the side.

Mint and Coconut Chutney

½ cup fresh mint leaves
6 tablespoons dried unsweetened
    coconut

1 tablespoon sesame seeds
¼ teaspoon salt
¾ cup plain yogurt

Roughly chop the mint leaves. Place all ingredients in a food processor or blender and process until smooth. Cover and chill before serving.

Up from Slavery by Booker T. Washington

Up from Slavery skillfully explains the political and psychological complexity that defined our nation in the years immediately following the Civil War. Booker T. Washington is an engaging, soulful writer, as well as an extraordinary individual and an indispensable leader—his writings and life continue to have a profound impact on readers, decades after his death.

Written in 1861, *Up from Slavery* is a timeless classic that is educational as well as inspirational. The insightful Washington writes: "I have learned that success is to be measured not so much by the position that one has reached in his life as by the obstacles which he has overcome while trying to succeed." This January, instead of only striving to follow a new set of New Year's resolutions, why not look back on all the obstacles you've conquered over the past year and celebrate all that you've overcome?

Up for Discussion . . .

- Why do you think Washington originally wrote this book? Who was his intended audience? What is the book's fundamental message?

- What did Washington consider the essentials of an effective education? What do you think are the essentials for an effective education? What is the difference between education and "schooling"?

- Why do you believe Washington was so critical of the preachers and teachers that worked during the Reconstruction period?

- Consider Washington's statement concerning the Tuskegee Institute: "We try to keep constantly in mind the fact that the worth of the school is to be judged by its graduates." How did this apply to the formation of Tuskegee? How would schools be different today if they lived by this teaching? *Do* some schools live by this teaching?

- Without question, General Samuel C. Armstrong was the person whose lifelong influence had the greatest effect on Washington. What did Armstrong do and what was the effect?

- Washington mentions that the following people also had a positive impact on his life: Viola Ruffner, Mary Mackie, Nathalie Lord, George Campbell, Lewis Adams, and J. F. B. Marshall. What was each person's contribution? How did that contribution impact Washington's life and work?

- We often hear the phrase "give something back to the community"; Washington may have been one of the first great leaders to conceive of this notion. What did he mean when he taught this? Does the phrase mean the same thing today?

- Here's another great Washington quote: "I believe that when one can grow to the point where he loves his work, this gives him a kind of strength that is most valuable." How was this ideal reflected in Washington's life? Have you gotten to the point of loving your work? If not, what do you think it will take for you to get there? If you have, how has it given you a valuable strength?

- How does Washington compare to today's self-help gurus? What lessons and teachings have they "borrowed" from him?

- Washington taught that the virtues of "patience, thrift, good manners and high morals" were the keys to empowerment. Explain how that statement hold true today.

- Washington says of his father, "I do not even know his name. I have heard reports to the effect that he was a white man who lived on one of the nearby plantations. But I do not find especial fault with him. He was simply another unfortunate victim to the institution which the nation unhappily had engrafted upon it at that time." What does this statement say about his character? If he were bitter and angry about his father's absence, how could his life have turned out differently?

Soul Food Supper

Somebody give me an Amen! I love soul food, and what better time to eat it than after reading a soulful book? The macaroni and cheese—not to mention the candied yams and string beans—is so filling that there won't be room in your stomach for a meat dish. I always come away from a soul food supper feeling stuffed, and I know these three recipes will be plenty for everyone!

Macaroni and Cheese

James Hemings, President Thomas Jefferson's slave chef, was among the first cooks in America to serve macaroni and cheese. His recipe was fairly simple; this is a more modern version.

6 cups water
1 tablespoon plus 1 teaspoon salt
2 cups elbow macaroni
¼ cup plus 2 tablespoons butter, softened, plus some for the dish
2 large eggs
2 cups evaporated milk

1 teaspoon salt
2 dashes Tabasco sauce
5 ½ cups extra-sharp cheddar cheese, grated
½ cup grated American cheese
½ teaspoon paprika

Preheat the oven to 350°F. Bring a large pot of water to a boil over a high heat. Add 1 tablespoon of the salt and slowly stir in the macaroni. Boil for 12 minutes, stirring constantly. The macaroni should be firm but tender. Pour the macaroni into a colander and rinse with cold water. Drain. Toss the macaroni with the butter and set aside.

In a medium bowl, beat the eggs until light yellow. Add the milk, remaining teaspoon salt, and the Tabasco sauce. Butter a large casserole, and alternate layers of the macaroni with layers of the cheddar and American cheese, ending with the cheese on top. Pour the egg mixture slowly and evenly over the macaroni and cheese. Sprinkle with the paprika. Bake for 30 to 40 minutes, or until the egg is set and the top is bubbly and golden brown.

Old-Fashioned String Beans

8 slices lean bacon, diced

1 cup thinly sliced scallions

2 pounds green beans, strings
   removed, ends snipped, and
   snapped in half

2 tablespoons cold water

2 teaspoons salt

½ teaspoon freshly ground black
   pepper

1 tablespoon red wine vinegar

¼ cup finely chopped fresh mint
   leaves

Fry the bacon in a large skillet over medium-high heat, turning the pieces frequently until brown and crisp, about 5 to 7 minutes. Drain on a paper towel. Lower the heat to medium and cook the scallions in the bacon fat for 3 to 4 minutes, until soft but not brown. Add the green beans to the skillet, stirring them until they are well coated with the bacon fat. Add the water and cover tightly. Reduce the heat to low and cook for 5 minutes, then uncover and continue to cook until the beans are crisp-tender. Sprinkle the beans with the salt and pepper, stir in the vinegar, and remove from the heat. Put the beans in a serving dish, crumble the bacon on top, and sprinkle the beans with the bacon pieces and mint.

Candied Yams

4 large yams or sweet potatoes,
   peeled and sliced ½ inch thick

2 teaspoons ground cinnamon

1 cup sugar

1 teaspoon ground nutmeg

¼ cup margarine or butter, plus
   some for greasing the dish

1⅓ cups evaporated milk

⅔ cup water

Preheat the oven to 350°F. Grease a baking dish and layer on half of the yams. Combine the cinnamon, sugar, and nutmeg in a small bowl. Sprinkle half of the sugar mixture over the yams. Dot the yams with half of the butter. Layer on the rest of the yams, sprinkle with the remaining sugar mixture, and dot with the remaining butter. Mix the milk and water together in a small bowl and pour over the yams. Cover and bake for 45 minutes. Increase the oven temperature to 400°F. Uncover the casserole and bake for another 10 minutes, or until the yams are golden brown and tender.

The Autobiography of Eleanor Roosevelt

by Eleanor Roosevelt

*I*f you were asked to think of one woman who changed our world, Eleanor Roosevelt would likely come to mind. She campaigned tirelessly for consumer welfare and civil rights; she improved urban and public housing; and she served as a delegate to the United Nations to set up the Commission of Human Rights.

With so many books about Eleanor Roosevelt to choose from (there are over five hundred on Amazon.com!) deciding on *one* was a difficult task. In the end, I went to the primary source herself: Mrs. Roosevelt, in her own words. In addition to chronicling the "big picture" of her life's course, Mrs. Roosevelt tells us intimate details about her private life. For example, after FDR passed away, she had to manage a budget on her own for the first time, and she tells us exactly how much money she received in life insurance and how she used it. She even discusses the income and inheritance taxes she had to pay.

Reading Mrs. Roosevelt's autobiography felt like hearing a good friend reveal her hidden fears, her vulnerabilities, and even her reactions to petty gossip. Despite having to overcome social and personal barriers, Eleanor Roosevelt managed to become one of the most influential women of the twentieth century and make the world a better place, especially for women and children. For me, that's enough inspiration to last for more than just one year.

Up for Discussion . . .

- How was Eleanor's life influenced by society's view of the role of women?

- How did Eleanor's perceived lack of beauty affect her self-concept and her relationship with her family?

- Why did Eleanor love her father so much, and how did his death affect her?

- From an early age, Eleanor was conscious and concerned about the fact that people around her were suffering—how did her compassion for others develop into her life's work?

- The fact that Eleanor's family was wealthy provided her with opportunities for travel and education that most women at the time did not have. Do you think that Eleanor would have become such a force of change without those opportunities? Why or why not?

- What personal traits did Eleanor have that made her as successful as she was in a world of powerful men?

- What does Eleanor reveal about her relationship with Franklin? What word would you use to describe their relationship?

- How did Eleanor's early experiences living a rather unconventional life prepare her for life in the White House?

- How would you describe Eleanor's emotional side?

- When asked who her role model is, Hillary Rodham Clinton names Eleanor Roosevelt. Why does this choice make sense to you?

- What differences did Eleanor Roosevelt make in the world?

World War II Coffee Klatch

Eleanor Roosevelt most likely had to attend her share of these during her years as First Lady. The recipes I've chosen are WWII–appropriate—they take into account the rations to which all families were allowed and the frugality that was an inherent part of living in times of war, without sacrificing flavor!

WWII Sugarless Brownies

Don't worry—these dark chocolate brownies aren't really sugarless. They use corn syrup and a little brown sugar to provide the sweetness that would normally be supplied by white granulated sugar.

1/3 cup vegetable shortening, plus some for greasing the pan
3/4 cup light corn syrup
1/3 cup packed light brown sugar
2 (1-ounce) squares unsweetened chocolate, melted

2 large eggs
2/3 cup all-purpose flour
1/2 teaspoon baking powder
1/4 teaspoon salt
1/2 teaspoon vanilla extract
1/2 cup chopped walnuts or pecans

Preheat the oven to 350°F. Grease a 9-inch square baking pan and set aside. In a large bowl, beat together the corn syrup, shortening, brown sugar, and chocolate using a handheld mixer until fluffy. Beat in the eggs, one at a time. Add the flour, baking powder, and salt. Beat until just smooth. Fold in the vanilla and walnuts. Spread the batter into the pan and bake for 25 to 30 minutes, or until a toothpick inserted in the center comes out clean. Cut into 16 squares while still warm. Cool to room temperature and serve.

Day-Old Bread Apple Brown Betty

1 teaspoon butter, melted, plus some for greasing the dish
2 cups day-old white breadcrumbs (from 5 to 6 slices of bread)
1/3 cup packed light brown sugar
1 teaspoon ground cinnamon

2 pounds cooking apples, peeled, cored, and thinly sliced
1/4 cup orange juice
1 (9-ounce) container frozen whipped topping, thawed, for serving

Preheat the oven to 400°F. Lightly grease a 1½-quart casserole or baking dish. Combine the breadcrumbs, brown sugar, and cinnamon in a medium bowl. Arrange one third of the apples on the bottom of the casserole; top with one third of the crumb mixture. Repeat once. Add the remaining apples, then drizzle the orange juice over the top. Combine the remaining third of the crumb mixture and the butter and sprinkle it evenly over the top. Bake until the apples are tender, 40 to 45 minutes. Cool 15 to 20 minutes, then serve warm with the whipped topping.

Gesundheit!

Bringing Good Health to You, the Medical System, and Society Through Physician Service, Complementary Therapies, Humor, and Joy

by Patch Adams, M.D., with Maureen Mylander

We have all been patients in a hospital or doctor's office at some point. I, myself, have worked in healthcare for the last eight years, namely because I love working with patients. I have also seen how HMOs and various government issues, such as Medicare's lack of prescription coverage, have slighted many people, myself included. Patch Adams saw these same shortcomings and dedicated his life to improving them. You may find that Dr. Adams' mandate seems a bit idealistic, especially if you've worked in healthcare and wince at the thought of spending hours just getting to know a patient (that would certainly throw payroll off!). And yet, the passion that Dr. Adams puts into treating the whole person, not just the disease, is truly inspirational. Plus, who knows—this book may just help you achieve that New Year's resolution to eat right and get more exercise!

Up for Discussion . . .

- How is Patch Adams different from your primary care physician?

- Would you prefer to have Patch Adams treat you (over your current primary care physician)? Why or why not?

- If you were diagnosed with a life-threatening illness, would you rather go mainstream in your treatment or go the alternative medicine route? Would you be open to trying a combination of both? Why or why not?

- What influence does your experience with past illnesses have on how you would handle a future one?

- What significance does your perspective on death have on how you would deal with a future serious illness?

- What kind of person does it take to change a firmly established system? Are you that kind of person? Why or why not?

- If you currently work in a healthcare setting—or have ever previously— what do you think of Dr. Adams' ideas? How do you think they would go over in your office or department?

- What type of person would benefit most from a system like Dr. Adams'? What type of person would benefit least?

- In the quest to see your dreams and plans realized, you will inevitably experience several setbacks. How do Patch and his team deal with setbacks? How would you deal with the setbacks Patch encountered?

- Do you think that a healthcare system like the one Patch Adams proposes would be easier to institute in a country such as the United States, or would it fare better in a struggling nation? Why? What cultural characteristics does a society need to have in order to embrace a healthcare system such as Dr. Adams'?

- Do you think the American public would embrace a system such as this if it were instituted in this country? Why or why not?

- What small parts of Patch's plan could we incorporate into our established system with little cost, little upheaval, and sizeable benefit?

Good for the Body and Soul

Because Patch Adams focuses on the complete person rather than just the disease, he is constantly preaching to his patients about the benefits of good nutrition. The dish below is packed with nutrients to keep you healthy and away from the doctor. It also tastes yummy, and pasta is almost always at the top of people's lists of comfort foods. Serve with baby spinach tossed in extra-virgin olive oil and balsamic vinegar to pack an even greater antioxidant punch!

Whole Wheat Fettuccine with Chicken and Broccoli Rabe

**Salt for cooking the broccoli rabe,
plus more to taste**
2 bunches broccoli rabe, chopped
1 pound whole wheat fettuccine
3 tablespoons extra-virgin olive oil
1 large red onion, chopped
6 large garlic cloves, minced
**2½ pounds boneless, skinless
chicken breasts, cut into 1-inch
strips**

**Freshly ground black pepper to
taste**
1 tablespoon Italian seasoning
½ cup dry white wine
2 heads radicchio, shredded
1 bunch fresh basil, chopped
**⅓ cup freshly grated Parmesan
cheese**

Bring a large pot of water to a boil over high heat, add salt, then drop in the chopped broccoli rabe. Cook for about 4 minutes, or until crisp tender. Remove the broccoli rabe from the boiling water with a slotted spoon and reserve in a bowl. Add the fettuccine to the boiling water and cook according to package directions.

Meanwhile, place a large skillet over medium heat and warm the oil. Add the red onion and garlic and cook for about 5 minutes, or until the onions are soft-ened. Add the chicken strips to the skillet and season with salt and pepper, then add in the Italian seasoning. Sauté until the chicken is cooked through, about 5 to 7 minutes. Add the wine, stirring, and scrape up the brown bits on the bottom of the skillet. Add the broccoli rabe and radicchio and cook for an additional 5 min-utes. Serve immediately over the fettuccine. Sprinkle the basil on top and serve the Parmesan cheese on the side.

FEBRUARY

♡ Be My Valentine

Romance, to me, is coming home to a clean kitchen.

My husband, Jim, is the best kitchen-cleaner in the country, if not the world. He gets down on his hands and knees and scrubs the floors, removes all mystery items from the refrigerator, and basically restores order to the chaos I've created while testing recipes. This usually prompts me to make him a lovely dinner (which is romantic to *him*), and the cycle starts all over again, keeping us in a constant state of marital bliss.

What is romance to you? Sinatra? The white knight in shining armor? Getting married on a whim in Las Vegas? Wherever you find romance, one thing's for sure: millions of people (er . . . *women*) turn to books. Romance novels are the highest selling genre of novel in the United States, and according to a recent internet poll on romantic times.com, the average romance novel buff reads twenty to twenty-five novels a month. Granted, this refers to the bodice-ripping Harlequin variety, but, twenty to twenty-five a *month*? (Yes, that amounts to almost one a day!)

During my visit to the Harlequin website (made strictly for research purposes, I swear . . .), I admit that I signed up to receive three free books and a free email newsletter. I read one of the free novels as soon as it arrived, and it wasn't altogether *horrible* . . . all right, I got a kick out of every bawdy word of it! Reading this novel inspired me to make a list of *proper* romance novels for the sensible reader, several of which you will find in this chapter.

What follows are some lovely selections for your group's Valentine's Day get-together. For the recipes, two of the selections are breakfast menus, which will leave your evenings free to dine with your Valentine!

Gone with the Wind by Margaret Mitchell

Gone with the Wind is far and away the best selling romance novel of all time. When released in 1936 it was hailed by critics and readers alike as a book that will not be forgotten—and they weren't kidding! *Gone with the Wind* has sold over *twenty-eight million* copies since its release. Its intriguing characters, dramatic (almost melodramatic) romantic scenes, and sweeping historical setting have made it a favorite of not only romance readers, but of historical fiction lovers as well.

Set during the Civil War and Reconstruction era in the South, this is one *long* epic novel. You'll be surprised at how quickly the novel reads, though—it's likely that you'll become so engrossed in the plot that you'll have to TiVo your favorite shows for a week! If you've already seen the movie, note that it's quite different from the book; while you're reading, keep an eye out for interesting twists that you may not expect. Finally, here's some trivia for you—*Gone with the Wind* is actually a bildungsroman (a novel that charts the maturation of the main character).

Up for Discussion . . .

- Would you rather live in the prewar South or in the postwar South? Why?

- What makes you like Scarlett O'Hara? What makes you dislike her?

- In what ways is Scarlett a feminist character? In what ways is she not?

- Why does Melanie always defend Scarlett?

- Do you think Melanie loved Scarlett in spite of her bad behavior, or was she simply too naive to understand Scarlett's motives?

- If you were Melanie, how would you have acted toward Scarlett?

- Why is Scarlett in love with Ashley? Is she just in love with the idea of him?

- In what ways does Ashley represent the prewar South?

- In what ways does Rhett represent the postwar South?

- Would you rather be married to Rhett or Ashley? Why?

- Were the other women jealous of Scarlett, or do you think they genuinely didn't like her? Why?

- How would Scarlett fair in modern times? Do you think she would adapt better than Melanie or Sue Ellen?

- What characteristics does Scarlett get from her father?

- What characteristics does Bonnie get from Scarlett?

- Why do you think that Mitchell couldn't portray Scarlett as a doting mother?

- What do you think about the portrayal of the slaves? Is it realistic or racist?

- What would have improved Scarlett and Rhett's relationship besides eliminating the Scarlett/Ashley issue?

- Do you think Scarlett will be able to win back Rhett's love? How will she do it?

- Is land the most important thing in a person's life today? Then?

- What gives you as much comfort as Tara gives Scarlett?

- How does the book compare to the movie? What parts of the book were left out of the movie? Why do you think the screenwriter didn't include these parts?

Brunch at Tara

Put on your hoop skirt and head out to the terrace! I can't think of anything with more Southern charm—or more romantic flair—than this big brunch. These Georgian delights are best served with lots of sweet iced tea or unsweetened iced tea with plenty of lemon.

Eggs O'Hara

**2 tablespoons butter, plus some
for greasing the baking dish**
2 tablespoons all-purpose flour
2 cups milk
**Salt and freshly ground black
pepper to taste**
1 cup shredded cheddar cheese

12 large eggs, beaten
¼ cup chopped onion
½ cup sliced white mushrooms
1 teaspoon chopped fresh parsley
½ cup buttered breadcrumbs
1 teaspoon paprika

Butter a 12 by 7-inch glass baking dish and set aside. Preheat the oven to 350°F. Melt the butter in a medium saucepan over medium heat. Stir in the flour to make a paste. Slowly whisk in the milk, incorporating it completely. Cook, stirring constantly, until the sauce thickens, about 3 minutes. Add the cheese, stirring to melt. In a large skillet over medium heat, scramble the eggs just until soft set (no more than half done). Season with the salt and pepper. Add the onions, mushrooms, parsley, and milk-cheese mixture and stir to combine. Transfer to the baking dish; top with the breadcrumbs and paprika and bake for about 30 minutes, or until the breadcrumbs are golden brown. Serve hot.

Georgia Peach Bread

**½ cup vegetable shortening, plus
some for greasing the pans**

**2 cups all-purpose flour, plus some
for dusting the pans**

1½ cups sugar

2 large eggs

2¼ cups pureed peaches (you can use canned or frozen, just make sure the canned are drained and the frozen are defrosted before using)

1 teaspoon vanilla extract

1 teaspoon ground cinnamon

1 teaspoon baking powder

1 teaspoon baking soda

¼ teaspoon salt

1 cup finely chopped pecans

Grease and flour two 9 by 5-inch loaf pans. Preheat the oven to 325°F. Cream the sugar and shortening together in a large bowl. Add the eggs and mix thoroughly. Stir in the peach puree and vanilla. In a separate bowl, combine the flour, cinnamon, baking powder, baking soda, and salt. Incorporate the flour mixture into the peach mixture until well blended. Fold in the pecans. Pour the batter into the pans and bake for 50 minutes to 1 hour, or until a toothpick inserted into the center comes out clean. Cool for 15 minutes before removing the bread from the pans to cool completely on wire racks.

Frankly My Dear, I Don't Give a Ham

4 (8-ounce) country-side ham slices

¼ cup brown sugar

1 cup strong black coffee

Soak the ham in a large bowl filled with water overnight in the refrigerator. In the morning, drain and pat dry with paper towels. Trim the fat from the ham. Cook the fat trimmings in a large skillet over medium-low heat for 6 to 8 minutes, or until crisp. Discard the trimmings, reserving 2 tablespoons of the drippings in the skillet. Add the ham slices to the skillet. Cook for 9 to 10 minutes on each side, until brown. Remove the ham slices from the skillet, but keep the ham warm by covering with foil.

To make the gravy, stir the brown sugar into the drippings. Cook over medium heat, stirring constantly, until the sugar dissolves. Stir in the coffee. Bring to a boil and boil for 2 minutes, or until the gravy is slightly thickened and is a rich, reddish brown color. Serve the ham with gravy on top.

Melonies

2 ripe honeydew melons, balled
  (or cubed if you don't have a
  baller)
¼ cup fresh lime juice
3 tablespoons gin

¼ cup chopped fresh mint
Grated zest of 2 limes
Thin lime slices and mint sprigs,
  for garnish

Combine all the ingredients in a large serving bowl and toss until coated. Garnish with the lime slices and mint sprigs.

The Love Letter by Cathleen Schine

The Love Letter offers an interesting twist on the "May-December" romance—instead of portraying a love affair between an older man and a younger woman, the novel features a forty-something-year-old woman who falls for a college-aged man. The plot is set into motion when a mysterious love letter appears in Helen MacFarquhar's mailbox, inspiring a titillating search for its author and intended recipient; nobody in Helen's small town is free from suspicion. Cathleen Schine keeps the novel intelligent and witty while maintaining its feel as a light, romantic read. I found the book's primary setting—a small bookstore owned by Helen—especially charming.

Up for Discussion . . .

- If Schine were to write a sequel to *The Love Letter*, how do you think the story would continue? What would happen to Johnny and Helen? How would it pan out if they did end up together? Who would have approved? Who would have disapproved?

- If you were Johnny, how would the story continue? If you were Helen?

- Who did you think wrote the letter before it was revealed at the end?

- How long did it take you to warm up to Helen's character?

- How believable did you find this love affair?

- Why do people find an older man/younger woman relationship more acceptable than an older woman/younger man relationship?

- Do you think that Lillian and Miss Skattergoods' relationship would have been more socially acceptable to Pequot's residents than Helen and Johnny's relationship?

- Have you ever had a crush on your boss? What happened?

- Could you work—or have you ever worked—with someone you were romantically involved with?

- Do you think that Jennifer, Kelly, and/or Lucy knew about Helen and Johnny's affair?

- Would you rather live in Pequot or New York City? Why?

- If you could open a business in Pequot, what would you want it to be?

- Have you ever written a love letter? Have you ever received a love letter? Discuss the details with the group.

- Would you like to receive this love letter? If not, what kind of love letter would you like to receive? Would it be from a secret admirer? Your old high school flame? Your spouse?

- How is it possible for one love letter to cause so much confusion? How about this particular letter?

Breakfast at Horatio Street Books

When you're a busy bookstore owner having an affair with one of your employees, it's hard to find the time to have breakfast at home—especially when you meet your much-younger lover on the sly every morning! You'll just have to buy your breakfast on the road and bring it with you to work. Serve the following modern coffee shop delights with bagels from your local bakery and flavored cream cheeses.

Note: All of the drink recipes that follow serve 2.

When I Peel an Orange . . .

This smoothie is as delicious as the mysterious love letter that Helen finds.

**1 cup canned orange sections,
   drained and chilled**
**½ cup canned grapefruit sections,
   chilled**

½ cup strong brewed tea, chilled
¾ cup orange sherbet
2 ice cubes, crushed

Combine the oranges sections, grapefruit sections, and tea in a blender. Add the sherbet and ice. Blend until smooth, pour into 2 glasses, and serve.

Refreshing Morning Swim

Dive right in! This smoothie is just as exhilarating as Helen's morning swim.

1½ cups diced honeydew melon
½ cup plain yogurt

1 cup frozen blueberries
1 tablespoon chopped fresh mint

Combine the melon and yogurt in a blender, then add the blueberries and mint. Blend until smooth. Pour into 2 glasses, and serve.

Jennifer and Kelly's Starbucks Special

**1½ cups strong brewed coffee,
   cooled to room temperature
   (don't put it in the
   refrigerator—this will make it
   cloudy)**

¼ cup half-and-half
2 tablespoons chocolate syrup
Sugar to taste

Combine the coffee, half-and-half, and chocolate syrup in a small bowl. Sweeten with sugar to taste. Pour over ice in two glasses and serve.

Lillian and Miss Skattergoods' Orange Coffee for Two

1 cup strong brewed hot coffee
1 cup hot chocolate
2 orange slices

Whipped cream, for serving
Cinnamon, for serving

Mix together the coffee and hot chocolate. Place 1 orange slice in each cup. Pour the coffee mixture over the oranges. Top with whipped cream and a sprinkle of cinnamon and serve.

Mount Vernon Love Story

A Novel of George and Martha Washington

by Mary Higgins Clark

Originally published in 1969 under the title *Aspire to the Heavens*, this romance novel predates all of Clark's bestselling mystery novels—in fact, it was Mary Higgins Clark's first attempt at novel writing. The novel was reprinted under the current title in 2002, after it was discovered by a Washington family descendent.

Mount Vernon Love Story gives us a peek into George and Martha Washington's personal affairs, bringing the legendary couple to life for the reader. Although this is fiction, it is extremely well-researched—Clark based her story around historical events, then used her imagination to fill in the rest. And even though this isn't a mystery novel, you'll still be able to detect Clark's signature style and voice.

Up for Discussion . . .

- Compare this romance novel to Clark's more recent, popular mysteries. How does this book measure up?

- What are some similarities between this book and her mystery novels that you noticed? Some differences?

- How much of this novel do you think is based on fact?

- How does this book rate as a romance novel?

- Compare the relationship George had with his mother to the relationships he had with his stepchildren.

- Do you think George loved Sally more than Patsy? Why or why not? If given the chance, do you think he would have left Patsy for Sally?

- Why do you think George and Patsy never had children of their own?

- What do you think about the relationship between George and Patsy? Is it what you would have expected? If not, how is it different?

- I don't think I'd like to have Mary Washington as a mother-in-law. Everyone share an in-law horror story.

- What do you think about the fact that George and Patsy owned slaves? Do you think Clark romanticized the relationship between the Washingtons and their slaves?

- What is the most wonderful thing about coming home after a long journey?

Big, Southern Bar-B-Que at Mount Vernon

George Washington loved his home at Mount Vernon, and back in Washington's day it was customary for such a popular gentleman and his lady to entertain family, friends, and political allies with a big Southern bar-b-que. These ribs are great because they're (primarily) prepared in the oven, so you can get that scrumptious bar-b-que taste without freezing your buns off trying to grill in February!

All-American Ribs

4 cups unsweetened pineapple
    juice
2 cups brown sugar
2 tablespoons powdered mustard
½ cup ketchup
⅓ cup red wine vinegar
2 tablespoons fresh lemon juice
3 tablespoons soy sauce

¾ teaspoon ground cloves
1 tablespoon ground ginger
6 garlic cloves, minced
¾ teaspoon cayenne pepper
2 (2-pound) slabs baby back pork
    ribs
2 (12-ounce) bottles of your
    favorite barbeque sauce

In a large glass bowl or dish, stir together the pineapple juice, brown sugar, mustard, ketchup, vinegar, lemon juice, and soy sauce. Mix in the cloves, ginger, garlic, and cayenne. Cut the ribs into serving size pieces and place in the marinade. Cover and refrigerate, for 8 hours, or overnight, turning occasionally.

Preheat the oven to 275°F. Place the ribs in a 9 by 13-inch baking dish and cover with marinade. Cook for 1½ hours, turning occasionally to ensure even cooking. Preheat an outdoor grill to medium heat. Cook the ribs on the grill for 15 to 20 minutes, or until heated through and slightly charred on the tips, basting with barbeque sauce and turning frequently.

Colonel Washington's Corn Pudding

2 tablespoons butter or
    margarine, melted, plus some
    for greasing the baking dish
3 large eggs
2 cups frozen corn kernels

¼ cup all-purpose flour
1 tablespoon sugar
1 teaspoon salt
½ teaspoon white pepper
2 cups light cream

Grease a 1½-quart baking dish and set aside. Preheat the oven to 325°F. Beat the eggs well in a large bowl and stir in the corn. Mix the flour, sugar, salt, and pepper together in a separate bowl and add to the corn mixture. Stir in the butter and cream and mix thoroughly. Pour into the baking dish. Place the dish into a larger pan and pour hot water into the larger pan until it comes up to about half the height of the pudding dish. Bake for about 1 hour, or until firm and browned.

Welcome Home Pecan Pie

4 large eggs, lightly beaten
2 tablespoons heavy cream
½ cup granulated sugar
½ cup lightly packed brown sugar
4 teaspoons all-purpose flour
⅛ teaspoon salt
1⅓ cups light corn syrup

5 tablespoons butter, melted
1½ teaspoons vanilla extract
1 tablespoon bourbon
1½ cups lightly toasted pecans
1 (9-inch) frozen pie shell, thawed
Whipped cream, for serving

Preheat the oven to 325°F. Mix the eggs and cream together in a medium bowl. In a separate bowl, combine the granulated sugar, brown sugar, flour, and salt. Stir the flour mixture into the egg mixture. Add the corn syrup and 3 tablespoons of the butter. Do not overmix. Stir in the vanilla and bourbon. Pour the mixture into the thawed pie shell. Sprinkle the pecans on top and drizzle with the remaining 2 tablespoons melted butter. Cover the pie shell edges with foil to prevent burning. Bake for 1 hour and 15 minutes to 1 hour and 30 minutes; remove the foil and bake another 10 minutes.

Remove from the oven. The pie should still be a bit jiggly in the middle. Let cool on a wire rack and let stand for at least 3 hours before cutting. Serve warm with fresh whipped cream.

Emma by Jane Austen

Jane Austen was one of the first great romance novelists, and *Emma* is the author's most lighthearted work. *Emma* is also the only selection in this chapter with a rock-solid happy ending, so if you're looking for a sure thing, this book is the way to go.

Emma's plot unfolds through a comedy of errors, beginning when Emma, who was raised as a proper young lady, befriends Harriet Smith, a girl of questionable background. Emma attempts to train Harriet to act and behave just like her, and she encourages Harriet to try to snag a gentleman a bit out of her league. As Emma plays matchmaker, she ends up spreading rumors, hurting feelings, and spinning her social life out of control. Although the book is set and written in the early 1800s, Austen's wit and ironic insights are amusing—and applicable—to the modern reader.

If your group wants to see a highly contemporary film adaptation of *Emma*, the movie *Clueless* (Paramount, 1995) offers an adorable interpretation. The movie's modern twists are very creative—Mr. Martin's character, for instance, is portrayed as a kindhearted California skateboarder.

Up for Discussion . . .

- What did you think of Emma's character? Would you have been friends with her if you lived in Highbury?

- Would you let Emma set you up on a date?

- What do you think this story says about social status and love?

- Would you attempt to love someone because someone else told you it was a good idea?

- Why do you think Emma meddles in everyone else's affairs?

- How was Emma's insult to Miss Bates a turning point in her life?

- Why does Emma realize her love for Mr. Knightly only after Harriet discloses her feelings for him?

- What do you think of Austen's use of humor? What do you think is the funniest part of the novel?

- List as many of the misunderstandings between the characters in the novel as you can. What are the various causes of all these misunderstandings?

- Which character would suit you best for marriage?

- Would you enjoy living in the time period in which Emma was set? Why or why not?

High Tea at Box Hill

At this month's reading group get-together, try to refrain from insulting your group members as Emma did at her picnic at Box Hill—this *is* high tea, for goodness sake! What follows is a great traditional English tea menu that is best served around 3 or 4 P.M. (between lunch and dinner). I recommend serving it in the sunniest room in the house with pretty teacups and dessert-size plates, to chase away your winter blahs. Or if you're feeling especially festive, why not spring for a fancy floor picnic complete with a crisp linen tablecloth spread out on the floor for a bit of added flair?

Emma's Prim and Proper Cucumber Sandwiches

2 seedless cucumbers, sliced paper
   thin
1 teaspoon salt
¾ cup butter, softened
1 tablespoon chopped fresh
   tarragon

32 slices pumpernickel cocktail
   bread
Chopped fresh parsley, for garnish

Sprinkle the cucumber slices with the salt and allow to sit for 5 to 10 minutes. In a small bowl, mix together the butter and tarragon. Spread a thin layer of tarragon butter over each bread slice. Pat the cucumber slices dry with paper towels and layer them on the bread slices. Sprinkle the sandwiches with chopped parsley and serve.

Harriet's Cozy Bread Pudding

½ cup whipped cream cheese
4 slices dry cinnamon raisin bread
1¾ cups milk
4 large eggs, beaten

⅓ cup sugar
2 tablespoons bourbon
1 teaspoon lemon zest
Fresh whipped cream, for serving

Preheat the oven to 325°F. Spread the cream cheese on 2 slices of bread (that's ¼ cup per slice). Top with the remaining 2 bread slices (making 2 "sandwiches"). Cut the sandwiches into cubes and place in an 8 by 8-inch cake pan. In a medium bowl, mix together the milk, eggs, sugar, bourbon, and lemon zest. Pour the mixture over the bread cubes. Bake for 35 to 40 minutes, or until a knife inserted in the center comes out clean. Serve warm with fresh whipped cream.

Nerve Soothing Tea

For when a friend tries to set you up with the wrong person! This is also a good tea to help you sleep if you are anticipating a set-up . . .

8 thin lemon slices
3 tablespoons honey

1 freshly brewed pot of
chamomile tea

Place a lemon slice in the bottom of each tea cup and drizzle with a bit of honey. Pour the tea into the prepared cups and serve.

MARCH

Leprechauns and Blarney Stones

I don't know what St. Patrick's Day is like in your town, but until I met my partially Irish husband, Jim, I had never been fully exposed to the exorbitant revelry that is St. Patrick's Day (I'm of partial Scottish descent myself). The first year Jim and I were dating, he invited me to meet his family at the Irish Center in South Buffalo, New York (a sort of Elk Club or Moose Club for Irish-Americans—or for anyone who loves Guinness) for the annual St. Patrick's Day celebration. He also told me that I needed to wear something green—or green and orange, to match the flag of Ireland—to this celebration in order to partake; I discovered, however, that I didn't own anything suitable. (Jim, of course, had his token Ireland sweatshirt that his parents purchased for him on their first trip to the motherland.) So, at the last minute I rushed out to purchase something kelly green, which, as I quickly discovered, is nearly impossible to find in Buffalo on March the 17th. I bought what I thought was the find of the century: a kelly green velvet tunic shirt that I could wear with leggings and boots (it was the 90s . . .).

I later realized—much to my horror—that I had purchased a maternity shirt, and I spent the day alongside every Irish Catholic in Western New York, unwed and looking great with child. Nevertheless, my affection for Irish culture has grown ever since. I love making corned beef and cabbage every March, and Jim cannot get through the month without at least one loaf of his mother's soda bread (you'll find the recipe in this chapter).

My goal in this chapter is to offer your group alternate St. Patrick's Day entertaining ideas so you can avoid attending the crowded parades and wearing the dreaded "Kiss Me I'm Irish" pins in public. There are so many great Irish authors and novels that are set against the magical Emerald Isle; what follows are a few of my favorites. So, don yer green and break out the Guinness—let's celebrate the feast of St. Patrick!

Quentins by Maeve Binchy

*D*o you have a favorite restaurant in the place where you grew up? You know—the one where you went for special dinners with your parents, on your first date, or to celebrate milestone events and anniversaries? For me, it's Salvatore's Italian Gardens in Buffalo, a flamboyant, candle-lit Italian restaurant. I went there for birthdays, before my prom, and for every celebration in between. The food is always great, I know the menu, and the service is just about the best you could find anywhere.

Maeve Binchy's *Quentins* is the story of such a place in Dublin, where everyone goes to celebrate everything and anything, and there's enough history between its walls to fill a thousand books. *Quentins* offers a modern (fictional) look at Ireland, and I simply couldn't write a chapter about Ireland without including a Maeve Binchy book. Binchy is the bestselling Irish novelist who wrote such favorites as *Circle of Friends* (made famous by the 1995 HBO Studios movie based on the book starring Minnie Driver and Chris O'Donnell), *Scarlet Feather*, and *Irish Girls About Town: An Anthology of Short Stories*.

One of my favorite things about Binchy's novels is that the same cast of characters appears in every book, though the size of a particular character's role varies from book to book. Reading her books always makes me feel as if I am walking down the streets of a small town and seeing old friends walk by. If you've never read a Maeve Binchy book, though, don't worry—they aren't written as a series, so you won't feel lost.

Up for Discussion . . .

- Did you see Don Richardson's betrayal coming? At what point?

- If you were Ella, would you have waited so long to give the laptop to the police? Why, or why not?

- If you were Ella, would you have taken Don's money to get your parents out of debt? Why? Why not?

- What do you think Don's wife is doing throughout the novel? Do you think she knew about the stolen money? About Ella? What was her father's role?

- Would you be able to look the other way, like Don's wife, if your spouse was spending three nights a week at a lover's house?

- How would Quentins be different had Patrick and Brenda had children? Would it be different at all?

- Do you have a favorite restaurant that you have celebrated in over the years? How did it become your favorite restaurant? What's it like? Share some of your memories with the group.

- If you could go to any restaurant in the world and have a free meal, where would you go? A posh Beverly Hills spot to "star gaze"? A French bistro in Paris? A trendy sushi bar in Manhattan?

- If you could own and operate a restaurant and had unlimited capital to start, what would your restaurant be like? What kind of food would you serve? Would you have nightly entertainment? What would the atmosphere be like? What would you name it? Where would it be? If you could invite anyone you wanted (including famous people), who would be at your grand opening?

- Could you successfully run a business with your spouse? Your siblings?

Quentins' Early Bird Special

Ella and her girlfriends spent many wonderful evenings taking advantage of the Early Bird dinner at Quentins. Given that the restaurant serves modern Irish cuisine, the following dishes may very well be what they enjoyed!

Parsnip and Apple Soup

1 tablespoon butter
1 pound parsnips, thinly sliced
1 pound apples, peeled, cored,
    and thinly sliced
1 medium onion, chopped
1 large garlic clove, minced
2 teaspoons curry powder
1 tablespoon ground cumin

1 tablespoon ground coriander
½ teaspoon ground cardamom
6½ cups chicken stock
Salt and freshly ground black
    pepper to taste
⅔ cup heavy cream
Chopped fresh parsley, for garnish

Melt the butter in a large stockpot over medium heat. Add the parsnips, apples, and onion and cook until soft but not browned, about 5 to 7 minutes. Stir in the garlic, curry, cumin, coriander, and cardamom and cook for about 2 minutes. Add the chicken stock and stir until combined. Raise the heat to high and bring the mixture to a boil; reduce the heat to low, cover, and simmer for 30 minutes, or until the parsnips have softened. Taste and add salt and pepper.

Remove from the heat and cool slightly. Using a stick blender, process until smooth. If you don't have a stick blender, use a standing blender and return the soup to the pot (then ask for a stick blender for the next gift "getting" holiday!) If the soup seems too thick, add more chicken stock to thin it out. Add the cream and re-heat over medium-low heat—don't let it boil! Serve garnished with chopped parsley.

On the Lamb

1 tablespoon butter
4 Granny Smith apples, peeled,
    cored, and thinly sliced
Juice of 2 lemons
2 teaspoons sugar
1 tablespoon ground ginger
1 (5-pound) loin of lamb, boned
    (your butcher will do this for
    you if you ask nicely)

Salt and freshly ground black
    pepper to taste
4 garlic cloves, thinly sliced
2 (12-ounce) bottles hard cider (or
    3 cups regular apple cider)

Combine the butter, apples, lemon juice, sugar, and ginger in a medium skillet over medium heat. Cook until the apples are softened but not mushy, about 3 to 5 minutes. Remove from the heat and set aside.

Preheat the oven to 400°F. Season the lamb liberally on both sides with salt and pepper. Lay the lamb on a board, flat side down. Make small cuts in the lamb with the tip of a sharp knife and stuff a piece of the sliced garlic in each pocket. Spoon the apple mixture along the center, roll up the lamb, and secure with cooking string. Place seam side down in a roasting pan and roast in the oven for 40 minutes.

Meanwhile, heat the cider in a small saucepan or in a microwave-safe bowl. Pour the warmed cider over the lamb after the first 40 minutes of roasting. Reduce the oven heat to 350°F and roast for another 50 minutes to 1 hour, or until the internal temperature is 160°F, basting frequently. Transfer to a heated serving dish. While the meat is resting, skim off any excess fat from the pan juices and boil over high heat until mixture is slightly reduced. Serve with the pan juices on the side.

Colcannon

Salt, for cooking the cabbage and
   potatoes
1 medium cabbage, core removed,
   quartered
2 pounds unpeeled potatoes,
   cubed
2 medium leeks, chopped

1 cup milk
1 teaspoon ground mace
3 large garlic cloves, minced
½ cup butter
Freshly ground black pepper to
   taste

Bring a large stockpot filled with salted water to a boil over medium-high heat. Add the cabbage and cook until tender, 12 to 15 minutes. Drain the cabbage and chop it. Set aside. In the same stockpot, bring more salted water to boil. Add the potatoes and cook until tender, 15 to 20 minutes. Drain and set aside. Place the leeks in the stockpot and cover with the milk. Bring the milk close to a boil over medium heat and immediately turn down the heat to low and simmer for about 10 minutes, or until the leeks are tender. Add the mace, garlic, and ¼ cup of the butter to the pot. Allow the butter to melt, then add the potatoes to the pot. Mash well with a potato masher, taking care not to mash the leeks completely. Add salt and pepper. If the mixture is too dry, add a little more milk. Add the cabbage to the mixture and continue to mash. Preheat the broiler. Transfer the mixture to an ovenproof dish. Dot with the remaining ¼ cup butter and place under the broiler to brown (keep a close eye on it!).

Frozen Black Irish

A yummy adult desert. It's sometimes called a Whisper because it tastes so light and delicate in your mouth. Note: This recipe serves 1.

1 part coffee-flavored liqueur
1 part Irish Cream liqueur
1 part vodka

1 scoop coffee ice cream (you can substitute chocolate or vanilla if you wish)
½ cup ice cubes

Place all the ingredients into a blender and blend until smooth.

Angela's Ashes

A Memoir
by Frank McCourt

Awarded the 1997 Pulitzer Prize for nonfiction, *Angela's Ashes* is a powerful memoir that will make you think twice before whining that you have nothing to eat or nothing to wear. I saw the movie *Angela's Ashes* before I read the book (not a usual practice of mine, but I simply hadn't gotten around to reading it at the time of the movie's release), and after watching the movie, I put off reading the book for a very long time because the movie was just *so sad*. I did finally read it, though, and I'm glad that I did. While the book is moving and poignant, Frank McCourt has a wonderful voice, and his wit and wisdom manage to lift the book's mood, despite the dour circumstances. In the book, McCourt chronicles his tumultuous childhood as he and his family journey from New York City to Limerick, Ireland, and finally he returns alone—both triumphantly and bittersweetly—back to the United States. No matter what, *Angela's Ashes* will make you grateful for all that you have.

Up for Discussion . . .

- How do Frank and his brothers maintain a sense of humor despite their circumstances?

- Would you be able to survive living in the slums of Limerick as an adult?

- How would Frank's childhood have been different had he been raised in New York? How about in your town? What if he were raised in modern times?

- If you had to choose between growing up hungry and sick, but with unconditional love, or growing up healthy and with a full tummy, but with uncaring or intolerant adults, which would you choose? It's tough, but think and talk about what you would choose and why.

- Discuss the role of grace (defined as forgiveness and favor with no strings attached), or lack thereof, in Frank McCourt's life. How does it shape him? How does it shape his mother?

- How does the Franciscan brother to whom Frank finally confesses change his life? What would have happened if he had made the same confessions to his grandmother or Aunt Aggie?

- Discuss the role of the church in Limerick. What would happen to the residents if the church did not exist?

- Brainstorm as many examples of hypocrisy or false piety presented in the book as you can.

- The United States has many programs and systems in place to protect children, families, and workers. Which of these programs could Frank McCourt and his family have utilized to their advantage had they lived in the United States? How do you think their lives would have been different had they had access to such programs?

- If you could only right one injustice in this story, what would it be? Why is this your choice?

Bread and Soup Is All . . .

In the perpetual damp chill of Limerick, nothing would warm you up faster than this hearty soup. It's one of my husband's favorite recipes, and the bread is sweet and comforting—especially when you smear it with real butter.

Drunken Potato Soup

2 tablespoons plus ¼ cup butter
3 garlic cloves, minced
1 bunch green onions, chopped
1 stalk celery, chopped
6 cups potatoes, peeled, diced,
    and boiled in salted water for 15
    minutes
2 (12-ounce) bottles beer
1 tablespoon sugar

1 chicken bouillon cube
7 cups chicken stock or canned
    broth
Salt and freshly ground black
    pepper to taste
⅓ cup all-purpose flour
2 cups half-and-half
1 cup grated extra-sharp cheddar
    cheese, for serving

Melt 2 tablespoons of the butter in a large stockpot over medium-high heat. Add the garlic, green onions, and celery and sauté for 3 to 5 minutes, or until the celery is translucent. Add the potatoes. Using a potato masher, coarsely mash the potatoes, leaving plenty of chunks. Add the beer and bring to a boil. Reduce the heat to low, add the sugar, bouillon cube, chicken stock, salt, and pepper. Cover and cook for 30 minutes, or until nicely thickened.

To make a roux, in a separate saucepan melt the remaining ¼ cup butter over medium heat. Slowly add the flour, stirring constantly until a paste forms, about 1 to 2 minutes. Add the roux to the soup, 1 tablespoon at a time, until the soup thickens. Lower the heat under the soup to medium-low and cook for 20 minutes. Reduce the heat to low and slowly stir in the half-and-half. Taste and add more salt and pepper if needed. Continue cooking for another 15 minutes. To serve, ladle into bowls and sprinkle with plenty of grated cheddar cheese.

Barm Brack (Irish Farm Bread)

1 cup raisins or dried currants
1 cup freshly brewed black tea
Butter, for greasing the pan
½ teaspoon ground cinnamon
½ teaspoon ground cloves

½ teaspoon allspice
½ teaspoon freshly grated nutmeg
2½ cups self-rising flour
1 egg, lightly beaten

Place the raisins in a small bowl and cover with the tea. Allow to sit for 30 minutes. Preheat the oven to 375°F. Lightly grease an 8-inch cake pan. In a medium bowl, combine the cinnamon, cloves, allspice, nutmeg, and flour. Mix in the raisins, tea, and egg until just combined. Pour the batter into the pan and bake for 35 to 45 minutes, or until a toothpick inserted in the center comes out clean. Cool in the pan for 10 minutes, then turn out of the pan and cool on a wire rack until time to serve. Serve sliced with butter.

The Mammy by Brendan O'Carroll

Entertainment Weekly called *The Mammy* "*Angela's Ashes* on Prozac." This is a fitting description for this novel, namely because the characters maintain a great sense of humor about their circumstances and are able to laugh at themselves, as well as each other (making this a mighty cheerful read—some parts are even laugh-out-loud funny).

In *The Mammy*, O'Carroll depicts a large, boisterous Irish family that is managing to survive despite the loss of their father (and husband). Agnes Browne, the book's central protagonist, is a "fly by the seat of her pants" single mother, forced to care for kids with ages ranging from the teens all the way down the low single digits, showing tender devotion despite constant threats of calamity. The book can be read in one sitting on a Saturday morning (perfect for the reading group get-together that you don't have loads of time to prepare for), but it's just as satisfying as any four-hundred-page novel.

Up for Discussion . . .

- How does Agnes Browne keep from becoming completely depressed through all of her trials?

- In the novel, is ignorance bliss? Do you believe that ignorance can be bliss in real life?

- Would you rather be an only child, or one of seven? Why? Is your response because of or in spite of your own family situation?

- Have you ever had as good a friend as Agnes had in Marion? Tell the group about this friend.

- How can it be that Agnes never mentions Marion's cancer from the time she finds out until Marion's death, yet they still remain best friends?

- In the spirit of Agnes's "assault with a deadly cucumber" incident, what is one thing you would have liked for your mother to do to one of your nasty teachers? Who was this teacher and what made him/her nasty? Do you think Agnes's situation could have been handled differently, considering the circumstances?

- What was your worst punishment as a school child? For those of you who were goody two-shoes, what was the worst punishment you can remember a classmate getting?

- Mark's first kiss was less than romantic, but memorable. Agnes's first kiss with Pierre was a bit surprising. Recount your first kiss to the group—no one is excused from participation!

- When you were a child, would you have given up your confirmation money to buy your siblings gifts and your mother new carpet? Why does Cathy?

- Did you like the length of this novel, or did it leave you wanting more?

- Marion's only dream in life was to learn to drive before she died. Do you have a simple dream like Marion's?

Cliff Richard's Comin' for Tea!

Lord have mercy! Cliff Richard just showed himself at your doorstep! Here are some sweet treats to serve him before you get that first dance . . .

Irish Potato Cake

⅔ cup vegetable shortening, plus some for greasing the pan

2 cups all-purpose flour, plus some for dusting the pan

2 teaspoons baking powder
⅛ teaspoon salt
2 teaspoons ground cinnamon
2 teaspoons ground cloves
2 teaspoons freshly ground
   nutmeg

2 cups sugar
2 large eggs
2 cups mashed potatoes
¾ cup milk
1 cup chopped walnuts
1 cup raisins

Preheat the oven to 350°F. Grease and flour a 10-inch Bundt pan and set aside. In a medium bowl, combine the flour, baking powder, salt, cinnamon, cloves, and nutmeg. Set aside. In a large bowl, cream together the shortening and sugar using a handheld mixer. Beat in the eggs, one at a time. Add the flour mixture alternately with the potatoes and milk. Stir in the walnuts and raisins. Pour into the Bundt pan and bake for about 1 hour and 30 minutes, or until a toothpick inserted in the center comes out clean. Allow the cake to cool completely before inverting onto a serving plate. Slice and serve.

Talk About Luck! Four Leaf Clover Cookies

YIELDS 4 DOZEN

1 cup butter, at room temperature
1 cup confectioners' sugar, sifted
1 large egg
1½ teaspoons peppermint extract

2½ cups all-purpose flour
1 teaspoon salt
2 teaspoons green food coloring
¼ cup superfine sugar (fairy dust)

Preheat the oven to 375°F. In a large bowl, cream the butter with the confectioners' sugar using a handheld electric mixer. Stir in the egg and peppermint extract. Add the flour and salt and mix until a dough is formed. Add the food coloring and work it in until the dough turns green. Line baking sheets with parchment paper. For each cookie, roll 4 small pieces of dough (about ¼ teaspoon each) into little balls. Place together on the prepared baking sheet. Make a little stem by rolling ⅛ teaspoon of dough into a log. Press the cookie together with your fingertips. Make the cookies one at a time so the dough does not dry out. Bake for 8 to 10 minutes. When you remove the sheet from the oven, immediately sprinkle each cookie with a pinch of the superfine sugar. Transfer the cookies to a wire cooling rack to cool completely.

Leprechaun's Delight

SERVES 1

1 cup hot brewed coffee
1 ounce Grand Marnier
1 ounce Irish Cream liqueur

1 tablespoon whipped cream
½ teaspoon grated orange zest

Pour the hot coffee into a mug. Stir in the Grand Marnier and Irish Cream. Top with a dollop of whipped cream and sprinkle with grated orange zest.

The Moorchild by Eloise McGraw

I've always loved a fairy tale. When I was about eight or nine years old, the house that my family and I lived in sat at the edge of the woods. I loved Barbie in those days, as many girls that age do, and one afternoon, in those magical woods by our house I found a Barbie wedding gown in the mud. I brought it home, and my mother washed it for me. I was convinced for the rest of my childhood that a fairy like the ones in *The Moorchild* had left it there and that it was simply a coincidence that it fit Barbie.

I'm pretty sure this miniature wedding dress was the only possession I ever took care of, with the exception of my Cabbage Patch Doll (who came from the magical cabbage patch). Perhaps if my parents had told me that all my possessions came from the fairies in the magical woods, I would have felt a bit more compelled to clean my room on occasion.

So, if you're in the mood for an Irish fairy tale—one that will help you to escape for a day or maybe even inspire you to clean your house—this is a great choice. *The Moorchild* is the winner of the 1998 Parents' Choice Silver Honor Award and the Newbury Honor Award. McGraw weaves together elements of traditional Irish folklore to create a modern fantasy novel that appeals to all ages. The characters are not only complex enough to entertain both adults and children, but McGraw's descriptions of the magical moor and "The Mound" where all of the Moorfolk live are simply enchanting.

Up for Discussion . . .

- Does the fact that this book was written for children affect the lessons it aims to teach? How? Do the lessons apply to adults as well?

- Why do a variety of cultures use fairy tales and fables to teach children lessons? If you are a parent, what stories or fairy tales have you used to help teach your children? What stories or fairy tales were your favorites as a child?

- Would you rather live among "The Folk" or among the people of the village? Why didn't Saaski want to stay in the mound at the end? Do you think she could have stayed?

- The "glamourie" was a magical spell that made humans see the mound as a rich and magnificent place. Why do you think this spell was put into place? Would you rather see life through the "glamourie," or do you prefer a more realistic view? If you could place the "glamourie" spell on something so that people would see it as rich and magnificent, what would you put it on? Your house? Your cubicle? Yourself?

- Saaski loses herself in playing the bagpipes. What activity do you love so much that you tend to lose yourself in it?

- If you were an adult in the village, what would your reaction be to the children being hateful to Saaski? Why do parents sometimes turn their heads to children being mean to other children?

- Describe some specific situations in which you felt like you were different from everyone else. What did you do about it?

- Why do we sometimes fear people who are different from us? Can you site instances in history in which the fear or mistrust of different cultures brought about disaster or tragedy?

- If you were given magical powers, name three special things that they would enable you to do.

- Ireland is known worldwide for its fairy tales. Why do you think this culture is more focused on tales of magic than most?

A Mid-March Night's Feast

On Midsummer Night's Eve, the moorfolk feast on traditional Irish fare, just like many Americans do every March 17th for St. Patrick's Day. Since *The Moorchild* is such a classic example of Irish folklore—filled with magic, moors, and bagpipe playing—I've included the most classic of all Irish menus so that your group can celebrate Mid-March Night's Eve the way it should be!

Corned Beef and Cabbage with Horseradish Mustard

Okay, don't panic! If you don't want to corn your own beef, just buy the prepared corned beef at the supermarket—in the meat case of your local supermarket you will find beef brisket that has the corning spices right in the package—and just start with the directions after draining the brine, indicated by**.

For the Corned Beef and Cabbage:

1 pound kosher salt
2 gallons water
1 (8-pound) beef brisket, cut in half
6 bay leaves
8 black peppercorns
1 onion, chopped
1 medium cabbage, quartered

1 pound carrots, cut into ½-inch slices
1 turnip, chopped
8 potatoes, peeled and cubed

For the Horseradish Mustard:

1 cup prepared mustard (yellow or brown will do)
1 teaspoon to 1 tablespoon horseradish, according to taste

Combine the salt, 1 gallon of the water, and the brisket in a large stainless steel or cast iron pot. Cover and let sit for 7 days in the refrigerator. (Note: the brisket must be completely submerged, so double the salt and water if necessary.) After 7 days, drain the brine and ** add 1 gallon fresh water, the bay leaves, and peppercorns to the meat in the pot. Place over high heat and bring to a boil. Reduce the heat to low and simmer for 2 hours and 15 minutes to 2 hours and 45 minutes, or until the meat is tender. Add the onion, cabbage, carrots, turnip, and potatoes and continue to simmer for another 45 minutes, or until all the vegetables are tender. Transfer the meat and vegetables to a serving platter. To make the Horseradish Mustard, in a small bowl, combine the mustard and horseradish and serve with the Corned Beef and Cabbage.

Irish Soda Bread

This is my Irish-blooded mother-in-law's recipe—it's about as authentic and as delicious as you can get.

½ cup canola oil, plus some for greasing the baking dish
4 cups all-purpose flour, sifted, plus some for kneading the dough

2 tablespoons sugar
1 teaspoon baking soda
1 cup raisins
1 large egg
1 cup buttermilk

Preheat the oven to 350°F. Grease a 9-inch baking dish and set aside. In a medium bowl, combine the flour, sugar, and baking soda. Add in the oil, using a fork, until coarse crumbs form. Mix in the raisins. In a small bowl, beat the egg and stir in the buttermilk. Gradually add to the flour mixture until a soft dough forms. Turn the dough out onto a lightly floured surface and knead until smooth, about 10 times. Form the dough into an oval and place in the baking dish. Cut a cross in the center using the tip of a sharp knife. Bake for about 50 minutes, or until a toothpick inserted in the center comes out clean. Remove to a wire rack and cool completely. Serve sliced with butter.

Sassy Singletons

It's springtime—time to start dreaming about strappy sandals, flirty sundresses, and tanned legs. What better way to get yourself in the warm weather mood than to flip through the myriad women's magazines that hit the shelves this time of year boasting that they can give you a rock-hard bikini body in just three weeks and revamp your entire summer wardrobe for under $250? As predictable as these glossies are, they always speak to me come April, and my hunch is that they also speak to every woman who can't stand the thought of wearing another black wool suit to work, no matter how flattering the flared pants are.

In the spirit of these sassy magazines—and the notion that we're all a little sassier and sexier in the spring and summer—I've dedicated this chapter to some fabulous books starring feisty female characters. During the first few weeks of spring when the sun isn't yet shining, these lively selections will help your group look ahead to the sunnier and beach-ier days to come, and they'll certainly set the stage for some spirited girl talk.

Confessions of a Shopaholic by Sophie Kinsella

The first time I read this novel, I thought, "Oh my god, this book is about me!" Through the character of Rebecca Bloomwood, Kinsella magnificently reflects the "shopaholic" in all of us—if there weren't so many Rebecca Bloomwoods in the world, it's safe to assume that there wouldn't be so many TV shopping networks, strip malls, or internet boutiques. Sassy girls do often fall prey to becoming shopaholics, but the ones that get themselves out of debt and learn to be sassy *thrifty* girls are the ones to be admired.

Confessions of a Shopaholic was published in 2001, about three years after *Bridget Jones's Diary*, written by Helen Fielding, started the chick lit craze. As in most other chick lit favorites, *Confessions of a Shopaholic* stars flawed but loveable female characters to which the everyday single gal can relate. This one has an especially delightful ending.

Up for Discussion . . .

- Here is the question of the day: cut back or make more money? Which would you prefer? Why?

- If your answer was "cut back," what would be the first things to go?

- If your answer was make more money, how would you do it?

- After the Finnish incident and Luke Brandon luggage shopping disaster, Rebecca needed a little treat to cheer herself up. After a day like that, what would you treat yourself to?

- How would you handle realizing you had just picked out luggage for Luke Brandon's girlfriend?

- Would you (or have you ever?!) date someone because you knew he had money, even though you weren't attracted to him? Would you date someone you were very attracted to, but who had absolutely no money nor hope of ever getting any?

- If you had thirty seconds alone with a millionaire's checkbook, would you peek? Why? What would you say if you got caught?

- Rebecca tries to run from her problems by escaping to her parents' house. If you had to escape, where would you go? Or, how would you find the courage to face the music?

- Rebecca always wanted to be known as "The girl in . . ." (the gray sweater, the white coat, etc.). What would you like to be known as?

- Finish this sentence: If I was given a $10,000 shopping spree I would . . .

Better Than Becky's Homemade Curry

One of my favorite parts of *Shopaholic* is when Becky tries to cut back by making her own "take-away" curry. She spends tons of money on various spices, a gorgeous spice grinder, and all of the other kitchen items she feels are a necessary investment if she's going to start eating at home, and the results are disastrous! For the recipe below, I recommend purchasing the red curry paste, found in the Asian cooking section of most supermarkets. Sure, it's about a four dollar investment, but you'll be sure not to scorch your or your group members' mouths. Also, you won't need to buy the stainless steel spice grinder that you most likely don't have space to store in your kitchen anyhow.

Cut Back Shrimp Curry

Brits love take-away curry just as much as Americans love Chinese take out. If you are trying to cut back yourself and the shrimp is out of your budget, this is just as good with the veggies alone or you can substitute three cooked chicken breasts cut into cubes for the shrimp.

3 tablespoons peanut or sesame oil
4 garlic cloves, finely chopped
2 tablespoons red curry paste
1 (15-ounce) can coconut milk
4 tablespoons oyster sauce
24 large raw shrimp, shells
  removed, with tails intact

Finely grated zest of 3 limes
1 cup chopped fresh basil
4 cups freshly steamed vegetables
  (such as broccoli, snow peas,
  sliced carrots, or diced green
  and red peppers)
6 to 8 cups hot cooked basmati rice

Heat the oil in a large skillet over medium heat. Add the garlic and cook until fragrant, about 1 to 2 minutes. Stir in the curry paste and heat briefly. Stir in 1 cup of the coconut milk and the oyster sauce. Add the shrimp and cook for about 3 minutes, or until the tips turn opaque, turning them over once. Add the rest of the coconut milk and the lime zest. Continue cooking until the shrimp are completely cooked, about 5 to 7 minutes. Stir in the basil and steamed vegetables. Serve immediately over the rice.

Iced Mint Tea

This tea goes best with a pair of strappy sandals and a darling vintage sundress.

8 green tea bags
½ cup sugar
1 cup chopped fresh mint

1 orange, thinly sliced
1 lemon, thinly sliced
Mint sprigs, for garnish

Place the tea bags in a large heat-resistant pitcher, pour in 8 cups of boiling water, and let the tea steep for 5 to 7 minutes. Remove the tea bags with a long-handled spoon and gently stir in the sugar and mint until the sugar is dissolved. Add the orange and lemon slices. Chill for 1 hour. Serve over ice garnished with the mint sprigs.

Headhunters by Jules Bass

*G*oodness gracious, the women in *Headhunters* are sassy *and* desperate!—a combination that guarantees a harebrained, misguided adventure. *Headhunters* tells the story of four middle-aged friends from New Jersey who set their sights on scoring the wealthiest men in the world, by posing as the four wealthiest women in the world. They charge their credit cards to the max; they rent designer clothes and some serious jewels; and they fly to Monte Carlo to live it up until they find their meal-ticket lovers, run out of funds, or get caught! This is one of those great novels that sucks you in quickly yet demands the same amount of brainpower as watching an episode of *The Montel Williams Show*. I've kept the discussion light, and the recipes party style. *This* combination guarantees some rollicking revelry.

Up for Discussion . . .

- Put yourself in these ladies' shoes. Would you have the audacity to pull a stunt like this? What parts of the scam would you be able to pull off? What parts are just too outrageous for you?

- Do you think this stunt would be possible to pull off in real life? List as many ways that you can think of that the girls could have been caught.

- Do you think these men, with their knowledge of the upper crust, would have really fallen for the women's impersonations? What parts of the girls' con could you see right through?

- If this were made into a reality television series, what would you call it?

- Let's take a look at supermodels, movie stars, and socialites—what would happen if you took away all of the glitz and glamour? Would we still admire them in the same way, or do we simply admire what we cannot attain?

- If you thought the love of your life was a millionaire, and he came to you one day and told you he was a doorman, would you stay with him?

- If you had two weeks to live someone else's life, whose would you choose? Why did you choose the person you did? What if you had to swap lives with that person? How do you think he or she would do living your life?

- What do you think of all the profanity used in the book? Does it come with the territory, or was it unnecessary?

A Sassy Salsa Extravaganza

No need to travel all the way to Monte Carlo for a good time—why not just have your fun at home? Here we have four sassy salsas and four classy drinks to get your party going! Serve these salsas up with baskets of tortilla chips.

Strawberry-Tomato Salsa

2 cups quartered strawberries (from about 1 pint whole strawberries)
1 cup quartered red grape tomatoes
½ cup finely chopped red onion
2 tablespoons finely chopped jalapeño chile, seeds removed
¼ cup chopped fresh mint

2 tablespoons chopped fresh cilantro
1 teaspoon grated lime zest
2 tablespoons fresh lime juice
1 tablespoon balsamic vinegar
½ tablespoon coarse salt
¼ teaspoon freshly ground black pepper

Combine the strawberries, tomatoes, red onion, jalapeño, mint, cilantro, and lime zest in a large bowl and set aside. Whisk together the lime juice, vinegar, salt, and pepper in a small bowl and pour over the strawberry mixture. Toss gently to combine. Cover the bowl with plastic wrap and refrigerate for 1 hour before serving.

Apple Salsa

3 tablespoons sugar

1½ tablespoons cider vinegar

2 tablespoons fresh lemon juice

¼ teaspoon red pepper flakes

4 unpeeled apples (use a
combination of apple varieties
to create a unique texture),
cored and chopped

1 tablespoon chopped fresh
oregano

2 to 3 scallions, chopped

Mix all the ingredients together in a large bowl. Cover with plastic wrap and chill for 30 minutes before serving.

Spicy Tomato Salsa

4 medium tomatoes, diced

1 medium cucumber, seeds
removed and diced

¼ cup coarsely chopped fresh
cilantro

1 medium red onion, diced

½ jalapeño chile, seeds removed
and chopped

1 garlic clove, minced

Juice of 2 limes

Gently combine all the salsa ingredients in a large nonreactive bowl and set aside for about 30 minutes for the flavors to combine before serving.

Black Bean and Mango Salsa

2 (16-ounce) cans black beans,
drained and rinsed

1 (11-ounce) can Fiesta corn,
drained

1 (16-ounce) jar prepared salsa
(medium or hot)

¼ to ½ cup chopped red onion

1 handful chopped fresh cilantro

1 mango, peeled, pit removed,
and chopped

1 avocado, peeled, pit removed,
and chopped

Combine all the ingredients in a large bowl. Cover with plastic wrap and chill for 30 minutes before serving.

Gimlet

SERVES 1

3 parts gin
1 part fresh lime juice

Crushed ice
Lime wedge, for garnish

Stir the gin and lime juice together and serve over crushed ice. Garnish with a lime wedge and serve.

Orange Blossom

SERVES 1

3 parts gin
1 part orange juice

Crushed ice
Cherry, for garnish

Stir the gin and orange juice together and serve over crushed ice. Garnish with a cherry and serve.

Bee's Kiss

SERVES 1

1 shot light rum
1 teaspoon honey

1 teaspoon heavy cream
Ice cubes

Shake all the ingredients together with ice. Pour into a chilled glass and serve.

Sweetly Sassy

Nonalcoholic, for your designated driver or expectant group member.

Juice of ½ lime
Ice cubes
Purple grape juice

Ginger ale
Lime wedge, for garnish

Squeeze the lime juice over ice in a tall glass. Fill the glass half full with grape juice and top off with ginger ale. Stir, garnish with a lime wedge, and serve.

Valley of the Dolls by Jacqueline Susann

Sex, drugs, and glamour—is that what we want? According to the list of the best selling books of all time, it is! The *2004 World Almanac* lists *Valley of the Dolls* as the *only* novel on the top ten best selling books of all time list (only nine slots below the Holy Bible) and has sold over sixty million copies since it was first published in 1966. So what's the appeal? Is it the novel's *National Enquirer* tell-all style or the writer's talent? You be the judge! Needless to say, *Valley of the Dolls* is packed, cover to cover, with sassy girls doing fabulous things.

Up for Discussion . . .

- What's the verdict? Why is this such a popular book?

- What did you think of Susann's storytelling ability? How does it compare to other novelists whom you've read?

- Anne, Neely, Helen, and Jennifer's characters were rumored to be patterned after actual celebrities' lives. Can you guess who they were supposed to represent?

- Do you think Anne made a wise decision in leaving Allen Cooper? How would her life have turned out had she decided to marry him? What would you have done in this situation if you were in Anne's practical, but stylish, shoes?

- In order to be creative and talented, do you have to be crazy? Or, does the attention of others force people into self-destructive behavior? Can you think of any other celebrities that are rumored to have similar behavior to Neely? If you were one of these celebrities' personal friend or assistant, what advice would you offer?

- Why do celebrities like Helen and Neely behave so badly?

- Would you be able to survive the Hollywood scene? Would you able to do it sober? How?

- If Neely had abandoned show business after her treatment, do you think her tendency toward self-destruction would have subsided? Why or why not?

- Did Henry give Anne good advice regarding Lyon's affairs? What advice would you have given Anne?

- Why couldn't Jennifer live with only one breast?

- Name as many parts in the book as you can in which vanity and self-ishness played starring roles.

- What do you think will become off Anne? Neely? Lyon? Helen? Baby Jennifer?

Drinks and Dolls

Little bites that fill you up without ruining your figure, and some drinks to take the edge off! The following recipes are perfect for the Swingin' Sixties party girl; they're so easy to prepare that you can actually attend your own party . . . *or*, of course, keep an eye on your philandering husband who may be sneaking off with a starlet at any moment. And in case you're recovering from an alcoholic binge of starlet proportions, I've included a nonalcoholic beverage as well.

Temper Tantrums

1 pound hot Italian sausage
1 pound mild cheddar cheese, shredded

3 cups Bisquick

Preheat the oven to 350°F. Crumble the Italian sausage into a large bowl and mix in the cheese until well incorporated. Then stir in the Bisquick. Roll into 1-inch balls and place on an ungreased cookie sheet. Bake for 10 minutes, or until the sausage is no longer pink. Pierce with party toothpicks and serve.

Smooth as Seconals

1 8-ounce package cream cheese
4 ounces crumbly blue cheese
1 teaspoon Worcestershire sauce

¼ cup sweet pickle relish
¼ cup chopped pecans

Mix together all the ingredients except the pecans in a medium bowl. Form into 1-inch balls and roll in the chopped pecans. Place on a serving plate and chill for at least 30 minutes. Pierce with party toothpicks and serve.

Cover-ups

1 ripe cantaloupe, cut in half and seeds removed

¼ pound prosciutto, sliced wafer thin

Using a melon baller, cut the cantaloupe into balls. Cut the prosciutto into strips and wrap it around the balls. Secure with party toothpicks and serve.

Roll in the Sack

½ cup whipped cream cheese
½ cup prepared Major Grey's Mango Chutney

¼ pound pancetta, thinly sliced

Mix the cream cheese and chutney together in a small bowl. Spread the mixture on the slices pancetta and cut it into ½-inch strips. Roll up the strips and secure with party toothpicks. Chill for at least 30 minutes before serving.

Sweet Success

SERVES 1

Sugar cubes
Orange wedge

Lemon wedge
Iced Champagne

Place a sugar cube in the bottom of a champagne flute. Add 1 small twist of orange and one small twist of lemon. Fill the glass with the champagne and serve.

Opening Night

SERVES 1

1½ ounces light rum
Juice of ½ lime
1 teaspoon honey

Cracked ice
Iced Champagne

Shake the rum, lime juice, and honey with cracked ice. Strain into a highball glass and fill with the champagne. Stir slightly and serve.

Rehab Remedy

SERVES 1

Cracked ice
Splash grenadine
Splash orange juice

7 Up
Cherry, for garnish

Fill a highball glass with cracked ice. Add the grenadine and orange juice, then fill the glass with 7 Up. Garnish with a cherry and serve.

Chocolat by Joanne Harris

*I*f you've seen the Oscar-nominated film *Chocolat* (Miramax, 2000), prepare to be wowed by the book. Although the movie was excellent (it was nominated for five Academy Awards), the book presents a more complex and far more controversial version of the storyline. Both versions are set in a small French village during the season of Lent, but the major difference lies in our protagonist's nemesis: the book portrays the man as a controversial, self-righteous Catholic priest, while the motion picture opts for the more publicly acceptable "evil mayor."

In any case, *Chocolat* (both the book and the movie version) is a whimsical and enchanting story that deliciously explores temptation, indulgence, and hypocrisy with insight and artistry. The story takes place in modern Europe but is set in a lovely old town and retains a charming old world feel. In keeping with this chapter's theme of sassy single gals, Vianne, the proprietress of the chocolate shop, is just about the feistiest character you will ever read about: this outspoken gal spiritedly defends her right to serve chocolate to the ever-craving townspeople—now that's a cause that I can support!

Up for Discussion . . .

- If you were a resident of Lansquenet-sous-Tannes, would you rather go to a party hosted by the boat people or the church people? Why?

- Fear plays a major role in many of the characters' lives. Discuss the following characters' fears and how they affected each. (For example, Caroline had a fear of not being in control. This fear kept her in constant conflict with people and situations that she was not able to control, resulting in a strained relationship with her mother.)

  1. Roux
  2. Curé Reynaud
  3. Josephine
  4. Vianne
  5. Guillaume

- What is one of your hidden fears? How does it affect you?

- Put yourself in Reynaud's shoes. How would you have reacted to the chocolate shop and its owner?

- How would you have dealt with Josephine's husband, Paul-Marie?

- What do you admire most about Vianne?

- Why do you think Vianne wouldn't let Josephine run away from Paul-Marie?

- What do you think of Armande's "send off" party?

- Discuss the dangers and benefits of both self-indulgence and self-denial.

- Why did Reynaud end up gorging himself on the chocolate instead of trashing the shop? What could he have done to prevent himself from doing this?

- Have you ever had any experience with tarot cards? Do you believe in them or not?

- What would you order at La Céleste Praline?

Vianne's Luxuriant Chocolate Delights

At your next reading group get-together, will you be a naughty heathen, or will you be a saint? The choice is yours! This menu includes two decadent chocolate recipes, one for angels and one that's strictly for sinners. Also, if you'd like to serve some fabulous chocolate candy (you'll probably be craving it after reading this chocolate-saturated book), check out the following websites, recommended on the popular show *Food Finds* on the Food Network: coltschocolates.com, moonstruck chocolate.com, and chocolateblablabla.com. According to the show, these rank as some of the best chocolates in the United States.

Chocolate Saint Cake

A chocolate angel food cake with a more saintly calorie and fat count!

For the cake:

1¾ cups granulated sugar
1 cup cake flour
¼ cup Dutch processed cocoa
** powder**
15 large egg whites
½ teaspoon salt
1½ teaspoons cream of tartar
1 teaspoon coffee liqueur

¼ teaspoon vanilla extract

For the cream frosting:

3 tablespoons confectioners' sugar
2 tablespoons Dutch processed
** cocoa powder**
1 cup heavy cream
½ teaspoon crème de cacao

To make the cake: Position a rack in the center of the oven and preheat to 325°F. Combine the granulated sugar, flour, and cocoa in medium bowl and sift twice. In a large bowl beat the egg whites and salt with a handheld electric mixer at high speed until foamy. Sprinkle the cream of tartar over the top and continue beating until stiff peaks form. Gently fold in the dry ingredients until just mixed. Fold in the coffee liqueur and vanilla. Pour the batter into an ungreased 10-inch tube pan and spread evenly. Bake for 60 to 65 minutes, or until a toothpick inserted in the center comes out clean. Invert the pan onto a wire rack and cool completely.

To make the frosting, combine the confectioners' sugar and cocoa in small bowl. In a medium bowl, beat the cream to soft peaks using a handheld electric mixer. Fold in the dry ingredients, then fold in the crème de cacao. Chill for 30 minutes. Frost the cake just before serving.

Devilish Chocolate Dunk

⅔ cup sugar

¼ cup all-purpose flour

¼ teaspoon salt

½ teaspoon ground cinnamon

2 cups milk

4 tablespoons unsalted butter

3 (1-ounce) squares unsweetened
   chocolate, chopped

1 large egg

1 teaspoon vanilla extract

6 bananas, sliced

1 quart strawberries, hulled

1 store-bought pound cake, cut
   into 1-inch cubes

In a medium heavy saucepan, combine the sugar, flour, salt, and cinnamon. Stir in the milk, butter, and chocolate. Place over medium heat and cook, stirring constantly, until chocolate melts and the mixture boils. In a small bowl, beat the egg with a wire whisk. Add a small amount of the hot chocolate mixture to the egg and whisk to slowly raise the temperature of the egg to keep it from scrambling. Slowly pour the egg mixture into the hot chocolate and stir constantly to combine. Reduce the heat to low. Stir the mixture constantly for about 2 minutes (don't let it boil once you've put the egg in it). Remove from the heat and stir in the vanilla. Divide mixture into 8 little bowls and serve with the fruit and pound cake to dip into chocolate.

Forgotten Favorites— Classic Young Reader Novels

After a particularly hard work week, I love relaxing with a favorite book from my childhood. It brings me back to a time when I didn't have to worry about oil changes, getting the central air repaired, or how to invest my retirement funds. With this in mind, I have decided to dedicate an entire chapter to forgotten young reader favorites so that you, too, can escape, if briefly, the pressures of adult life this month.

In rereading several of these selections, I was amazed by how little I actually remembered about the books. Sure, I remembered the main plot and some facts about my favorite characters, but I'd forgotten most other details. When I read the books as an adult, I discovered layers of meaning that I wasn't able to recognize when I was younger, making the reading experience not only nostalgic but intellectually gratifying.

It goes without saying that the books in this chapter are wonderful selections to share with the kids in your life. And, if you're up to it, why not invite one or several of these kids to this month's book club get-together? Including them in the discussion— and creatively explaining to them the connections between the recipes and the books—will help to show them that reading is not just something people do in school, but an activity that can be enjoyed and savored for a lifetime. I've chosen four books that, although they are commonly used in school curriculums, won't leave you feeling like you've just read a children's book. They were written not only for the young reader, but also for the parent or adult that is reading the book to her or with her.

The Wind in the Willows by Kenneth Grahame

The Wind in the Willows is a charmingly simple read filled with wonderful lessons, applicable to both children and adults. From the dutiful friendship shared by Mole and Rat to a seemingly modern "intervention" for Toad, you will surely enjoy the many adventures of these animal characters. Grahame does an excellent job making the characters complex enough for adults to appreciate— you may even be able to liken the members of your group to some of the characters and award them new and irritating nicknames like "Ratty" or "Toadster."

One fact that I find particularly interesting about the author, Kenneth Grahame, is that he was part of the fashionable pagan movement of the late nineteenth and early twentieth centuries. To him, though, paganism simply represented his love for the countryside, an escape from what he referred to as "sordid humanity." So go—escape the "sordid humanity" of your offices, and take a trip to the countryside with Mr. Grahame in *The Wind in the Willows*.

Up for Discussion . . .

- What lessons could you teach a child using *The Wind in the Willows* as a guide? What lessons did you learn, or were you reminded of, as an adult?

- In the very beginning of the book, Mole sets out for a short vacation from his spring cleaning. It is said by our narrator, "After all, the best part of a holiday is perhaps not so much to be resting yourself, as to see all the other fellows busy working." Do you agree or disagree with this observation? What is your favorite part of taking a vacation?

- In the first chapter of the book Mole gets a little overzealous and becomes desperate to steer the boat, then ends up turning it over. He profusely apologizes to Rat, who extends grace so easily that Mole is moved to tears. Then, in the last chapter we see that Badger, Mole, and Rat fight valiantly to save Toad's house without much thanks. What can we learn about the role of grace and forgiveness in friendships from the above examples? Can you share a time when grace and forgiveness played a role in one of your friendships?

- Which animal/character do you most identify with? Why?

- Which one would you want as a best friend? Why?

- Do you have a friend that has similar characteristics to one of these animals? Tell the group about this friend.

- Now it's time to discuss Toad, a very challenging friend! Badger, Rat, and Mole decide to intervene in Toad's life to try to save him from his destructive behavior. How well do you think this technique works? Why? How does their intervention parallel modern day drug and alcohol interventions?

- Toad had many relapses into destructive behavior patterns, even after he escaped from prison. List some of them. Do you think that if there were a sequel to *The Wind in the Willows*, Toad would once again display these behaviors, or do you think that he really was a changed toad?

- What was Toad's greatest vice (besides motor cars)?

- What person or character in modern day society can you compare Toad to?

- In Chapter 2 Toad states, "Live for others! That's my motto in life!" What do you think Toad's real motto in life was? Everyone create a life motto of her own and share it with the group.

Rat's Riverside Picnic

One of my favorite things about *The Wind in the Willows* is all of the picnicking that goes on. My edition of the book has adorable illustrations, and one that I especially love depicts the animals sitting on the fragrant grass down by the riverside with their picnic baskets. For me, a traditional picnic includes fried chicken—served cold. However, since I'm not big on frying chicken in my house (I can't stand the way everything smells like fried food for days on end, and I also have no room in my kitchen to store either a large vat of oil or a fryer), I don't wish those things on you either. Instead, I've chosen some great picnic-style salads that you can serve with fried or roasted chicken from your local supermarket. This is a great way to enjoy your group's company on a weeknight when all of the end-of-the-school-year activities cut your time to a minimum.

Sweet Potato Salad

2 teaspoons salt, plus some for cooking the potatoes
2 sweet potatoes, peeled and cut into 1-inch cubes
1 pound unpeeled baby red potatoes, cut in half
1 pound Yukon gold potatoes, peeled and cut into 1-inch cubes
1 large red onion

1 garlic clove, minced
1 jalapeño chile, seeded and minced
¼ cup fresh lemon juice
1 cup mayonnaise
1 tablespoon curry powder
¼ cup chopped fresh parsley
¼ teaspoon freshly ground black pepper

Bring a large pot of salted water to a boil and boil all the potatoes until tender, 15 to 20 minutes. (Do not overcook the potatoes, or they will not hold up in the salad.) Drain and chill the potatoes overnight.

Place the potatoes into a large bowl. Thinly slice the red onion and place it in a colander. Sprinkle the 2 teaspoons salt over the red onion and let it sit in the colander for 30 minutes to drain. Squeeze the onion to remove excess water and add the red onions to the potatoes. Mix in the garlic, jalapeño, lemon juice, mayonnaise, curry powder, parsley, and pepper and chill for at least 6 hours before serving.

Rich Big Bowl Salad

8 slices bacon
4 cups chopped broccoli

4 cups chopped cauliflower
4 cups chopped celery

2 cups frozen green peas, thawed
1¼ cups sweetened dried
    cranberries
⅓ cup sugar
1¼ teaspoon salt
1 tablespoon plus 1 teaspoon
    white wine vinegar

3 onions, grated
⅓ cup grated Parmesan cheese
1½ cups light mayonnaise
1¼ cups raw Spanish peanuts

Place the bacon in a large, deep skillet. Cook over medium-high heat until evenly brown. Drain on paper towels, crumble, and set aside. In a large bowl, combine the broccoli, cauliflower, celery, peas, and cranberries. In a small bowl, whisk together the sugar, salt, vinegar, grated onions, Parmesan cheese, and mayonnaise. Pour the dressing over the salad; add the peanuts and bacon and toss well. Chill for at least 2 hours before serving.

Blueberry Jell-O Salad

2 (3-ounce) packages blackberry
    Jell-o
2 cups boiling water
1 (15-ounce) can blueberries in
    light syrup
1 (8-ounce) can crushed
    unsweetened pineapple,
    drained, with juice reserved

1 (8-ounce) package cream cheese,
    softened
½ cup sugar
1 cup sour cream
½ teaspoon vanilla extract
½ cup chopped pecans

Place the gelatin in a large bowl and pour the boiling water over it to dissolve. Drain the liquid from the canned blueberries and pineapple into a measuring cup and add enough water to make 1 cup of liquid. Stir the juice mixture, blueberries, and crushed pineapple into the gelatin and pour into a 2-quart mold. Refrigerate until firm, about 3 hours. In a medium bowl, mix together the cream cheese, sugar, sour cream, and vanilla and spread over the gelatin mixture. Top with the chopped pecans. Chill for about 30 minutes, then invert and serve.

Treasure Island by Robert Louis Stevenson

Treasure Island is the quintessential pirate novel: mysterious treasure chests, the peg-legged Long John Silver and his parrot, mutineers, and plenty of action—it's all there, making this one of the greatest sea adventure tales ever written. I think the reason this book has remained so popular with young readers is that it's an exquisite imagination stimulator—after all, Stevenson was inspired to write it when his stepson challenged him to write something "interesting." Thus, you won't find much symbolism or metaphor in this one, only page-turning action. I actually never read this when I was young because I thought it was too much of a "boy book," but I loved it so much as an adult that I now wish that I had borrowed it from my brother.

Up for Discussion . . .

- Name as many modern-day references to the characters and events of *Treasure Island* as you can. Start with the restaurant Long John Silver's.

- If you found a treasure map, would you put your life on hold to go on an adventure to find the treasure? Would you tell anyone? Who would you tell? Who would you take with you?

- If you had to write a sequel to *Treasure Island*, what would happen to Jim? Long John Silver? Would you have Jim or Long John Silver go back to retrieve the rest of the treasure?

- What would it be like at your place of employment if your coworkers had "pirate mentality" and you could trust no one? Would you be a mutineer?

- In what ways do you think Long John Silver served as a role model for Jim?

- What does Jim gain from his relationship with Long John Silver?

- How would the story be different had Jim's father not died?

- Why does Jim focus on the design and nationality of the coin rather than the value of the treasure?

- *Treasure Island* has always been spun as a classic "boy's book"—how is it also appealing to a female audience? Describe how modern girls are more likely to relate to the characters in the book than girls growing up in the 1930s.

Argh . . . A Hearty Fish Pasta Matey!

I don't think that I would want to get the recipes for *anything* served on a pirate ship, for obvious reasons. So, instead, I chose a great one-dish salmon pasta to go along with the sea theme of *Treasure Island*. This is my husband's favorite fish dish—I make it at least once a month. You will be surprised at how quickly this comes together, even though it tastes like you've slaved over it all day! And unlike most fish dishes, this pasta makes great leftovers. Serve this dish with a fresh loaf of crusty bread and butter and a tossed green salad.

Creamy Salmon Pasta

2 tablespoons extra-virgin olive oil

1½ pounds salmon fillets, skinned (you can have this done at the fish counter of your local supermarket) and cut into medium-size chunks

1 large sweet onion, chopped

1 large carrot, grated

1 large garlic clove

¼ cup chicken broth (or substitute white wine)

1 tablespoon butter or margarine

2 tablespoons plus 1 teaspoon all-purpose flour

2 cups 1% lowfat milk

3 tablespoons cooking sherry (or substitute white wine)

Juice of 1 lemon

1 tablespoon dried dill

Grated zest of 1 lemon

Salt and freshly ground black pepper to taste

½ cup sour cream (you can use fat free; it works just as well as full fat)

10 to 12 ounces hot cooked spaghetti (you can also use linguine)

Lemon wedges, for serving

Heat the oil in a large skillet over medium heat. Cook the salmon chunks for 8 to 10 minutes, turning them over once. Remove the salmon from the skillet and reserve. In the same pan, add the onion, carrot, garlic, chicken broth, and butter. Cook for about 6 minutes, stirring frequently. Stir in the flour to make a smooth paste. Gradually whisk in the milk—make sure you stir constantly to keep the mixture smooth. Add the sherry and lemon juice, continuing to stir constantly until both are incorporated. Add the dill, lemon zest, salt, and pepper. Simmer for 4 to 6 minutes, stirring constantly, until the sauce thickens. Flake the salmon and gently fold it into the sauce. Stir in the sour cream. Reduce the heat to low and cook for an additional 5 minutes. To serve, divide the pasta into individual bowls and spoon over the sauce. Serve with lemon wedges.

Anne of Green Gables by L. M. Montgomery

*A*nne of Green Gables, originally published in 1908, is perhaps one of the most widely read young reader novels in North America. On top of that, it's been translated into over seventeen languages, and according to Danielle Allard, author of *Making Avonlea: L. M. Montgomery and Popular Culture*, it sits at the very top of young Japanese girls' favorite books to read (who'd have thought?). Mark Twain referred to Anne's character as "the dearest and most loveable child in fiction since the immortal Alice," and *I* love this book because Anne tends to speak before she thinks, something that I can closely identify with. Anne also has a keen sense of fashion, always wanting to wear her puffy-sleeved dresses—who can't admire a girl for that? If you've never read *Anne of Green Gables*, you'll be touched by its simplicity and charmed by Anne's vivid imagination and her seemingly uncontrollable tendency to talk.

Up for Discussion . . .

- *Anne of Green Gables* was written almost a century ago, yet it continues to capture the hearts of girls of all ages. What qualities in the writing style or story can explain the universal, timeless appeal of this young adult novel?

- Which personality traits of the young characters in the novel seem different from those commonly found in today's youth? Which seem similar?

- Compare and contrast Marilla's relationship with Anne to Matthew's relationship with Anne. How did each relationship change as Anne matured?

- The role of women in society is a common theme throughout the book. How does Anne's upbringing with the Cuthberts parallel society's perception of women? (Keep in mind that the arrival of Miss Stacy as the first woman teacher in Avonlea is referred to as a "dangerous innovation" by Mrs. Lynde at the end of Chapter 22.) Do the Cuthberts allow Anne to grow beyond the normal barriers of women at that time?

- Throughout the novel, Anne often compares her clothing to that of her friends and other people in town. What does fashion represent to Anne and why is it so important to her?

- Discuss the development and progression of Anne's independence, beginning with her arrival at Green Gables, continuing through her friendships at school, and ending with her move to town to attend Queen's. How does she progress beyond what would be expected of someone who spent most of her life without strong family support?

- Anne has a fascination with imagination, and with helping others to develop a vivid one. How did Anne's imagination benefit her? How did it cause problems?

- Why is it so important to Anne that everyone spells her name with an "e" at the end? Why does her name mean more to her than to other characters in the book?

- Describe Anne's relationship with Gil Blythe. What is the turning point in the book in which her feelings toward him soften?

- The story of *Anne of Green Gables* has been seen on the movie screen in many different versions, including several cartoon versions. If you have seen any of these, how much of the original story is typically preserved? What other book-based movies have you seen, and which did you prefer, the book or the movie?

Use the Raspberries for Cooking— Not for Drinking!

Anne and Diana get themselves in a bit of a pickle when Diana drinks the raspberry cordial. In honor of her unexpected inebriation, I've compiled some great dishes with the raspberry taking center stage. While we'll be using the berries to enhance the taste of our meal instead of using them to get drunk, if you're really feeling in the spirit of the book and wish to follow Diana's lead, be my guest!

Chicken Salad with Raspberry Vinaigrette

For the raspberry vinaigrette:

1 cup extra-virgin olive oil
1 cup raspberry wine vinegar
½ cup sugar
¼ cup Dijon mustard
½ teaspoon dried oregano
Salt and freshly ground black
    pepper to taste

For the chicken salad:

4 pounds cooked chicken, cut into
    bite-size pieces

1 large red onion, diced
4 large celery stalks, diced
3 unpeeled Granny Smith apples,
    cored, seeded, and diced
¼ cup unsalted sunflower seeds
½ cup chopped walnuts
8 cups baby field greens
1 cup crumbled Danish blue
    cheese

To make the raspberry vinaigrette: In a jar with a tight fitting lid, combine the oil, vinegar, sugar, mustard, oregano, salt, and pepper. Shake well.

To make the chicken salad: Combine the chicken, red onion, celery, apples, sunflower seeds, and walnuts in a large bowl. Pour enough dressing over the mixture to lightly coat but not drench. Toss lightly. Reserve the extra dressing to serve on the side. Serve the chicken salad over the baby field greens and sprinkle with the blue cheese. Don't forget the dinner rolls and butter!

Delicious Dinner Rolls

2 teaspoons active dry yeast
2½ cups lukewarm milk
2 tablespoons sugar
6 cups all-purpose flour, plus some
   for kneading the dough and

dusting the pans
½ teaspoon salt
¼ cup butter, melted and cooled,
   plus some for greasing the bowl
   and pans

In a small bowl, dissolve the yeast in the milk and add the sugar. In a large bowl, sift the flour and salt together and stir in the butter. Add the yeast mixture to the flour mixture, then turn out onto a floured counter and knead until the dough is smooth and elastic, about 2 to 3 minutes. Place the dough in a greased bowl, cover with a clean towel, and let rise in a warm, draft-free place for 45 minutes until doubled in size. Preheat the over to 425°F. Grease and flour two 9-inch square pans and set aside. Turn the dough out onto a freshly floured board and shape into 18 balls. Place the dough balls into the pans and cover with a towel. Let them sit for another 15 minutes to rise again. Bake for 15 to 20 minutes, or until browned and puffed. Split the rolls open and serve warm.

Raspberry Chocolate Bars

Serve these rich bars with a pot of fresh coffee.

1 cup all-purpose flour
¼ cup confectioners' sugar
½ cup butter
½ cup raspberry jam
3 ounces cream cheese, softened
2 tablespoons milk

1 cup white chocolate chips
2 (1-ounce) squares semisweet
   chocolate
1 tablespoon vegetable
   shortening

Preheat the oven to 375°F. Lightly spoon the flour into measuring cup and level it off. Combine the flour and sugar in a large bowl. Cut in the butter with a fork and mix well. Press the mixture into a 9-inch square pan. Bake for 15 to 17 minutes, or until lightly brown. Allow to cool completely.

To make the fillings, spread the jam evenly over the baked crust. In a small bowl beat the cream cheese and milk together until smooth. Melt the white chocolate chips in a small saucepan over low heat and add to the mixture. Beat until smooth. Drop the cream cheese mixture by teaspoons evenly over the jam. Spread carefully and refrigerate for at least 2 hours.

To make glaze topping, cut the chocolate squares into small pieces and melt with the shortening in a small saucepan over low heat, stirring constantly. Spread over the white chocolate layer. Cool completely. Cut into bars and store in refrigerator.

A Tree Grows in Brooklyn by Betty Smith

*I*n 1943, the year this book was published, everyone was reading it. My guess is that during the cold, dark days of World War II, the country welcomed a novel as uplifting and triumphant as this. Betty Smith tells the compelling story of Francie Nolan, a resilient and introspective girl, as she grows up in the early part of the twentieth century in Brooklyn, in a family that struggles with poverty, a common literary theme in those days. It's a classic for school reading because it demonstrates how having values and strong personal character will help you triumph over adversity. Oprah Winfrey has it on her list of the ten books that have deeply affected her life, and the New York Public Library ranks it among the best books of the twentieth century. This is Smith's first and most beloved book.

Up for Discussion . . .

- Describe—using only one word—each of the following characters in the Nolan family: Francis's mother, father, brother Johnny, Katie, Francie, and Neely. For each character, why did you select the word you did?

- How does Francie's love of reading affect her life?

- Young Francie recognizes that she is poor, and she views this with a degree of acceptance. What makes her sad about being poor? Where does she still find joy in her life?

- Why did the Union mean so much to Johnny Nolan? What role did it have in his decline?

- What character outside of the Nolan family did you find most interesting or amusing? How does that character affect the members of the Nolan family?

- How does Smith deal with sexuality in this book without using the graphic descriptions found in some contemporary fiction?

- Why do you think pride is so important to the Nolans? How do they (occasionally) have to compromise their pride in order to survive?

- What qualities of Francie's character are developed early in her life? How do those qualities provide her the strength to triumph in the end?

- Describe the relationship between Francie and Neely. How do they support each other through childhood?

- Why is owning property and being educated so valued by the Nolan family? Do we, in contemporary society, value both as much as they did?

- How is Francie like the Tree that Grows in Brooklyn, the "Tree of Heaven"?

- Why do you think this book made Oprah's top ten list of most inspirational books?

Hard Times Brooklyn Buffet

The Nolans didn't have much, but they made do with what they did have. Here is a supper they might have enjoyed on a regular basis—it can be made with just some meaty soup bones and a stale baguette. The results are a hearty beef barley soup with delicious, giant garlic Parmesan croutons for dipping.

"Nothing But Bones"
Beef Barley Soup

2 beef soup bones
2 tablespoons kosher salt
5 stalks celery, chopped
1 onion, chopped
1 bouquet garni (3 stalks fresh parsley, 1 sprig fresh thyme, 1 sprig fresh rosemary, and 1 large bay leaf tied together with kitchen string)

½ teaspoon freshly ground black pepper
½ pound baby carrots
¼ cup chopped fresh parsley
11 garlic cloves, peeled and halved
1 cup barley
Stale Bread Soup Croutons (recipe follows)

Place the beef bones in a slow cooker. Add the salt, celery, onion, bouquet garni, pepper, carrots, parsley, and garlic. Fill the slow cooker within 2 inches of the top with hot water and cook on high heat for 6 hours, covered, stirring occasionally. Add the barley and cook for 2 more hours, stirring occasionally, until the meat can easily be removed from bones. Remove and discard the bouquet garni. Transfer the bones to a cutting board and remove the meat from the bones, being careful not to take off cartilage or gristle. Place the meat back into the soup, stir, and serve with Stale Bread Soup Croutons.

Stale Bread Soup Croutons

1 baguette (day old is fine)
½ cup olive oil
Salt and freshly ground black pepper to taste

½ cup grated Parmesan cheese
1 tablespoon garlic powder

Preheat the oven to 400°F. Using a sharp serrated knife, slice the baguette into ¼-inch rounds. Place a single layer on a parchment paper–lined baking sheet. Brush each bread round with oil, season with salt and pepper, sprinkle on Parmesan cheese, and top with a pinch of garlic powder. Place in the oven and bake for about 5 minutes, or until golden brown. Watch carefully—the croutons burn quickly if you forget about them! Serve with the Beef Barley Soup.

 ## Something Borrowed, Something Blue

Now that I've been married for over seven years, I can finally laugh at myself and the many others who have been—or are currently—caught up in bridal hysteria. I am amazed by the ever-expanding genre of magazines, websites, and books (both fiction and nonfiction) devoted to the wedding fantasy of young women, preying on the female desire for a fairy tale and calling out to engaged brides-to-be: *your wedding will be a disaster if you don't buy me now!*

My February wedding was supposed to be small and simple, but, as weddings are prone to do, it quickly turned into a three-ring circus. Thankfully, my sister-in-law Debbie helped me retain my sanity throughout the planning stages by inviting my now-husband, Jim, and me over for drinks (strong drinks) on a regular basis. Debbie was also the one to arrive at the church with the two things every bridal emergency kit should be equipped with: a bottle of white wine and a plastic cup. She helped me to laugh off things like my six-year-old cousin Madeline stubbornly and loudly appointing herself flower girl at the last minute, complete with plans to use my toss bouquet, or the fact that the priest refused to sign the marriage certificate because I hadn't written two checks, one for the church and one for the organist. My wedding was such a whirlwind that, like many brides, I didn't even eat at my reception. When Jim and I got home at 3 A.M., I actually cooked us dinner while he opened the cards. That is my favorite memory of my wedding day.

So, now that the chaos has long been put behind me and I realize that marriage is a lot more fun than the wedding itself, I can objectively provide some great wedding-related selections for those of you who are tying the knot, who have tied the knot, who *want* to tie the knot, or who have recently survived being a bridesmaid.

Diary of a Mad Bride by Laura Wolf

*T*his book is perfect for any bride-to-be (and her close friends and relatives) who is irrationally blinded by the stress of planning a wedding while working a full-time job. I remember it well: the seven-page lists, the temper tantrums over the most miniscule details, and the realization after the event that *no one even noticed that I bought the envelopes lined with Japanese lace!* (I actually cried over wanting this lace, and my husband nearly had a heart attack when he saw how much I spent on it. . . .)

Diary of a Mad Bride is, as you would suspect, written in diary format, which makes it easy to read and also allows the reader a voyeuristic glance into the protagonist's life. Throughout the book, we travel alongside Amy Sarah Thomas, the bride-to-be and a magazine editor residing in New York City, as she discovers that everything she needs for her wedding is way overpriced and out of her reach, and that there is inevitably never enough time (or money) to create a wedding as perfect as the ones described in the popular wedding manuals. I especially loved reading Amy's notes from the middle of the night. (Anyone who has ever planned a wedding knows about the crazies that strike in the wee hours of the morning.) *Diary of a Mad Bride* is a light, fun, fictional read that you can finish in a weekend.

A note: The author, Laura Wolf, followed this novel with Diary of a Mad Mom-to-Be, *which stars the same main character from* Mad Bride *(Amy Sarah Thomas). Instead of imbuing her with wedding hysteria, though, she gives her the baby crazies. A great follow-up for any expectant newlywed!*

Up for Discussion . . .

- Did you find the book's diary format enjoyable or distracting? What about the footnotes?

- Take a look at Amy's wedding to-do list (look only at the longest version—it should have seventy items on it). With your group, go through all seventy items (if you have the patience) and decide which items would stay on the list if you were planning a wedding on a budget, and which items you wouldn't bother with. Discuss some of the items you crossed off the list. Why did you think these items weren't necessary? What items would you keep on the list if you had an unlimited amount of money?

- Have you ever been in a situation in which your boss asked you to assist him/her with his/her personal affairs? Did you do it? If you were Kate, would you have reacted as she did toward Amy? How would you have acted differently? Have you ever asked your assistant at work to help you with personal tasks?

- If you were Amy, how would you have handled the delicate wedding dress issue? Would you have had the courage to tell your mother that it was the ugliest dress you had ever seen? What would you have done after you found out she also offered it to your sister, who refused to wear it?

- Shoes were the hardest thing for Amy to choose. What wedding-related decision would you spend (or did you spend) the most time on? The food? The dress?

- Amy's grandmother is obviously trying to make the whole wedding experience difficult for Amy. Why? How should Amy have handled her grandmother's antagonism from the beginning? Has anyone in your family (including in-laws) tried to steal the show on your big day?

- Lucy is Amy's favorite relative—she stands by Amy throughout the entire wedding experience and gives her levelheaded advice when she needs it most. Do you have a friend or relative like Lucy? How has she or he come to your aid in the past?

- Amy has some interesting stress-related dreams leading up to her nuptials. What do you think they meant? If you had such dreams, to whom could you confide in about them? When you are under extreme stress, what do you dream about? Missing final exams? Showing up naked on the first day of school or work?

- Amy is very disturbed by the memory of the girl in her freshman English class who married just for the sake of wanting to be married.

Does this thought/situation disturb you as well? Explain to the group.

- When shopping for my wedding dress, there was a girl in the dressing room next to mine who was also trying on wedding dresses. The girl confessed to me, though, that she was single, with no potential groom candidates; she simply wanted to have her dress ready when the time came. Why do you think some women do this? Analyze and explain to the group.

- Mandy is a bridesmaid of superhuman proportions. How would Amy have survived without her? What are some major predicaments Mandy bailed her out of? If you needed a guerilla-warfare maid of honor, who would you chose? Why? Who would be the worst candidate for the job?

Jeb's Crazy Indian Wedding Feast

When Amy can't scrounge up the funds to hire a proper caterer, Lucy suggests Jeb, a culinary renegade who will make Amy's wishes of an interesting Indian-themed wedding menu come true. What follows are my favorite Indian dishes, both to prepare and eat. Look past the glass-jarred spice section in your supermarket for these spices—if you cruise over to the specialty foods section, you will most likely find either bulk spices or little cellophane bags filled with spices. Although theses bags will not keep fresh in your pantry for long (making them loads cheaper than the glass jarred variety), they do the job just fine when you need several spices for one menu and don't feel like forgoing a week's worth of groceries for expensive jarred spices you won't use everyday.

Kesari Bhaat (Sweet Saffron Rice)

¾ teaspoon saffron threads
3 cups plus 2 tablespoons boiling
    water

2 tablespoons butter, melted
6 cardamom pods, bruised with a
    blunt object (but not crushed)

6 whole cloves
1 cinnamon stick
¾ teaspoon black peppercorns
2½ cups jasmine rice
Finely grated zest of 1 orange
1 cup freshly squeezed orange
   juice

1 teaspoon salt
2 tablespoons golden raisins
2 tablespoons sliced blanched
   almonds
2 tablespoons pistachio halves

Soak the saffron in 2 tablespoons of the boiling water for 10 minutes (allow the remaining 3 cups water to cool slightly). Heat the butter in a large heavy saucepan over medium heat. Add the cardamom, cloves, cinnamon, and peppercorns and sauté for 2 minutes, or until fragrant. Add the rice and sauté for 2 minutes, stirring constantly to mix well. Add the remaining 3 cups hot water, the orange zest, orange juice, salt, saffron, and saffron water. Stir well and bring to a boil. Cover, reduce the heat to low, and cook for 12 minutes, or until the liquid is absorbed and the rice is tender. Scatter the raisins over the rice, cover, and cook for 2 minutes more. Transfer to a serving dish. Garnish with the almonds and pistachios and serve.

Cucumber Raita

This is served on the side as a condiment to cool your mouth when necessary.

½ cucumber
1 green chile, seeded and finely
   chopped

1¼ cups plain yogurt
¼ teaspoon salt
¼ teaspoon ground cumin

Dice the cucumber finely and place it in a medium bowl, then stir in the chile. Beat the yogurt with a fork until smooth, then stir into the cucumber and chile mixture. Stir in the salt and cumin. Cover and chill before serving.

"Rogan Josh" (Curried Lamb)

3 tablespoons fresh lemon juice
1 cup plain yogurt
1 teaspoon salt
2 garlic cloves, crushed
1-inch piece ginger root, grated
2 pounds lamb, cut into 1-inch
   stew cubes
4 tablespoons olive oil
½ teaspoon cumin seeds

2 bay leaves
4 cardamom pods
1 onion, finely chopped
2 teaspoons ground coriander
2 teaspoons ground cumin
1 teaspoon cayenne pepper
1 (14-ounce) can diced tomatoes
2 tablespoons tomato paste
⅔ cup water

In a large bowl, combine the lemon juice, yogurt, salt, 1 garlic clove, and ginger. Add the lamb cubes and place in the refrigerator to marinate overnight.

Heat the oil in a large skillet over medium heat. Cook the cumin seeds for about 2 minutes, or until they start to sputter. Add the bay leaves and cardamom pods and cook for another 2 minutes. Add the onion and remaining garlic clove and cook for 5 minutes, or until the onion is soft and translucent. Stir in the ground coriander, ground cumin, and cayenne and cook for 2 minutes. Add the marinated lamb and cook for 5 minutes, stirring occasionally. Add the tomatoes, tomato paste, and water. Bring to a boil, cover, and reduce the heat to low. Simmer for 1 hour, or until the meat is tender. Serve with rice.

Burfi (Sweet Nut and Milk Cake)

This is one of my favorite exotic desserts. I first had it at an Indian restaurant when I was a little girl. At the time, I ordered it because I thought it had a funny name; once I tasted it, though, I fell in love with it!

½ (4 tablespoons) stick butter
1 (13-ounce) can evaporated milk
1 cup ground almonds

1 cup ground unsalted cashews
1 cup sugar

Melt the butter in a large heavy skillet over medium heat. Add the evaporated milk. Bring to a boil, stirring constantly. Reduce the heat to low and cook until the milk thickens, about 3 to 5 minutes. Add the almonds, cashews, and sugar and continue to stir constantly. Cook for 10 minutes. Pour the mixture into a shallow dish and spread evenly with the back of a spoon. Allow to cool, then cut into small squares and serve.

Lucy Sullivan Is Getting Married

by Marian Keyes

*D*on't let the pink cover and cutesy title fool you—this book actually has substance. It's far more realistic than most "chick lit" tends to be, as it tackles topics such as alcoholism and clinical depression with sensitive humor. The plot is kicked into action when Lucy and her girlfriends visit a fortune-teller who predicts that Lucy that will be married within the year. When her other friends' predictions start to come true, Lucy understandably begins to wonder about her own. The combination of silly and serious in this book makes it a highly memorable read.

Up for Discussion . . .

- In the opening chapter of the book, Lucy and her friends prepare for a trip to the fortune-teller. Lucy states that this "was the kind of thing [she and her friends] did, even though [none of them] believed the fortune-tellers. At least none of [them] would admit to believing them." Have you or someone you know had any experience with fortune-tellers or psychics? What happened?

- Do you think that a person's destiny can be changed by what he or she hears about the future, regardless of whether this individual believes that the psychic powers of fortune-tellers are real? How? Why do you think some people consult psychics on a regular basis?

- Chapter 1 closes with Lucy reflecting on nice guys and not-so-nice guys. She decides that "it's (nearly as) bad when the guy you thought was an unreliable heartbreaker turns out to be uncomplicated and nice." Does this accurately describe her relationship with Daniel? At what point does he go from "heartbreaker" to "uncomplicated and nice"?

- This book vividly shows us how rumors can get started and spread at a frightening pace. Describe Lucy's reaction to the wedding rumor. Would you have reacted differently? How so? Would it have bothered you more or less than it seemed to bother Lucy? Why?

- Describe how Lucy views her relationship with Gus, and contrast that with how it appears Gus views his relationship with Lucy. What compels her to give him one more chance once it becomes clear that he is not relationship material?

- Many of Lucy's decisions are based on how she thinks her roommates will react. Handling the delicate balance between girlfriends and a potential love interest is a task most young women struggle with at some point in their life. Can you point to some situations in which Lucy made sacrifices in order to keep the peace with her girlfriends? Ultimately, do you think she made the best decision for her love life at the expense of friendships, since her friendships often suffered as a result of her love life? What would you have done if you were in her shoes?

- In Chapter 31, Lucy ponders whether honesty is the best policy: "I was all for bluntness. Well actually, that's a complete lie. I thought it was one of the most overrated things I had ever heard of. But Karen behaved as if being blunt was a great virtue, the kindest act she could do for you. Whereas I felt there were some things that didn't need to be said or shouldn't be said." Do you feel that complete honesty is always the right path to take, regardless of how it might be received? Why or why not?

- While the tone of the novel is playful and entertaining, many passages cause the reader to pause and/or to think more deeply about a situation. In Chapter 34, Gus and Lucy are walking through Camden Town and encounter some homeless people. In an effort to help them, Lucy wonders whether it is better to "give all [her] change to one person so that he could do something decent with it like get something to eat or drink, or . . . to share it among as many people as possible so that lots of people get a few pennies." What would you do in a situation in which you were faced with that decision? Why?

- As Lucy waits for a phone call from Gus at the end of Chapter 41, she contemplates the emptiness that she is feeling: "He had come, filled the gap, and when he left, he took more than he arrived with." Do you think that Lucy truly ended up with less as a result of her relationship with Gus? If so, how did that end up being the case? Do you think she ended up with less because Gus took something or because she gave something up?

- Chapter 48 contains some relationship psychology: "Popular myth has it that women are desperate to trap men, that men are afraid of being trapped, so the best way to trap them is to pretend that you don't want to trap them." What truth might there be to this myth? Where and when did this image of women being the aggressive pursuer of relationships originate? In your current relationship were you the pursuer or the pursuee?

- Toward the end of the book, Lucy is thankful to both Gus and her father for "being so horrible to [her]. For pushing [her] into a place where [she] didn't care about them anymore." How did Lucy's negative experiences help to lead her into a positive relationship?

Lucy Sullivan Needs Some Wedding Cake!

Lucy and her friends know how to fight the blues—by eating! Since Lucy is an unusual girl, here are some unusual ideas for "wedding" cakes, or cakes that you can eat while reading and talking about weddings. . . .

Better Than Wedding Cake

1 package devil's food cake mix
1 cup sweetened condensed milk
¾ cup caramel ice cream topping,
   plus some for garnish

3 bars (1.4 ounces) chocolate-
   covered toffee (like Heath),
   chopped
1 (9-ounce) container frozen
   whipped topping, thawed

Bake the cake according to the package directions for a 9 by 13-inch pan and cool on a wire rack for 5 minutes. Using a sharp paring knife, make slits across the top of the cake; make sure not to go through to the bottom. Combine the sweetened condensed milk and caramel topping in a small saucepan over low heat, stirring until smooth and blended. Slowly pour the warm topping over the top of the warm cake, letting it sink into the slits, then sprinkle some of the chopped toffee bars across the entire cake while still warm. Let the cake cool *completely* (if you don't, you will have a whipped topping disaster—and I speak from experience!). Frost with the whipped topping. Garnish the cake with more chocolate toffee bar chunks and swirls of caramel topping. Refrigerate for 1 to 2 hours before serving.

Piña Colada Party Cake

For the cake:

¼ cup vegetable oil, plus some for
   greasing the pans
1 package white cake mix
1 (4-ounce) package instant
   coconut pudding mix
4 large eggs
¼ cup water
⅓ cup dark rum
1 cup flaked sweetened coconut

For the frosting:

1 (8-ounce) can crushed
   unsweetened pineapple in juice
1 (4-ounce) package instant
   coconut pudding mix
⅓ cup dark rum
1 (9-ounce) container frozen
   whipped topping, thawed

To make the cake: Preheat the oven to 350°F. Grease 2 nonstick 9-inch cake pans and set aside. In a large bowl, combine the cake mix, pudding mix, eggs, water, rum, and oil and beat with a handheld electric mixer at medium speed for about 4 minutes, or until well combined. Fold in the coconut. Pour the batter into the cake pans and bake for 25 to 30 minutes, or until a toothpick inserted in the center come out clean. Cool in the pans for 15 minutes, then remove the cakes from the pans and cool completely on wire racks.

To make the frosting: In a medium bowl, combine the pineapple, pudding mix, and rum. Beat with a handheld electric mixer until well blended. Fold in the whipped topping. Frost the cooled cake and serve.

Autobiography of a Fat Bride by Laurie Notaro

This book is a collection of hilarious essays written by Laurie Notaro, humor columnist for the *Arizona Republic*. Notaro's first book, *The Idiot Girl's Action Adventure Club* (also a collection of essays) was published in 2002 and quickly became a bestseller. Notaro writes with hysterical self-deprecating candor, and she has been praised for her ability to relate to the average thirty-something American woman who neither is a size four nor has escaped the phenomenon of adult acne—in other words, most of us!

The essays in this book follow Notaro's bumpy path from "dating to newlywed"—about a two-year journey in all. In the beginning, we learn about Notaro's horrific dating experiences; by the end, we witness her life as a married woman battling plumbing problems. Notaro has a fantastic ability to look at mundane, everyday happenings with outrageous humor. Get out the tissues—I laughed so hard I cried!

Up for Discussion . . .

- What do you think of Notaro's self-deprecating humor? Do you think that one has to have a solid sense of self-esteem to make fun of herself in this way, or do people who are constantly self-deprecating sincerely feel bad about themselves? Is there perhaps a gray area?

- What did you think about the "everything is discussable—even bodily functions" content? Are there any tidbits of information you could have done without, or do you think Notaro manages to successfully pull off talking about anything and everything?

- The dating nightmare stories in this book are of legendary proportions. Which of Laurie's boyfriends did you think was the worst? Why? Everyone has at least one horrific dating or relationship story—share yours with the group!

- Notaro is very open about her relationship with her mother, candidly discussing its ups and downs. Since this is obviously not fiction, what do you think her mother thinks of this book?

- What do you think your daughter or son would say about you if he or she were going to write a book like this? What would you say about your mother or father? How would they react to being a part of a tell-all type book about your family life?

- Would you like to be friends with Notaro? Why or why not? Would you like to be her spouse? Why or why not?

- What makes Notaro and her husband so compatible? Are there aspects of their relationship that are similar to your relationship with your spouse/significant other?

- If you could register for wedding gifts today, what are the top five items you would want? When invited to a wedding, do you typically buy a gift from the registry, pick out a (non-registry) gift yourself, or just give money?

- Notaro points out that we are simply never ready for some aspects of adulthood. What part of adulthood do you find to be the most challenging or tedious, and why? Taxes? Home improvement? Credit ratings?

- What about adulthood do you find to be the most fun? Staying out and up as late as you want? Not having to swim in gym class? Understanding the world more fully than you did as a kid?

- Which of Laurie's anecdotes did you find the funniest? Which one did you most closely identify with?

Cutlet Mania

Laurie boasts that the only wifely skill she possesses is cutlet making. So, the obvious choice of menu for this selection was, of course, cutlets. (I chose

Chicken Piccata because it's my favorite.) Serve this meal with crusty French bread and a bottle of Chardonnay.

Chicken Piccata

16 chicken cutlets (see Note)
Extra-virgin olive oil
Salt and freshly ground black
pepper to taste
1 cup all-purpose flour
1 cup dry white wine
5 garlic cloves, minced

2 cups chicken broth
½ to ¾ cup fresh lemon juice,
according to taste
¼ cup capers, drained
½ cup butter
2 lemons, sliced into thin rounds

Warm about 1 tablespoon extra-virgin olive oil in a large skillet over medium-high heat. Preheat the oven to 300°F and have a 9 by 13-inch baking dish ready to place the cutlets in. Season each cutlet liberally with salt and pepper, then dredge each cutlet in the flour and shake off any excess. When the oil is hot but not smoking, add in as many cutlets as your skillet will allow without having them touch. Sauté the cutlets for about 3 minutes, or until nicely browned, then flip and sauté for about another 2 minutes. Remove the cutlets from the skillet and place in the baking dish, cover with aluminum foil, and place in the oven to keep warm. Add more oil to the skillet if necessary and repeat the sautéing process with the remaining cutlets.

After finishing all the cutlets, deglaze the empty skillet with the wine, stirring constantly. Add the garlic and continue to cook until the wine is reduced by half. Add the chicken broth, lemon juice, and capers. Cook for 3 to 4 minutes, stirring occasionally. Stir in the butter and lemon slices and cook until the butter has melted. Pour the sauce over the warmed chicken cutlets and serve.

Note: To make chicken cutlets, take half of a skinless, boneless chicken breast, remove the tenderloin, and cut it in half. Place the halves between 2 pieces of plastic wrap. Using the smooth side of a mallet (or the bottom of a wine bottle covered in plastic wrap) pound the chicken pieces until they are an even ¼ inch thick all over. This will ensure that they cook evenly.

Lemony Asparagus

2 pounds asparagus (I recommend the very thin ones—I think they taste better)
2 tablespoons extra-virgin olive oil
Juice of 1 lemon
Salt and freshly ground black pepper

2 jarred roasted red peppers, sliced into very thin strips
¼ cup chopped fresh flat-leaf parsley

Preheat the oven to 350°F. Snap the tough ends off of the asparagus and place the stalks in a baking dish. Drizzle the oil and lemon juice over the stalks and season liberally with salt and pepper. Toss to coat. Layer the roasted red pepper strips over the asparagus and place in the oven. Bake for about 15 minutes, or until the asparagus is tender but still retains its bright green color. Toss with the chopped parsley and serve.

Note: You can make this dish before you start the cutlets and then cover with aluminum foil and place in the warm oven with the chicken cutlets until you're ready to serve.

The Princess Bride by William Goldman

I originally chose this book because I've seen the 1987 MGM movie (which I adore) about fifty times. I had always hoped that the movie was based on a book, and I was pleased to learn that it was. Interestingly, though, the only version of the book that is available for sale is an abridged version. The author of this abridged version, William Goldman, says that his father read him the unabridged version when he was a child, and he loved the book so much that, as an adult, he decided to publish the "best parts" version. Goldman also wrote the screenplay for the movie.

According to Goldman, the unabridged version of the book was written by an S. Morgenstern. There is controversy among fans, however, as to whether this S. Mogenstern ever existed—you can search the internet for hours, and you will never find a copy of the "original." If Goldman *did* in fact write the initial *Princess Bride,* the Morgenstern myth only speaks to Goldman's creative brilliance.

The Princess Bride is a classic fairy tale, filled with true love, revenge, good guys, bad guys, miracle makers, and scary creatures—all the components of a modern wedding-planning experience!

Up for Discussion . . .

- What do you think about Goldman's "abridged" version of *The Princess Bride*? Would the story be as good unabridged?

- What did you think about Goldman's "interruptions"?

- Have you ever been in love as deeply as Buttercup and Westley are?

- If you were kidnapped by the Turk, the Spaniard, and the Sicilian, which one would you be the most afraid of? Why?

- Do you think you'd ever want to avenge a loved one's death as Inigo did?

- What do you think about a life devoted only to seeking revenge?

- Have you ever felt the need to seek revenge? Did you get your revenge or did you decide to forgive? In either or both cases, how did you feel afterward?

- What do you think about the book's ending? Does the end ruin the "fairy tale"?

- If Miracle Max offered you one free miracle pill, what would you want it to do?

- If you were Buttercup, would you rather live with the Prince or die with Westley? Why? Could you learn to love the Prince?

- Could you live your life without romantic love? How?

Inconceivable! Frittatas

The frittata is an egg dish similar to an omelet that is popular in Europe and usually eaten as a light supper. Frittatas are not only easy to make but they are also very inexpensive—you can use just about any veggie you have on hand. That said, if you're a crook with no one to plunder, you can still afford to make one or more of these for your hungry group members.

The Sicilian

3 tablespoons olive oil
½ cup chopped red onion
1 cup diced tomatoes
1 large portobello mushroom cap, sliced thin
8 large eggs

½ cup grated Parmesan cheese, plus some for serving
1 tablespoon dried Italian seasoning
1 teaspoon salt
1 teaspoon freshly ground black pepper

Heat the oil in a 12-inch skillet over medium heat. Add the red onions and cook until transparent, 4 to 5 minutes. Add the tomatoes and mushroom slices and cook until just tender, about 3 to 5 minutes.

Meanwhile, in a medium bowl, beat the eggs. Stir in the Parmesan cheese, Italian seasoning, salt, and pepper. Pour the egg mixture over the vegetables in the skillet and gently mix. Cover and cook over medium-low heat until firmly set, 10 to 15 minutes. Remove from the heat. Allow to stand for a few minutes before slicing into wedges and serving. Serve with grated Parmesan cheese.

The Turk

½ cup red onions
3 cups fresh spinach leaves
½ cup pitted and chopped
   kalamata olives
8 large eggs
¾ cup crumbled feta cheese

2 tablespoons fresh oregano
1 teaspoon grated lemon zest
1 teaspoon salt
1 teaspoon freshly ground black
   pepper

Heat the oil in a 12-inch skillet over medium heat. Add the red onions and cook until transparent, 4 to 5 minutes. Add the spinach and olives and cook until just tender, about 1 to 2 minutes.

Meanwhile, in a medium bowl, beat the eggs. Stir in the feta cheese, oregano, lemon zest, salt, and pepper. Pour the egg mixture over the vegetables in the skillet and gently mix. Cover and cook over medium-low heat until firmly set, 10 to 15 minutes. Remove from the heat. Allow to stand for a few minutes before slicing into wedges and serving.

Buttercups

½ cup butter, chilled and cut into
  pieces, plus some for greasing
  the pan
2 cups all-purpose flour, plus some
  for kneading the dough
1 cup yellow cornmeal
3 tablespoons baking powder

½ teaspoon salt
2 tablespoons light brown sugar
1½ cups buttermilk
1 cup finely chopped fresh basil
1 cup frozen corn kernels,
  defrosted and drained
1 cup grated cheddar cheese

Preheat the oven to 400°F. Lightly grease 1 large or 2 medium baking sheets. In a large bowl, stir together the flour, cornmeal, baking powder, salt, and brown sugar. Cut in the butter with a pastry blender until the mixture resembles small crumbs. Add the buttermilk, basil, and corn and stir until just blended. Turn the dough onto a lightly floured surface and knead about 10 times, until the dough no longer sticks. Roll the dough out to a thickness of about 1½ inches and sprinkle it with cheese. Cut the dough into 2-inch rounds using a 2-inch biscuit cutter or 2-inch round cookie cutter, and place them on the baking sheet about 1 inch apart. Refrigerate for 30 minutes to chill the butter in the dough. Bake for about 15 minutes, or until golden brown, and serve warm.

The Spaniard's Sangria

1 lemon
1 lime
1 orange
1½ cups rum

1 (750 milliliter) bottle dry red
  wine
1 cup orange juice
½ cup sugar

Have the lemon, lime, orange, rum, wine, and orange juice well chilled. Slice the lemon, lime, and orange into thin rounds and place them in a large glass pitcher. Pour in the rum and sugar. Chill for 2 hours so the flavors can develop. When ready to serve, crush the fruit lightly with a wooden spoon and stir in the wine and orange juice. Add sugar if necessary to adjust the sweetness to taste.

JULY

✈ Travels to Remember . . . or Forget

My family and I are beach people, and when I was a kid, my parents took my siblings and me on countless road trips every year. Time and time again Mom and Dad would wake us up at 3 A.M., carry us out to our red station wagon, and begin the trek from Western New York to Rehoboth Beach, Delaware; Ocean City, New Jersey; or Emerald Island, North Carolina. Looking back, I have no idea how my parents survived those long trips to the beach. Our station wagon had black vinyl interior—we were always in danger of getting third degree burns on the backs of our thighs—and no air conditioning, and we were usually accompanied by several of my mother's six sisters, their significant others, my cousins, grandparents, and/or assorted family friends. We would all pack into one damp wooden beach house that never had enough bathrooms, beds, or space in general, but we always managed to have the greatest time. On rainy days, my renegade grandmother would let my siblings, cousins, and me eat cookies for lunch and teach us to be proper card sharks by initiating game after game of pinochle and black jack.

These days, between conflicting work schedules, budget constraints, and other roadblocks, the only vacations I take are in my imagination via books. So if you're stuck in your hometown this summer, why not read one of these great travel stories—you can experience faraway places without having to wait in line at the airport, max out your credit cards, or deal with lost luggage!

Travels with Charley

In Search of America
by John Steinbeck

*I*f you've never read a John Steinbeck novel for fear that Steinbeck's style might be a bit heavy for your taste, give *Travels with Charley* a try. The book will give you a glimpse of Steinbeck's distinct and critically praised voice, but the subject matter is a lot lighter than, say, *The Grapes of Wrath*. In *Travels with Charley*, Steinbeck chronicles a cross-country trip that he took in a camper with his dog, Charley. Steinbeck made this trip after publishing most of his popular novels, namely because he felt that he had become disconnected from the America he had written about in his earlier works and saw this trip as a means to reconnect. Critics regard *Travels with Charley* as one of the greatest American travelogues ever written.

Steinbeck made his trip in the 1960s, and in his travelogue he presents an eclectic picture of what life was like in this era. He introduces the reader to people from all walks of life, from eccentric Maine residents who give poor directions, to party-loving Texans. Steinbeck even drives past crowds protesting the historic Brown v. Board of Education outcome.

Up for Discussion . . .

- Why is the travelogue such a popular genre? What other books can you compare this to?

- How has the country changed since Steinbeck wrote *Travels with Charley,* published in 1962?

- Why is there often a letdown near the end of such a trip like Steinbeck's?

- What are some of the predictions Steinbeck makes? Have they come true?

- Where would you go today to find "America"?

- What could you learn on a road trip that you couldn't learn in your own backyard?

- Would you have wanted to accompany Steinbeck on his trip? Why or why not?

- Have you ever read any of Steinbeck's novels? How does *Travels with Charley* compare?

- There's a section in the book in which Steinbeck is staying at a campground owned by a man who is having great difficulty with his son. Steinbeck speaks to the son privately and then convinces the father that it's okay for the son to study hairdressing. Why does Steinbeck get involved? Is his description of the relationship between a woman and her hairdresser accurate? In what ways?

- If Steinbeck mentioned visiting your town or region, or a part of the country that you have visited before, how do you feel about his description of the area? The people? How would you have described the area? The people?

- Share your worst road trip experience with the group, then share your best road trip experience.

- If you were going to be traveling across the United States, what would you want your vehicle to be equipped with? What treasured possessions (like Steinbeck's books) would you want to bring along?

- If you had unlimited resources and space, what luxury items would you want to bring with you on the road?

- What would this trip be like if you took your family pet? If you don't have a pet, what type of pet would you bring with you on a cross-country road trip if you had the chance?

- Would you be able to take the trip by yourself (or, without any human companions . . .) as Steinbeck did, or would you prefer to bring a friend or loved one? If so, who would you bring? If you could pick a celebrity to tour the country with, who would it be and why?

- What would you name your vehicle? Why?

Supper with Charley in Rociante

In *Travels with Charley* Steinbeck is always cooking with the canned goods he packed for his long journey. If you've had a hectic month, the menu below is a great one to choose because the recipes are unbelievably simple, and they call only for canned goods and ingredients that you most likely already have in your house.

Rociante Supper Stew

This is actually what I cooked for my husband after our wedding, after arriving home at 3 A.M. It seems an apt choice for *Travels with Charley*, since it could have been made with the provisions Steinbeck brought along, most of which you'll find in your pantry or freezer.

2 tablespoons olive oil
2 pounds stew beef, cubed
2 (16-ounce) cans stewed
   tomatoes with juice
1 envelope dry onion soup mix
1½ cups water
1 tablespoon chili powder

1 (11-ounce) can Fiesta corn,
   drained
2 large carrots, chopped
2 celery stalks, chopped
2 large unpeeled Russet potatoes,
   diced

Heat the oil and brown the beef cubes in a large skillet over medium-high heat. Add the stewed tomatoes, onion soup mix, water, and chili powder and stir until well combined. Reduce the heat to low and simmer for about 30 minutes, or until beef is cooked through, stirring occasionally. Add corn, carrots, celery, and potatoes, cover, and cook for about 45 minutes, or until nicely thickened. Serve with crusty bread and a salad.

Canned Cobbler

¼ cup butter, melted
1½ cups sugar
1 cups all-purpose flour
2 teaspoons baking powder
¾ cup milk

1 (16-ounce) can pitted sour pie
cherries (you can find them in
the canned fruit aisle in your
local supermarket)
Whipped cream, for serving

Preheat the oven to 325°F. Pour the melted butter into an 8-inch square baking pan. In a medium bowl, combine 1 cup of the sugar, the flour, baking powder, and milk. Stir until well blended. Pour over the melted butter in the baking pan—do not stir. Pour the can of cherries, including all the juice, on top of the flour mixture—again, do not stir. Sprinkle the remaining ½ cup sugar over the cobbler. Bake for 1 hour, or until the cobbler is golden brown on top. Serve warm, with whipped cream.

Coffee Without the Coffeemaker

SERVES 8

¼ cup instant coffee
½ cup boiling water
½ cup honey

1½ cups cold water
Milk, to top off

Dissolve the instant coffee in a small saucepan with the boiling water. Stir in the honey and mix well. Add the cold water and pour over ice in 8 glasses. Top off with milk.

The Story of a Shipwrecked Sailor

by Gabriel García Márquez

I couldn't possibly write a travel chapter without including a book about a journey gone awry. If you've never read anything by this Nobel Prize–winning author, *The Story of a Shipwrecked Sailor* is a great place to start. Much like *Travels with Charley* by Steinbeck, this is probably García Márquez's lightest work, but his brilliance and talent are still vividly apparent. García Márquez originally wrote this tale in 1955 as a series for the Columbian newspaper *El Espectador*, before he became a world famous author, and it wasn't published as a book until 1970, after he'd become very successful. García Márquez did not view the book's publication as any cause for celebration; he felt that it was published not for its quality, but simply because he was a celebrity author.

García Márquez masterfully tells this story—so well, in fact, that I had a hard time putting it down. And if you ever go on a cruise and something Titanic-like happens, this story will have taught you many survival tips for being lost at sea!

Up for Discussion . . .

- Would you be able to survive ten days alone at sea?

- If you were Luis, what would the scariest moment of this journey have been for you?

- If you had to spend ten days alone at sea, what four things (or people) would you want on the boat with you?

- What if you could only have three of these four items (or people)—which ones would you choose? What if you could only have two? Only one?

- Why did Luis kill the seagull? Do you think he will always regret killing it?

- Luis said that he had a strange premonition that something wasn't right. Have you ever had an experience when you felt that something wasn't quite right? What happened?

- When people who are alone at sea have hallucinations, do they have them because they are going mad, or do the hallucinations cause them to go mad?

- Every time Luis describes a new day, he begins by saying, "My third (or fourth or fifth, and so on . . .) day was one of hunger, thirst and desperation." How did he find the strength to go on when every day and night began and ended the same?

- Which do you think was worse for Luis, the day or the night? Which would have been the worst for you?

- After spending ten days at sea with no food, what would be the first thing you would want to eat? Who would be the first person you would want to see?

A Welcome Home Feast

Luis didn't eat much in this story, but we can imagine he had an incredible welcome home feast. Paella is a traditional Hispanic meal, often served at family celebrations, and it is cooked in homes from South America to Central America to Spain, the recipe often varying a bit from region to region. Serve it with warm crusty bread with butter.

Paella

¼ cup extra-virgin olive oil
1 tablespoon balsamic vinegar
2 garlic cloves, minced
1 teaspoon dried marjoram, crumbled
1 teaspoon dried thyme, crumbled
¼ teaspoon salt
½ teaspoon freshly ground black pepper
1 whole chicken (about 2½ pounds), cut into serving pieces
1½ pounds unpeeled medium shrimp
Meat from one 2-pound lobster, chopped
½ pound sea scallops
2 chorizos or hot Italian sausages
1 onion, chopped

½ cup drained chopped canned tomatoes
2 tablespoons capers, rinsed
1 teaspoon saffron threads, crumbled
1 teaspoon sweet paprika
3½ cups chicken broth
½ cup dry white wine
2½ cups uncooked long grain rice
Salt and freshly ground black pepper to taste
1 unpeeled head of garlic
1 pound mussels, scrubbed and debearded
16 to 20 small clams, scrubbed
½ cup frozen peas
1 (4-ounce) jar of pimentos, drained

Combine 1 tablespoon of the oil, the vinegar, garlic, marjoram, thyme, salt, and pepper in a small bowl and rub onto the chicken pieces. Let the chicken stand for at least 30 minutes, or up to 24 hours in the refrigerator.

Heat 1 tablespoon of the oil in a large skillet (or paella pan, if you have one) over medium heat until hot but not smoking. Add the shrimp and sauté for 2 minutes, or until just firm and opaque. Remove and reserve (peel and devein the shrimp, if desired). Add another tablespoon of the oil to the skillet and sauté the lobster pieces for about 2 minutes, then remove from the skillet and reserve. Add the remaining tablespoon oil and sauté the scallops for 3 minutes, or until opaque. Remove them and reserve. Add the sausages and sauté for 15 minutes, or until cooked through. Remove them from the pan, cool slightly, slice, and reserve.

Add the chicken pieces to the pan and cook for about 8 minutes, turning frequently, until browned all over. Stir in the onion, tomatoes, capers, saffron, and paprika. Stir in the chicken broth, wine, rice, salt, and pepper. Wedge the unpeeled garlic head into the center of the pan. Bring to a simmer, reduce the heat to low, and simmer, covered, for 10 minutes.

Add the mussels and clams and about ¼ cup of water. Replace the cover and simmer for an additional 5 minutes. When the rice is done, discard the garlic head and any clams and mussels that do not open. Add all the reserved ingredients and the peas. Cook for 5 minutes, stirring frequently. Add a little more water if all the liquid has been absorbed; the rice should be moist, but there should not be any excess liquid when the rice is completely cooked. Garnish with the pimentos and serve.

Tres Leche Cake

This is a traditional Hispanic dessert. Translated, it means Three Milk Cake because it uses condensed milk, evaporated milk, and regular milk. This is very sweet and filling, so cut and serve accordingly!

For the cake:

Butter, for greasing the pan
1 cup self-rising flour, plus some
for dusting the pan
5 eggs
¾ cup sugar
2 teaspoons vanilla extract
1 cup sweetened condensed milk

1 cup evaporated milk
¾ cup milk

For the Meringue Frosting:

3 egg whites
¾ cup sugar
1 teaspoon vanilla extract

Preheat the oven to 350°F. Grease and flour an 8 by 12-inch pan and set aside. Separate the 5 eggs and beat the egg whites in a large bowl. Slowly add the sugar to the egg whites, beating constantly. Add the yolks, one at a time, beating well after each addition. Stir in 1 teaspoon of the vanilla. Sift the flour, and and stir it into the egg mixture. Pour the batter into the pan. Bake the cake for 20 minutes, or until a toothpick inserted in the center comes out clean. Using a skewer, poke holes all over the cake. In a large bowl, combine the sweetened condensed milk, evaporated milk, milk, and the remaining teaspoon of vanilla. Pour the syrup over the warm cake.

To make the meringue frosting: In a large bowl, beat the egg whites to soft peaks. Gradually add the sugar and beat until stiff peaks form. Stir in the vanilla. Frost the cake and place back in the oven until the meringue turns a light brown, 6 to 8 minutes. Chill completely before serving.

Variations

You can also make the *Tres Leche* Cake using the same recipe, but with a flavored cake mix (devil's food cake tastes fantastic) instead of making the cake from scratch. Prepare the cake as directed on the package and proceed with the rest of the recipe.

American Pie

Slices of Life (and Pie) from America's Back Roads
by Pascale Le Draoulec

Having moved a number of times as a child, I know that the experience can be either faced with fear or viewed as an adventure. Pascale Le Draoulse, currently a restaurant critic for the *New York Daily News*, decided to make her move from San Francisco to New York an adventure. Instead of flying, Pascale chose to drive, using only back roads to see the "real America"; she also decided that her journey would revolve around the search for the best pie and pie makers, wherever it took her. So, with several recommendations from friends, her good friend Kris, and a sedan named Betty, Pascale set out on her quest. At one of her first stops, a motel manager says quite matter-of-factly, "bet you're finding a lot more than pie." She certainly does—and so will you when you read this incredible travelogue.

Up for Discussion . . .

- When was the last time you had and/or made homemade pie? Where was it and whom did you share it with?

- What is the "taste of family heritage" to you? What memories do you connect with those tastes?

- Why is homemade pie becoming an "endangered species"? What are some of the dangers of homemade traditions becoming extinct? What can you do in your family to prevent this from happening?

- What emotions connected with homemade pie did Pasacle find throughout her search?

- Which pie maker in the book was your favorite? What did you find interesting or endearing about that individual?

- Why are we willing to settle for less-than-homemade? Is "good enough pie" better than no pie at all?

- What are the differences between a pie made from hand and a pie made from the heart?

- What did Pascale find on her trip beyond pie?

- One piece of advice given by a pie maker was "talk to your grandmother." Why is this important?

- Does this book inspire you to travel? If so, where would you like to go? Does it inspire you to bake a pie from scratch? If so, what kind?

- One of the last chapters begins with a quote from Alexis de Tocqueville: "I confess that in America I saw more than America; I saw the image of democracy itself, with its inclinations, its characters, its prejudices and its passions, in order to learn what we have to fear or hope from its progress." How does this quote relate to the book?

Nothing Is Finer Than Pie at the Diner!

After reading this book, you're going to want to make (or at least eat) pie—there's no question about it. Below are two of my favorites. I love the Apple Shortbread Pie because it's not just your standard old apple pie, and the Lemon Meringue Pie is like summer sunshine on a plate!

Apple Shortbread Pie

2 cups plus 1 tablespoon all-purpose flour
½ cup granulated sugar

¼ teaspoon salt
¾ cup butter, chilled and diced
2 large egg yolks, beaten

**1¼ pounds Granny Smith apples,
peeled, cored, and cut into
¼-inch slices**

**¼ cup packed light brown sugar
½ teaspoon ground cinnamon
½ teaspoon ground nutmeg**

Preheat the oven to 400°F. Sift 2 cups of the flour, granulated sugar, and salt into a large bowl. Cut in the butter until the mixture resembles coarse crumbs. Fold in the egg yolks (the mixture will be crumbly). Remove one quarter of the mixture, and set aside. Press the remainder onto the bottom and sides of an 8-inch pie plate.

In a large bowl, combine the apples, brown sugar, remaining 1 tablespoon flour, the cinnamon, and nutmeg. Place the apples over the crust and sprinkle the reserved crumb mixture evenly over the top. Place the pie plate on a baking sheet and bake for 15 minutes. Reduce the heat to 350°F and continue baking 20 minutes, or until the top is golden brown and the filling is bubbling. Allow to cool and serve.

Lemon Meringue Pie

**1⅓ cups sugar
3 tablespoons cornstarch
1½ cups cold water
3 large egg yolks, lightly beaten
Grated zest of 1 lemon**

**¼ cup fresh lemon juice
1 tablespoon butter
1 (9-inch) frozen pie shell, baked
according to package directions
3 large egg whites**

Combine 1 cup of the sugar and the cornstarch in a medium saucepan over medium heat. Gradually stir in the water until smooth. Stir in the egg yolks. Continue to stir constantly and bring to a boil. Boil for 1 minute, then remove from the heat. Stir in the lemon zest, lemon juice, and butter. Cool. Pour into the prepared pie shell.

Preheat the oven to 350°F. In a large bowl, beat the egg whites with a handheld electric mixer until foamy. Add the remaining ⅓ cup sugar, 1 tablespoon at a time, beating well after each addition. Continue beating until stiff peaks form. Spread some meringue around the edge of the pie shell, then cover the pie completely with meringue. Bake for 15 minutes, or until lightly browned. Cool and serve at room temperature.

Cuppa Coffee with That Pie, Darlin'?

ONE GENEROUS SERVING (LARGE CAPPUCCINO MUG)
OR TWO REGULAR COFFEE CUPS

4 teaspoons chocolate-flavored syrup
½ cup whipping cream
¾ teaspoon ground cinnamon

¼ teaspoon freshly grated nutmeg
1 tablespoon sugar
1½ cups strong hot coffee

Drizzle 1 teaspoon of the chocolate syrup into the bottom of the cup. Mix the cream, ¼ teaspoon of the cinnamon, the nutmeg, and sugar in a large bowl. Whip with a handheld electric mixer until soft peaks form. Combine the coffee and remaining ½ teaspoon cinnamon. Pour into the prepared cup and stir gently. Top with the spiced whipped cream.

Ciao, America!

An Italian Discovers the U.S.

by Beppe Severgnini

Ciao, America! offers a look at the United States and Americans through the eyes of a visiting Italian journalist, Beppe Severgnini. Beppe is a columnist for the *Economist* as well as for the Italian newspaper *Corriere della Sera*. I chose this book because if we're going to look at travel it can be interesting to examine how travelers from other nations view our home.

Because I live in a tourist town (Sarasota, Florida), I live with non-American visitors on a daily basis, and I regard them with both affection and curiosity. My husband and I can spot them easily enough—most of them wear strangely matched outfits and Speedo bathing suits, and the tourists from Great Britain are normally burnt to a crisp. Some women even show up topless to our conservative public beaches—now *these* tourists are easy to spot!

Ciao, America! provides some insight about what visiting tourists think of Americans, from our outrageous eating habits to the way our waiters and waitresses try to charm you into a bigger gratuity. By the time you're done reading this book you'll be asking yourself questions like, *why do we like our coffee so scaldingly hot?* and *why are Americans so obsessed with ice and air conditioning? Ciao, America!* is Beppe's second book using the theme of an outsider's perspective of a foreign culture. His first book, *Inglese,* offers his thoughts on Great Britain, and it is a bestseller in that country.

Up for Discussion . . .

Discuss each of the quotations below from *Ciao, America!,* and for each quote, try to answer the following questions: How accurate are these observations? Is this how we (as Americans) see ourselves? Which quotes show that Americans are often misunderstood? If Beppe were sitting in your group right now, how would you explain to him why Americans act as they do? Based on these observations, what are some things that we tend to take for granted? Why do you think things are so different here than they are in other parts of the world?

- "Americans are impeccably well mannered."

- "Your urge to control the outside world (from Bosnia to Korea, to death, to the weather)—I explain to any Americans who are willing to listen—is well-known and widely admired. In America, air-conditioning is not simply a way of cooling down a room. It is an affirmation of supremacy."

- "Americans crave new experiences and experiment endlessly."

- "Knowing the exact quantity of discomfort—being able to say exactly how badly you feel and why—is the first step toward the goal of every U.S. citizen: to feel good."

- "The importance of showering—in a country convinced that natural body odor is identical to the smell of shower gel—cannot be overestimated."

- "American restaurant staff . . . They are the Red Guards of Good Intentions always on the lookout for someone to make happy . . . Certainly nothing upsets the digestion like a Georgetown freshman counting how many mouthfuls of your hamburger are left before swooping from behind to whisk away your plate."

- "For Italians who are used to getting away with a few thousand lira (when dining out) at home, leaving 15 or 20 percent of the bill as a tip is yet another psychological trauma. I have guests from home who would stare at the pile of dollars on the table, as if they were abandoning their first born."

- "In America, government ministers see nothing embarrassing in sipping their coffee from a receptacle with *I BOSS! YOU NOT!* written on the outside. Captains of industry can flaunt a personal mug bearing the likeness of the Three Little Piglets and still look their peers unswervingly in the eye."

- "Americans tell you more about themselves in one hour than the British do in ten years."

- "One of the favorite topics of conversation among Europeans in America is how big people are. Transatlantic obesity is a continual source of wonder. You don't need statistics to see that this is a Big Country. Just take a walk through any mall. Happy smiling couples clutching doughnuts that resemble truck tires fill the corridors. Literally."

- "Lighting up (a cigarette) at a table in the States isn't impolite. It's an act of aggression. You'd be better off trying to blow your nose on the tablecloth, drink from the fingerbowl, or stare openly down your hostess's cleavage. You're more likely to get away with it."

Georgetown Welcomes "The Nice Italian Man"

One of my favorite parts of *Ciao, America!* is when Beppe decides to volunteer at the Georgetown Community Clean-up. Every woman there tells him her life story—perhaps if these women had something to chew, like this delectable Italian party sandwich, they wouldn't be so inclined to share their intimate details with our poor Italian guest.

Beppe's Community Clean-up Picnic Sandwich

SERVES 8

1½ teaspoons Dijon mustard
1 tablespoon balsamic vinegar
¼ cup extra-virgin olive oil
2 tablespoons warm water
Salt and freshly ground black pepper to taste
1 large loaf of round bread (It's best to use one with a softer crust, as thick-crusted loaves are sometimes a bit hard to chew.)
½ cup prepared black olive paste

2 jarred roasted red peppers, cut into strips
8 ounces fresh goat cheese
8 ounces marinated artichokes
6 ounces prosciutto, thinly sliced
¼ pound peppered salami, thinly sliced
2¼ cups loosely packed mixed fresh herbs, such as basil, cilantro, or parsley

In a medium bowl, combine the mustard and vinegar. Gradually whisk in the oil, then whisk in the warm water and the salt and pepper, and set the vinaigrette aside.

Slice the loaf of bread lengthwise. Spread the olive paste on the bottom half, then top with the red pepper strips. Crumble the goat cheese on top of the peppers. Arrange the artichokes over the goat cheese. Drizzle half of the vinaigrette on top. Arrange the prosciutto and salami over the artichokes. Drizzle with the remaining vinaigrette. Scatter the herbs on top and place the top half of the bread loaf on the sandwich.

Wrap the sandwich tightly with plastic wrap. Set a weight such as a brick or large cast-iron skillet on top for at least 1 hour. When ready to serve, slice the sandwich into 8 pieces.

Green Bean Salad

My husband is a card-carrying green bean hater, but this salad is so good he will eat the entire bowl if left unsupervised.

1 pound fresh green beans, strings removed, ends snipped, and cut in half	**¼ cup extra-virgin olive oil**
	Salt and freshly ground black pepper to taste
½ cup very thinly sliced red onion	**Balsamic vinegar to taste**

Bring a medium saucepan of water to a boil. Add the green beans and blanch for 2 minutes, then immediately place in a nonreactive bowl filled with ice water. Chill for 30 minutes. Dry off the chilled beans, transfer to a serving bowl, and combine with the red onion. Drizzle the oil on top and toss gently. Season with salt and pepper, then add balsamic vinegar, 1 tablespoon at a time, and tossing. Allow the salad to marinate for about 30 minutes before serving.

AUGUST

☀ Not-So-Lazy Summer Reads

Every August, my office becomes eerily quiet, my friends leave Sarasota for exotic vacations, and I finish renting all the DVDs on my must-see list—making these long, hot, dog days of summer the best time of year to stimulate my mind with a thought-provoking book. All of the selections in this chapter are written by phenomenal authors, and each requires more brainpower and reflection than your typical beach book. If your children are returning to school in the fall, or you are a teacher preparing for another hectic year, these books will help rev up your mind for the whirlwind back into reality and the busy fall and holiday seasons ahead. I've also found that reading a mentally satisfying book can help to slow life down a bit, and since no one ever wants summer to end, reading one of these great novels will help you to savor every last minute!

To Kill a Mockingbird by Harper Lee

I read this book once every year, usually in the late summer, in the evening, and with the windows open so I can hear the crickets. This atmosphere really helps to bring this story of the South to life.

In *To Kill a Mockingbird,* Scout, an innocent child growing up in a Southern town, narrates and poignantly describes the racial injustice that surrounds her. After reading the book, it's easy to understand why it won the Pulitzer Prize in 1961—its characters are complex and multidimensional; its Southern vernacular gives the book realism and immediacy; and the lessons it teaches are both ageless and timeless. A must-read for any book group.

Up for Discussion . . .

- How does this book fit the Pulitzer Prize criteria of being a distinguished piece of fiction by an American author, dealing with American life?

- What is the most meaningful lesson you learned from this story?

- What would you like about living in Maycomb? What would you dislike?

- How is the title *To Kill a Mockingbird* relevant to the plot of the novel?

- What does Miss Maudie mean when she says "sometimes the Bible in one man's hand is worse than a whiskey bottle in the hand of another"? Can you think of a true-life example of this?

- Describe Jem's growth and maturity from the beginning of the novel to the end. How does his relationship with Scout change?

- Describe Scout's growth and maturity from the beginning of the novel to the end.

- Is Atticus an ideal father? Elaborate.

- Why does Boo give Jem and Scout gifts? Why does Boo's father put a stop to it?

- What is the significance of Mrs. Dubose's character?

- How would Tom Robinson's trial be different if he were tried today?

- What would have happened in Maycomb had Tom been found not guilty?

- Who is responsible for Tom's death? How do you think each character would respond to that question?

- Some critics say the African American characters in the novel are too one-dimensional. Discuss.

- Do you feel sympathy for Mayella Ewell? Why or why not?

- Why did Heck Tate decide to file a false report regarding Bob Ewell's death?

Missionary Society Dessert Table

I couldn't resist including this perfect recipe for Lane cake—Scout refers to it so often throughout *To Kill a Mockingbird* that I find myself craving it every time I read it! And you might want to make two batches of the butterscotch treats recipe—they disappear quickly, and everyone always asks if there are extras for them to take home.

Miss Maudie's Famous Lane Cake

For the cake:

1 cup butter, plus some for greasing the pans
6 large egg whites, at room temperature
2 cups sugar
2 ¾ cups cake flour
1 cup milk
1 tablespoon baking powder
1 teaspoon salt
1 teaspoon vanilla extract

For the filling:

8 large egg yolks
1 ¼ cups sugar

½ cup butter
½ cup shredded coconut
1 cup chopped pecans
1 cup chopped candied cherries
1 cup chopped raisins
⅓ cup bourbon

For the frosting:

1 ½ cups sugar
½ cup water
2 large egg whites
1 tablespoon light corn syrup
1 teaspoon vanilla extract
½ teaspoon salt

To make the cake: Preheat the oven to 375°F. Grease two 9-inch cake pans and line the bottoms with parchment paper. Grease the parchment paper and set aside.

In a large bowl beat the egg whites with a handheld electric mixer until soft peaks form. Gradually add the sugar while beating at high speed. Continue beating until stiff peaks form. In a large bowl mix the flour, milk, butter, baking powder, salt, and vanilla at low speed; increase to medium when combined and continue to beat for another 4 minutes. Fold in the egg whites with a rubber spatula. Pour the batter into the pans and bake for 35 minutes, or until a toothpick inserted in the center comes out clean. Cool for 10 minutes in the pans, then turn out onto a wire rack to cool completely.

To make the filling: Combine the egg yolks, sugar, and butter in a large saucepan over medium heat. Cook, stirring constantly, until thickened, about 5 minutes. Remove from the heat, stir in the coconut, pecans, candied cherries, raisins, and bourbon. Set aside.

To make the frosting: Place all the frosting ingredients in the top of a double boiler and beat with a handheld electric mixer at high speed for about 1 minute. Place over rapidly boiling water and beat at high speed until soft peaks form. Pour into a large bowl and beat until thick enough to spread. Set aside.

Cut each cake layer in half horizontally (making 4 layers). Place the first layer on a serving plate and spread a third of the filling on top. Repeat with the remaining layers, then frost the cake on the top and sides.

Boo Radley's Butterscotch Bars

¼ cup butter, melted, plus some
   for greasing the pan
1 cup packed light brown sugar
1 large egg
¾ cup all-purpose flour

1 teaspoon baking powder
½ teaspoon salt
½ teaspoon vanilla extract
½ cup chopped walnuts

Preheat the oven to 350°F. Grease an 8 by 8-inch baking pan and set aside. In a large bowl, stir the brown sugar with the melted butter until blended. Stir in the egg. In a small bowl sift together the flour, baking powder, and salt. Incorporate the flour mixture into the butter and egg mixture until well combined. Mix in the vanilla and walnuts. Spread the batter into the pan and bake for 25 minutes, or until a toothpick inserted in the center comes out clean. Cool completely and cut into squares to serve.

Founding Brothers

The Revolutionary Generation
by Joseph J. Ellis

*F*ounding Brothers isn't your typical history book. In this book Joseph Ellis expertly portrays the larger-than-life men of the revolutionary generation—George Washington, Thomas Jefferson, Benjamin Franklin, and John Adams, among others—as real people, as he outlines six key events that shaped our nation into what it is today. The events include the deadly Hamilton-Burr duel, Washington's Farewell Address, the partnership of John and Abigail Adams, and the debate over where to establish the nation's capital. What's especially amazing about these events is that the players involved most likely didn't realize their significance at the time. To quote Ellis, "They were making it up as they went along, improvising on the edge of catastrophe." Incredible! The founding brothers were brave and brilliant visionaries who sacrificed their lives so that we can live as freely as we do today. When it was published in 2001, *Founding Brothers* was a big bestseller and the winner of that year's Pulitzer Prize.

Up for Discussion . . .

- What do you think about the practice of dueling? What did it prove or solve?

- Of our current politicians, who would be most likely to engage in a duel, and why?

- What is a modern counterpart to dueling—lawsuits? Tabloid slander? Is the modern counterpart more or less effective than dueling?

- If you were Alexander Hamilton, would you have agreed to duel? If not, how would you have avoided it?

- Do you think Burr wasted the shot (i.e., intentionally shot into the air away from Hamilton), or did he intend to kill Hamilton? What was his motive if he intended to kill, and do you think he felt it was worth it in the end?

- If Congress had to agree upon a city to move the capital to today, what city or area do you think they would choose?

- Why do you think it's a good idea to keep the capital city separate from the financial center of the country?

- Do you think the relationship between John and Abigail Adams was similar to the relationship between Bill and Hillary Clinton? FDR and Eleanor Roosevelt? Can you think of another president and first lady who had a similar "professional" relationship?

- How do you feel about the First Lady being highly involved in political and policy decisions? How do you think the general public feels about it?

- Do you think the Constitution would have been ratified if the Northern states had insisted on the abolition of slavery? What are the reasons the Northern states didn't push for the abolition of slavery at that time?

- Do you think the farmers of the Constitution made the Civil War inevitable because of their choice not to discuss slavery? How would things have been different if the issue of slavery was kept on the table for congressional debate?

- What do you think was the most profound statement in Washington's Farewell Address?

- How do you feel about Washington's comments relating to isolationism? What would the benefits of isolationism be? Do you think that the concept has relevance in the modern world?

- Is it still possible today for politicians to have personal friendships with members of a different political party?

- How would today's elections be different if it was still in bad taste for candidates to campaign for themselves? What would the ads be like?

An All-American Meal

After reading about the birth of our nation, you may be in the mood for an all-American meal. And since you probably won't want to prepare a turkey in your oven in the hottest month of the summer, why not enjoy a turkey burger instead? (Don't scrunch your nose—these are the best I've ever tasted, and my husband likes them better than the beef ones!) I've paired them with two other all-American picnic favorites: potato salad and bean salad.

Thankful for the Turkey Burgers

3 pounds ground turkey
¼ cup seasoned breadcrumbs
¼ cup finely diced onion
2 egg whites, lightly beaten
¼ cup chopped fresh parsley

1 garlic clove, minced
1 teaspoon salt
¼ teaspoon freshly ground black pepper
1 tablespoon olive oil

In a large bowl, mix together the ground turkey, breadcrumbs, onion, egg whites, parsley, garlic, salt, and pepper. Form the mixture into 12 patties. Cook the patties in a skillet greased with the oil over medium heat, turning once, until the internal temperature reaches 180°F, 5 to 7 minutes on each side.

Jefferson-Adams Perfect Partnership Potato Salad

Salt, for cooking the potatoes, and to taste

3 pounds unpeeled russet potatoes

1½ cups mayonnaise

3 tablespoons sweet pickle relish

1 tablespoon sugar

¼ cup chopped Vidalia (sweet white) onion

1 tablespoon prepared mustard

2 teaspoons white wine vinegar

1 celery stalk, chopped fine

1 tablespoon minced pimento

1 small carrot, grated

1 teaspoon dried parsley

½ teaspoon freshly ground black pepper

Bring a large pot of salted water to a boil. Add the potatoes and cook until tender but still firm, about 15 minutes. Drain, cool, and chop. In a large bowl, combine the potatoes, mayonnaise, pickle relish, sugar, onion, mustard, vinegar, celery, pimento, carrot, parsley, pepper, and salt and mix well. Chill for at least 4 hours before serving.

Dueling Beans

⅔ cup apple cider vinegar

¾ cup sugar

⅔ cup vegetable oil

1 teaspoon salt

Salt and freshly ground black pepper to taste

1 (16-ounce) can cut green beans

1 (16-ounce) black beans

1 (16-ounce) can garbanzo beans

1 (16-ounce) can yellow wax beans

1 (16-ounce) can kidney beans

½ cup chopped celery

½ cup chopped green pepper

½ cup chopped onion

1 (16-ounce) can black olives

In a medium bowl, combine the vinegar, sugar, oil, salt, and pepper. Chill for 2 hours. Drain and rinse all of the beans. Combine the beans in a large bowl and toss gently. Add the celery, green pepper, onion, and olives. Pour the chilled dressing over the top and toss to coat. Chill overnight before serving.

The Tortilla Curtain by T. C. Boyle

*I*n this subtly satirical novel, Boyle weaves together a thought-provoking story line with elements of suspense and humor. Aiming to unveil hypocrisy on many different levels, *The Tortilla Curtain* gives us a compelling look at the intersections between the lives of illegal Mexican immigrants and white "liberal" suburbanites. Boyle is best known for his novel *The Road to Wellville*, published in 1993, a spoof on turn-of-the-century health spas that was later made into a popular movie (Columbia/Tristar, 1994) starring Anthony Hopkins, Matthew Broderick, and John Cusack.

Up for Discussion . . .

- Below are three quotes and statistics that shed light on immigration. Discuss.

—In November 1994, California passed by a 59% to 41% vote Proposition 187, a bill that denies certain social privileges, mainly welfare, public schooling, and nonemergency medical care, to illegal immigrants. (*The New York Times*, November 11, 1994) Do you think that this is fair?

—All Americans . . . are rightly disturbed by the large numbers of illegal aliens entering our country . . . We are a nation of immigrants, but we are also a nation of laws. It is wrong and ultimately self-defeating for a nation of immigrants to permit the kind of abuse of our immigration laws we have seen in recent years, and we must do more to stop it. (President Clinton, "We Heard America Shouting," Address to Joint Session of Congress, January 25, 1995)

—About 800,000 people follow the rules and enter the United States legally as immigrants each year. An additional 200,000 to 300,000 come to the country illegally. (*San Francisco Chronicle*, December 5, 1995)

- Do you think that Delaney and Kyra are living "the American Dream"? Why or why not?

- How do you think T. C. Boyle would describe "the American Dream"?

- What is "the American Dream" to you?

- Discuss the following quote: "History suggests that those who truly yearn to come to America and stay will find a way to do it." (*Newsweek*, August 9, 1993)

- Would you be able to live like Cándido and América? Would "the American Dream" be enough incentive to go without common comforts as they did?

- Is Cándido just unlucky? Is there anything he could have done to change his luck?

- Boundaries—both real and imagined—play a large role in the novel, especially the front gate at Arroyo Blanco Estates. Where else do boundaries appear in the novel, and what do they represent? What roles do the different characters play in constructing these boundaries?

- What similarities do you see between Cándido and the coyotes?

- There were many cultural misconceptions in *The Tortilla Curtain*. For example, Delaney and Kyra thought that illegal immigrants like América and Cándido were given government assistance, therefore "freeloading" off of taxpaying citizens. We see that this wasn't the case. Can you think of other cultural misconceptions that characters on both sides had?

- What is the significance of Dominick Flood's character? Why is he, as a convicted criminal, more accepted in society than the Mexican immigrants?

- In the beginning of the novel, Delaney hits Cándido with his car, and at the end, Cándido starts to pull Delaney out of the mudslide. How have both characters come full circle?

- If you were to write the sequel to *The Tortilla Curtain*, how would you continue the story?

A Chicken in Every Pot

Arroz con Pollo is another traditional, Hispanic, family-style meal served in homes from Santo Domingo to Madrid, and it is one of my absolute favorites. This was one of the first dishes I ever cooked for my husband when we were dating—I'm not sure if it made him fall in love with me, but he does request it on a regular basis. It tastes even better the next day! The Goya products can be found in your local supermarket in the ethnic foods section.

Arroz con Pollo

¾ cup plus 1 tablespoon olive oil

10 garlic cloves, finely chopped

7 scallions, finely chopped

1 bunch fresh cilantro

3 ½ teaspoons dried tarragon, crushed

Salt to taste

16 medium pieces (such as thighs or drumettes) of chicken

1 cup dry white wine

Freshly ground black pepper to taste

4 packets Goya Sazón seasoning with coriander and annatto

2 packets Goya powdered chicken bouillon

1 teaspoon ground cumin

11 cups water

1 (8-ounce) package frozen sweet peas, thawed

6 Spanish chorizos (Goya's are delicious and easy to find in most grocery stores)

3 ½ cups long-grain rice

1 (9.5-ounce) jar Goya Manzanilla Spanish olives stuffed with minced pimentos, drained

¼ cup capers, drained

6 red peppers, cored, seeded, and cut into strips

In a 10-quart stockpot, heat ½ cup of the oil over medium heat. Add 6 of the garlic cloves and sauté for 2 minutes. Add 4 of the scallions, 4 sprigs of the cilantro, 2 teaspoons of the tarragon, and a few pinches of salt and sauté for another 2 minutes. Add the chicken pieces and cook for about 4 minutes on each side, or until nicely browned. Add the wine, simmer for 1 minute, then add the pepper and 2 packets of the Sazón seasoning, 1 packet of the chicken bouillon, and ½ teaspoon of the cumin and stir thoroughly. Add the water and salt to taste and simmer for about 45 minutes, or until the chicken is completely cooked through.

Remove the chicken from the pot and set aside. Pour the broth into a separate container and set aside as well. In a separate medium saucepan cook the sweet peas in water with ½ clove of the garlic and a few pinches of salt for 5 to 7 minutes. Remove from the heat and leave the peas in the seasoned water until it is time to add them to the rice. Cut the chorizo into ¼-inch thick slices and sauté them in a large skillet placed over medium heat (they will cook in their own fat). When nicely browned, about 5 to 7 minutes, remove from the skillet and place on a paper towel–lined plate to drain. In the same skillet (with the chorizo drippings), add 1 tablespoon of the oil and sauté the peppers for 2 to 3 minutes, or until softened. Remove the peppers from the pan and set aside with the chorizo.

Heat ¼ cup of the oil in the 10-quart stockpot over medium heat. Add the remaining garlic, scallions, 3 sprigs of the cilantro, remaining tarragon, 2 Sazón packets, 1 packet chicken bouillon, cumin, and pepper. Sauté for 2 to 3 minutes, or until the scallions are soft, then add the rice and sauté for about 1 minute, stirring constantly.

Preheat the oven to 350°F. Add the chicken pieces and 8 to 9 cups of the reserved broth (if you have less than this simply add water and salt to taste) and stir well. Bring to a boil, reduce the heat, cover, and simmer for 15 minutes. Remove the cover and simmer for an additional 6 to 8 minutes, or until the rice is tender and the mixture is moist but not watery. Place the rice and chicken in a large baking dish. Gently fold in the drained peas, chorizo, olives, and capers. Spread the red peppers over the dish and heat through for 5 to 10 minutes. Serve family style.

Mint-Garnished Mojito

½ **teaspoon confectioners' sugar**
½ **lime, juiced**
1 sprig fresh mint, finely chopped,
    plus 1 spring for garnish

½ **cup crushed ice**
2 ounces white rum
½ **cup club soda**

Combine the sugar and lime juice in a tall glass. Add the chopped mint. Add the ice and pour the rum on top. Top off with club soda, stir, garnish with a mint sprig, and serve.

Busman's Honeymoon by Dorothy L. Sayers

*Y*ou'll be hard-pressed to find a more delightfully quirky detective than Lord Peter Whimsey. In *Busman's Honeymoon*, Lord Whimsey is on his honeymoon with his bride, Harriet Vane, but when a dead body turns up in the cellar of the farmhouse in which they're staying, we realize that this isn't going to be much of a vacation for the lovebirds. With the addition of some splendidly ignorant village people and a constantly annoyed butler, we have a recipe for fiasco!

This mystery novel is perfect for those who love both modern fiction and the classics, as Sayers skillfully alludes to classic literature and laces the book with witty high-society sarcasm. Lord Peter and Harriet do have a tendency to speak to each other in French, but don't let that scare you off—you can skip over this dialogue without missing a beat.

As a final note: Dorothy L. Sayers was one of the first women ever to be awarded a degree from Oxford University (she received her degree in 1915), and she is considered to be one of the greatest mystery writers of the twentieth century. *Busman's Honeymoon* was published in 1937, and it is the final book in the Lord Peter series (the series has eleven books total).

Up for Discussion . . .

- What do you think of Lord Peter and Harriet's love affair? How does it compare to more traditional marriages of the 1930s?

- At what point did you know "who done it"? What clued you in?

- At what point did you know how it was done? Do you feel that the author, Mrs. Sayers, held back too much vital information for anyone to figure it out?

- If you were Joe Sellon, would you have paid the blackmail? If not, how would you have handled that situation?

- This was certainly a high-jinx honeymoon for Lord and Lady Peter. Would you have been as mild-tempered as Lady Peter?

- Please share your honeymoon or vacation horror stories.

- If you could have Bunter the butler for one week, please share what you would have him do.

- If you were Superintendent Kirk, would you have gone to such lengths to prove your employee's innocence?

- At the end of the book, Lady Peter has an encounter with a ghost in the Duchess's library. What do you think about the concept of ghosts that look as real as people? Does anyone have a real-life ghost story to share?

- How do you think this book compares with modern day detective stories, both in the form of books and TV shows? How do you feel about the absence of gratuitous violence and sex from the book?

Frank Crutchley's Two Tart Picnic

Our boy Frank had a little two-timing going on, so we've followed suit with recipes for two rustic tarts (of the food—not female—variety!). Bunter might have served these at the impromptu lunch at the Talboys if only he had a properly stocked pantry. If you'd prefer to serve this menu as a lunch or light dinner rather than a snack, just make two of the vegetable tarts.

Miss Twiterton's Roasted Vegetable Tart

You can substitute virtually any of your favorite veggies in this recipe. Also, try using other types of cheese—just make sure that the cheese is melted before serving.

1 pound red peppers, cored,
  seeded, and sliced
1 pound portobello mushrooms,
  sliced
1 pound zucchini, sliced
½ pound red onions, quartered
2 garlic cloves, minced
2 tablespoons Dijon mustard
2 tablespoons balsamic vinegar
¼ cup olive oil
2 teaspoons dried oregano

Salt and freshly ground black
  pepper to taste
1 frozen puff pastry sheet, thawed
  according to package
  instructions
½ cup crumbled feta cheese
2 tomatoes, sliced thin
¼ cup pine nuts
Fresh oregano leaves, for garnish
  (optional)

Preheat the oven to 400°F. Combine the red peppers, mushrooms, zucchini, red onions, garlic, mustard, vinegar, oil, oregano, salt, and pepper in a shallow baking dish. Place in the oven and roast, stirring once, until the edges of the vegetables turn a deep brown, about 15 minutes. Pour off any excess liquid from the mushrooms. Reduce the oven temperature to 375°F.

Line one 9-inch shallow pie dish or a tart pan (if you happen to have one) with the puff pastry. Layer the roasted vegetables and feta cheese in the tart shell. Top with sliced tomatoes and then with the pine nuts.

Bake the tart for 40 minutes, or until the edges of the crust are golden. Serve hot, garnished with fresh oregano leaves if you wish.

Polly Mason's Rustic Apple Tart

All-purpose flour, for rolling out
  the puff pastry
1 frozen puff pastry sheet, thawed
  according to package
  instructions
1 pound Granny Smith apples,
  peeled, cored, and sliced thin
3 tablespoons sugar
2 teaspoons ground cinnamon

½ teaspoon ground ginger
½ teaspoon freshly ground
  nutmeg
2 tablespoons butter
1 large egg, beaten
Sugar and cinnamon, for
  sprinkling the dough
Fresh whipped cream (or Cool
  Whip), for serving

Preheat the oven to 400°F. On a lightly floured surface, roll out the puff pastry to ⅛-inch thickness. Line a baking sheet with parchment paper. Place the puff pastry centered on the paper—it will be too big to fit (we're going to fold it later). Place the apples in the center of the dough, overlapping them slightly, and leaving about 2 inches of dough on each side. Sprinkle the apples with the sugar, cinnamon, ginger, and nutmeg. Dot with the butter. Fold the sides of the dough over the apples. It will not completely cover. Brush the top of the dough with the beaten egg and sprinkle with sugar and cinnamon. Bake for 25 to 30 minutes, or until the apples are bubbly and the dough is golden. Remove from the oven. Using the sides of the parchment paper as your grip, transfer the tart to a cooling rack. When the tart has completely cooled, transfer to a serving plate. Serve topped with whipped cream.

SEPTEMBER

 ## Celebrate Banned Books Week

Banned Books Week—a week designed to celebrate books that groups or individuals have tried to ban over the years—has been observed in the United States every September since 1982. While most would-be "book banners" have been unsuccessful, their intentions are troubling—these challengers aim to completely remove various books from school and public libraries.

I can't comprehend why residents of a country that celebrates freedom of expression would want to ban a book from the public. In the face of such threats, most librarians simply adhere to the American Library Association's *Library Bill of Rights,* which asserts that "Librarians and governing bodies should maintain that parents—and only parents—have the right and the responsibility to restrict the access of their children—and only their children—to library resources."

According to a study found on the American Library Association's website, based on information compiled by the Office for Intellectual Freedom between 1990 and 2000, the books that have been most challenged contain "sexually explicit" material, closely followed by books that contain "offensive language." (If you want your teenager to put down the remote and pick up some literature, just tell him that he can't read a certain book because of its sexual content and offensive language—you'll have a reader on your hands in no time!)

For this chapter's selections, I've chosen four titles from the list of the top 20 most challenged books of 1990 to 2000. So, let's be rebels, don our leather jackets, and set off to read some books that some people find so offensive they not only don't want their teenagers to read them, but they don't want us to read them either!

The Color Purple by Alice Walker

Coming in at number eighteen on the top twenty list of most challenged books is a Pulitzer Prize–winning novel about an African American woman and the self-realization she reaches after years of neglect and abuse. The chief objections to this book have been its violence, sexual themes, and offensive language—all elements that are, in my opinion, vital to the book's setting and plot. Walker does an amazing job keeping the novel incredibly realistic, especially the main character Celie's dialect. Best of all, despite the hardships each character faces, Walker blesses them all with happiness in the end.

Up for Discussion . . .

- Is the violence in *The Color Purple* crucial to the story line, or is it gratuitous? Do you think it's worth challenging? Explain why you feel the way you do. How does it compare to the violence found (or not found) in other books?

- Are the sexual themes necessary to the plot? Why or why not? How would the book be different without these themes? How would the characters' lives be different? If you removed them, would the book still be worthy of the Pulitzer Prize?

- Is the offensive language worth challenging? Why or why not? How would your perception of the various characters change if they didn't use offensive language? Since we all know that many people do speak this way in real life, do you think that Walker could have avoided using such language? How?

- How does the language in this book compare to PG-13-rated movies you have seen? R-rated movies?

- Would you let your teenager read this book? Why or why not? If you would allow him or her read it, what lessons do you hope that he or she would learn from it?

- Why do you think that Celie and Nettie turned out so differently from one another? Trace their lives from childhood to adulthood to see the different paths on which life took each character.

- When you read each of their letters, it's obvious that Nettie has received far more schooling than Celie. Do you think that had she been schooled, Celie would have been just as intelligent as Nettie?

- How did having children at such a young age—and by the man whom she thought was her father—make Celie less likely to succeed?

- If Harpo had not been influenced by his father's style of being a husband, how would his relationship with Sofia have been different? Do you think that if Harpo had been different (i.e., he did not attempt to be so controlling), Sofia would not have gotten herself into trouble with the mayor? Why or why not?

- Do you think that a different, more outspoken personality would have allowed Celie to overcome her societal status as an unattractive, sterile, unschooled woman? How did each of these traits shape her?

- Do you think that Celie was born a homosexual, or did her experiences with men push her into this lifestyle?

- Do you think that Shug was a bisexual by nature, or did circumstances steer her in that direction?

- What is the significance of Celie starting a business that makes pants for women?

- There are so many amazing coincidences in this book. For example, Nettie goes on a missions trip with her niece and nephew and eventually becomes their stepmother, and Celie and Nettie inherit their stepfather's land and store, and so on. Which coincidences do you feel were believable and which ones did you find to be unrealistic?

- Do you think that the ending is realistic? Why or why not? Considering each character's life circumstances, is it really feasible for this story to have a happy ending?

Happy Southern Endings

Here are two sweet Southern desserts in honor of the happy ending Alice Walker gives us. At Celie and Nettie's Fourth of July barbeque reunion, these goodies may very well have been the sweets to end the feast!

Harpo's Fountain 7 UP Cake

1 cup butter, at room temperature, plus some for greasing the pan
3 cups cake flour, plus some for dusting the pan
½ cup vegetable shortening

3 cups sugar
5 large eggs
1 tablespoon lemon extract
1 cup 7-UP
½ teaspoon salt

Preheat the oven to 325°F. Grease and flour a Bundt pan and set aside. In a medium bowl, cream the butter and vegetable shortening using a handheld electric mixer. Add the sugar, ½ cup at a time. Beat until the mixture is creamy, about 2 minutes. Add the eggs, one at a time, and beat an additional minute. Fold in the lemon extract. In a separate bowl sift together the flour and salt. Gradually add the flour, alternating with the 7 UP, and beat until all the flour is well blended. Pour into the Bundt pan and bake for 1 hour and 10 minutes, or until a toothpick inserted in the center comes out clean. Let cool for about 20 minutes before removing the cake from the pan.

Henrietta's That-Better-Not-Be-Yams! Sweet Potato Pie

1 (1-pound) unpeeled sweet
  potato
½ cup butter, softened
1 cup sugar
½ cup milk
2 large eggs

½ teaspoon freshly ground
  nutmeg
½ teaspoon ground cinnamon
1 teaspoon vanilla extract
1 unbaked 9-inch prepared pie
  shell

Preheat the oven to 350°F. Boil the sweet potato whole in a medium pot of water for 40 to 50 minutes, or until soft. Run cold water over the sweet potato and remove the skin. In a medium bowl, break apart the sweet potato. Add the butter and mix well using a handheld electric mixer. Stir in the sugar, milk, eggs, nutmeg, cinnamon, and vanilla. Beat on medium speed until the mixture is smooth. Pour the filling into the unbaked pie shell and bake for 55 to 60 minutes, or until a knife inserted in the center comes out clean. Allow to cool completely before serving.

Harry Potter and the Sorcerer's Stone

by J. K. Rowling

*T*his seemingly innocent book—the first in the Harry Potter series—ranks number seven on the most challenged list for promoting Satanism and the occult, and also for "anti-family" themes. Despite such objections, I love the entire Harry Potter series, namely for its far-fetched setting and action-packed story lines, and I'm not alone, judging from its phenomenal success. According to the BBC, the books in the Harry Potter series have been translated into more than forty-seven languages and have sold over one hundred million copies, 49 percent of those sold in the United States. *Harry Potter and the Order of the Phoenix* (Scholastic, 2003) sold over one million copies in the United Kingdom alone on its first day of sales, making it the fastest-selling book in history.

In terms of the book's adversaries, I suppose we are dealing with the age-old, powerful fear of witchcraft (remember Salem, Massachusetts?). The book *is* about kids learning to be witches and wizards, so the question is, is it simply fun and creative, or does it really promote Satanism? You be the judge. Let's take a look at what makes this book, and the rest of the series, so wildly popular.

Up for Discussion . . .

- Does this book promote Satanism? Explain.

- Does the book promote the occult? Does it glamorize witchcraft to the point that children will try to cast spells on their teachers, enemies, or friends?

- Do you think this book is inappropriate for classroom reading? Why or why not?

- Why do you think the series has become so popular that readers line up at bookstores (often until midnight!) the night before a new addition to the series is released?

- What do the kids in your life think about the series? When this title was first released, were there any stirrings in your hometown? What do you think of the parents who are trying to ban it from public school use? Why do you think they feel it is harmful for their children?

- What types of anti-family values does this book portray? Should we be supportive of a family such as the Dursleys? What about the Weasleys?

- Discuss Harry's character. Is he a typical eleven-year-old? How does he handle his newfound celebrity? How about his newfound identity? How do you think his life would have turned out had he never been made aware of his wizarding abilities? What if he were never removed from the Dursleys?

- Most of the characters are portrayed either as good guys or bad guys. Do you think that the characters are too one-dimensional or are they appropriately complex for the target audience? In what ways does Professor Snape straddle the lines between good and bad?

- If everyone who comes out of the Slytherin house is evil, then why do they allow that house to be in the school at all? Is it safer to keep all the "bad eggs" in the same house, or should everyone be mixed up? Why?

- There are obvious suggestions of racism throughout the book when characters refer to Muggles and (or versus) Wizards. What could you teach a child about racism using this story?

- Which of the teachers would be your favorite? Why?

- Harry, Ron, and Hermione break the school rules several times, but for good reason. Do you think that this book encourages kids to be rule-breakers? Why or why not?

- How do you pronounce "Hermione"?

- What character did you most resemble growing up—Harry, Ron, Hermione, Draco, or Neville?

- My favorite quote in the book is said by Dumbledore, about Neville: "It takes a great deal of bravery to stand up to our enemies, but just as much to stand up to our friends." Discuss this quote. Have you ever had to courageously stand up to a friend? Under what circumstances should kids stand up to their friends?

- If you had magical powers, name three things that you would use them for.

Dinner at the Leaky Cauldron

While shopping in Diagon Alley for your robes, wand, and other Hogwarts necessities, you may work up quite an appetite. If you decide to replenish yourself at the Leaky Cauldron, though, beware of shady dragon egg dealings and discussions regarding "You-Know-Who." Cottage (or Shepherd's) Pie has been a traditional family meal in England and Scotland for centuries; it's also very popular in taverns and pubs.

Mini Cottage Pies

It's easy to make these pies in the disposable tin baking dishes you can find in the grocery store. (Plus, no clean-up!) The 6-ounce size comes in an eight-pack for about $2. You also can use 6-ounce mini-casserole dishes if you have them on hand.

For the filling:

3 tablespoons olive oil
2 garlic cloves, minced
1 large onion, finely chopped
2 celery stalks, chopped
2 medium carrots, chopped
Salt and freshly ground black pepper to taste
1 cup sliced white mushrooms

1 pound ground sirloin
1 pound ground lamb
2 tablespoons all-purpose flour
1 cup beef stock
3 tablespoons tomato paste
1½ teaspoons dried thyme
½ teaspoon dried marjoram
¼ teaspoon dried mustard

¾ cup grated sharp cheddar
cheese

For the topping:

**4 cups Yukon gold potatoes,
peeled and cubed**

1 cup milk
5 tablespoons butter or margarine
2 teaspoons garlic powder
½ teaspoon onion powder
**Salt and freshly ground black
pepper to taste**

To make the filling: Heat the oil in a Dutch oven over medium heat. Add the garlic and cook until fragrant. Add the onion, celery, and carrots. Season with salt and pepper and cook until softened, 5 to 7 minutes. Add the mushrooms and cook until they give off some liquid, 3 to 4 minutes. Add the sirloin and lamb, continually breaking it up so that big chunks don't form. Season with salt and pepper. Cook until the meat is browned, about 5 to 7 minutes. Stir in the flour. Add the beef stock, tomato paste, thyme, marjoram, and mustard. Raise the heat and bring to a boil. Reduce the heat and allow gravy to thicken and absorb into the meat and vegetables, about 20 minutes (too much gravy will make the pies overflow in the oven). Divide the mixture into 8 mini-casserole dishes or 8 disposable tins. Place them on cookie sheets to cool slightly.

To make the topping: Preheat the oven to 375°F. Put a pot of water on the stove to boil. Peel and chop the potatoes, then store them in a big bowl of iced water until the water is boiling. Cook until tender, 12 to 15 minutes. Drain. Put the potatoes back into the pot. Add the milk, butter, garlic powder, and onion powder. Mash away. Season with salt and pepper.

To assemble: Spread the mashed potatoes on top of each casserole and sprinkle with the grated cheese. Bake on the cookie sheets for 15 to 20 minutes, or until the tops are slightly browned. Serve hot.

Crispy Cabbage Salad

This is a crunchy, refreshing accompaniment to the savory Cottage Pies. The savoy cabbage has a wonderful light texture and taste.

1 medium savoy cabbage
¼ cup olive oil
2 tablespoons cider vinegar
2 tablespoons Dijon mustard

½ teaspoon Worcestershire sauce
1 garlic clove, minced
**Salt and freshly ground black
pepper to taste**

Slice the cabbage into thin shreds. In a large bowl whisk together the oil, vinegar, mustard, Worcestershire sauce, and garlic. Add the cabbage and toss. Season with salt and pepper. Serve immediately—the cabbage will get soggy if it sits too long.

Hagrid's Potent Potion

3 cups water
6 orange pekoe tea bags
2 cinnamon sticks
4 whole cloves

⅔ cup sugar
3 cups cranberry juice cocktail
2 cups Burgundy wine

Bring the water to a boil in a large saucepan. Remove from the heat and immediately add the tea bags, cinnamon sticks, and cloves. Cover and set aside to brew for 5 minutes. Remove the tea bags and add the sugar, cranberry juice cocktail, and wine. Heat through, stirring for the sugar to dissolve. Remove the cinnamon sticks and cloves and serve hot.

The Adventures of Huckleberry Finn

by Mark Twain

The Adventures of Huckleberry Finn ranks fifth on the list of most challenged books—it's been challenged repeatedly since its debut in 1884, and it's namely targeted for what opponents label "racism" and "offensive language." While I'll admit that this book does use racial slurs that are offensive to the modern ear, if parents and/or community leaders are worried about what it will teach impressionable young readers, I recommend that they view the book as an opportunity to teach the lesson that it's offensive and hurtful to use the words and names that we see in *Huckleberry Finn*. The book is such a piece of Americana that it would be a shame to see it banned from school reading lists— and thereby allow the sensitive issue of racism to go undiscussed.

Ernest Hemingway called *Huckleberry Finn* "the best book we've had," and he also said, "All modern American literature comes from [this book]." Twain not only inspired Hemingway, but also such classic American writers as William Faulkner, F. Scott Fitzgerald, and J. D. Salinger. His folksy voice and re-alistic descriptions of the sounds and smells of the mighty Mississippi should be known not just for their controversy but for the way they influenced the course of American literature.

Up for Discussion . . .

- What can you learn about pre–Civil War Americana in the South by examining the mannerisms and vernacular of the three main charac-ters—Huck Finn, Jim, and Tom Sawyer?

- Why do you think Twain used a boy, instead of a man, as his pro-tagonist?

- The "N" word is used repeatedly throughout the *Huckleberry Finn*; however, the book wouldn't have been an authentic reflection of its time and place had this word been sidestepped. Have your group members individually describe the book's use of the "N" word and the word's effect on them.

- I want to believe that society is now better able to understand the role of provocative themes in literature; however, this book continues to be challenged. Why do people still have issue with it, and what would the effect of banning a book like this be?

- Huck and Tom are masters at cooking up schemes and getting out of sticky situations, and their success is largely the result of their amazing ability to be creatively deceptive. Which incidences best demonstrate Huck's and Tom's inventiveness? Do you have any stories from your childhood or high school days when you were able to creatively get out of trouble?

- Mark Twain's years as captain of a steamer are obvious in his rich descriptions of the Mississippi River. What did you learn about the river in this book—its physical features? Its role in transportation? What symbolic function does the river play in the story and the development of its themes?

- The characters in *Huckleberry Finn* all have very distinct ways of speaking. How can language and dialect develop a character for the reader?

- The Duke and Dauphin, whose behavior ranges from comic to cruel, are important to the development of the book. What beliefs and practices, common at the time that the book was set, were exposed through these characters? Aside from eventually being tarred and feathered, what do you think became of them beyond the end of the story?

Fish from the Mighty Mississippi

The river plays a central role in *The Adventures of Huckleberry Finn*, and every time I've seen an illustration of Huck, he's holding a makeshift fishing pole in his hand. So, catfish—a fish widely served in the restaurants on the banks of the Mississippi—is the perfect choice for this menu. Enjoy!

Riverboat Catfish

¼ cup extra-virgin olive oil, plus some for greasing the baking dish

4 pounds catfish fillets

¼ cup Old Bay seasoning

2 lemons, juiced

1 cup dry white wine

2 large tomatoes, chopped

Preheat the oven to 350°F. Lightly grease a 13 by 9-inch baking dish. Brush both sides of the catfish fillets with oil. Rub both sides of the fillets with the Old Bay seasoning. Heat a large skillet over medium-high heat, add the fillets, and cook about 2 minutes on each side, until slightly blackened. Arrange the blackened fillets in a single layer in the baking dish. Pour the lemon juice and wine over the fish and sprinkle the tomatoes over the top. Loosely cover with aluminum foil and bake for 30 to 35 minutes, or until the fish is easily flaked with a fork. Serve immediately.

Rice and Corn

3 tablespoons butter

1½ cups basmati rice

2⅔ cups water

3 cups frozen corn kernels, thawed

5 large shallots, thinly sliced

½ teaspoon sugar

Salt and freshly ground black pepper to taste

3 tablespoons chopped fresh mint leaves

Melt 1 tablespoon of the butter in a medium saucepan over medium heat. Stir in the rice, add the water, and bring to a boil. Reduce the heat, cover, and simmer for 16 to 18 minutes, or until the water is absorbed and the rice is tender. Meanwhile, melt the remaining 2 tablespoons butter in a large skillet over medium heat. Stir in the corn, shallots, sugar, salt, and pepper. Cook, stirring occasionally, for 4 to 6 minutes, or until tender. In a serving bowl, combine the cooked rice, corn mixture, and chopped mint. Serve with the Riverboat Catfish.

The Catcher in the Rye by J. D. Salinger

The Catcher in the Rye is the gold standard to which all coming-of-age stories are compared, and because of its notorious reputation for badness—complete with true-to-life teenage anger, profanity, and sexual thoughts—I can't imagine it ever coming off the banned list. It's currently ranked at number thirteen on the most challenged books for "offensive language," "sexual content," "occultism," and "violence."

The Catcher in the Rye is an important book for adolescents to read because Holden Caulfield, the sixteen-year-old narrator, is a character that many can identify with. The book makes me grateful that I'm not a teenager anymore—I would gladly forego being a size two again to avoid going through the awkward and often painful experience that adolescence can be. This is a great book for reading groups because it's fun to share, unload, and commiserate about our own coming of age.

Up for Discussion . . .

- How does the sexual content in *The Catcher in the Rye* compare to that in contemporary fiction?

- Holden displays mostly typical types of adolescent behavior—lying, swearing, sexual promiscuity, and cynicism. As an adolescent, do you think that you would have identified with Holden?

- Did you know or attend school with any guys like Holden? If so, tell the group about them. If you have since seen these guys in adulthood, what has become of them?

- What do you think becomes of Holden after the story ends?

- What causes adolescents like Holden to act as they do? What are their motives?

- Why does Holden have such a difficult time dealing with adults? Why does he have trouble dealing with his peers? Who in the book has a positive effect on him, and what differentiates these characters from the rest?

- After Holden's late night visit with Phoebe, he visits Mr. Antolini. The visit ends abruptly when Holden bolts from the apartment fearing that Mr. Antolini may have made a sexual advance toward him. What is the significance of this scene? What effect does this have on Holden? Was it really a sexual advance? If not, what was it?

- Compare and contrast Mr. Antolini and Mr. Spencer. What does Holden think about each of them?

- Salinger doesn't tell us much about Holden's parents nor his relationship with them. Does Holden view his parents as he does all adults, as "phonies"? Do you find his parents to be supportive? Helpful? Aware? Do you think the Caulfields were a "normal" family? Why or why not?

- What effect did the following women have on Holden: Jane Gallagher, Sally Hayes, Sunny (the prostitute), Faith Cavenish, the three women visiting New York from Seattle, and the two nuns that hoped to be teachers?

- In what ways does Phoebe assist and support Holden? Why is she so important to him?

- Why do you think *The Catcher in the Rye* should be required reading for high school teachers, guidance counselors, and school therapists? Is it a good book for parents of teenagers to read? Why or why not?

Dinner with the Antolinis and the "Buffaloes from Buffalo"

I was thrilled to see that, in Chapter 24, the Antolinis were entertaining some folks from Buffalo, New York—the city where I grew up! Mrs. Antolini refers to these guests as the "buffaloes from Buffalo," and if the Antolinis entertained these buffaloes correctly, they probably would have served a menu similar to the one below. Schwables', one of my favorite restaurants in Buffalo, serves the ultimate version of one of the city's famous culinary delights, Beef on Kimmelweck (or Kummelwick—depending on what suburb you live in, or what generation you belong to!). A Kimmelweck roll is simply a Kaiser roll dressed with kosher salt and caraway seeds. In the chilly months (which can be abundant), Schwables' also serves Tom and Jerrys, a variation of eggnog that was very popular in the 1930s and '40s. The Tom and Jerry was invented in the 1820s by British author Pierce Egan to publicize his book, *Days and Nights of Jerry Hawthorne and his Elegant Friend Corinthina Tom.* To make his famous Tom and Jerrys, Mr. Egan simply poured brandy into the eggnog, adding to the popularity of the drink as well as the book!

Roast Beef on Kimmelweck

3 pounds beef rump roast
1 (10.5-ounce) can condensed beef broth
1 cup water
Freshly ground black pepper to taste

Kimmelweck Rolls, split (recipe follows)
Prepared horseradish, for serving

Place the rump roast in a slow cooker. Pour in the condensed beef broth and water and season with the pepper. Cook on low setting for about 8 hours, or until the roast is completely cooked and tender.

Remove the roast from the slow cooker and place it on a cutting board. Allow the roast to rest for about 5 minutes before carving. Skim the fat off the remaining liquid in the slow cooker and transfer it to a small saucepan. Bring to a boil over medium heat. Allow to cool slightly. Gently dip the inside of the half of each Kimmelweck roll into the beef drippings. Carve the roast into thin slices and serve in the Kimmelweck rolls with prepared horseradish.

Kimmelweck Rolls

8 to 10 large kaiser rolls
2 large egg whites

⅓ cup kosher salt
3 tablespoons caraway seeds

Preheat the oven to 350°F. Place the rolls on a baking sheet and brush the top of each with egg white. In a small bowl combine the kosher salt and caraway seeds. Sprinkle this mixture liberally on top of each roll. Bake in for 3 to 5 minutes, or until the salt and caraway seeds are nicely stuck to the Kaiser rolls.

Hot German Potato Salad

2 teaspoons salt, plus some for
boiling the potatoes
9 white potatoes, peeled
6 slices bacon, cooked and
crumbled, drippings reserved
¾ cup chopped onion
2 tablespoons all-purpose flour

2 tablespoons sugar
½ teaspoon celery seed
Freshly ground black pepper to
taste
¾ cup water
⅓ cup distilled white vinegar

Bring a large pot of salted water to a boil. Add the potatoes and cook until tender but still firm, about 25 minutes. Drain, cool, and thinly slice. Heat the bacon drippings in a large skillet over medium heat. Add the onions and sauté until golden brown. In a small bowl, whisk together the flour, sugar, 2 teaspoons salt, celery seed, and pepper. Add to the onions and cook for 3 to 5 minutes, stirring constantly, until the onions are transparent, then remove from heat. Stir in the water and vinegar, then return to the stove and bring to a boil, stirring constantly. Boil for 1 minute, continuing to stir. Reduce the heat and carefully add the bacon and sliced potatoes to the hot vinegar, stirring gently until the potatoes are heated through. Allow to cool slightly, then serve.

Tom and Jerry

6 large grade AA eggs (individuals who are pregnant, elderly, or those with serious medical conditions should avoid consuming any raw or undercooked animal products.)

½ cup plus 2 tablespoons confectioners' sugar
1¼ cups brandy
12 cups milk
Freshly ground nutmeg, for garnish

Separate the eggs into 2 large bowls. Using a handheld electric mixer, beat the egg whites until frothy. Whisk in ½ cup of the confectioners' sugar and beat until stiff peaks are formed. In a separate bowl, beat the egg yolks with the remaining 2 tablespoons confectioners' sugar and 4 to 5 tablespoons of the brandy until light and lemon colored. Fold the egg whites into the egg yolks and refrigerate. In a large stockpot, heat the milk until hot, but do not boil. Reduce the heat and keep the milk hot. Add 2 tablespoons brandy (or more to taste) and 1 large heaping tablespoon of the egg mixture to each of 8 mugs. Fill the mugs with hot milk and stir. Place another tablespoon of the egg mixture on top, sprinkle with nutmeg, and serve.

OCTOBER

Fright Night

Who says Halloween is just for kids? While I'm not exactly into dressing up like Cher or a French maid, or putting any kind of mask on my face unless it's made of seaweed or clay, I do love to celebrate Halloween. The pumpkins, the chocolate, my neighbors' complete lack of restraint when decorating with that horrendous fake spider webbing—it's all right up my alley.

I can't think of a better way to celebrate a holiday that's filled with legend and superstition than to read a good ghost story. Ghost stories, it seems, have been around since the dawn of the campfire, and even in today's world of high tech entertainment, we never seem to grow tired of hearing (or reading) them. In this chapter I've chosen three classic fiction titles and one nonfiction (if you wish to classify it as such) look at hauntings across the United States. If you want to give your group's gathering a more eerie ambience, why not dim the lights or eat by candlelight? If the candles blow out on their own, though, don't try to put on a brave face—run like hell!

The Hound of the Baskervilles

by Sir Arthur Conan Doyle

To me, Holmes and Watson are the best mystery-solving duo of all time. Sir Arthur Conan Doyle wrote four full-length novels and fifty-six short stories starring this dynamic duo. Doyle also wrote *The Lost World*, the original book about dinosaurs living in a hidden, modern-day jungle.

The Hound of the Baskervilles has all of the components of a great ghost story—eerie moors, a family fortune, a curse, greedy neighbors, and a scary house that was, most likely, very drafty. This is a great book to read when the smell of fall leaves is in the air and it's finally cool enough to wear a sweater. It is the least scary of the four titles, so if you're in a group full of scaredy cats, this is the one you should choose!

Up for Discussion . . .

- How does this rate as a ghost story, in terms of "scariness"?

- How does Sherlock Holmes's method of deductive reasoning differ from plain old guessing? Do you think anyone could *really* be as good as Holmes at solving a crime?

- Do you think Holmes is a "know it all"? If so, do you think he has good reason to be?

- If you were Watson, how would you feel about being Holmes's friend? What would happen if Watson were given a healthy dose of self-esteem? How would that change their relationship?

- In what ways is Watson important to Holmes? In what ways is Holmes important to Watson?

- What would happen to the story if it were narrated by Holmes instead of Watson?

- What is appealing about Holmes's character? Would you like to work with him?

- What are some similarities between the female characters in the story? If this story were written in modern times, how do you think the women would be portrayed? What would that do to the story?

- Do you think that it's possible to die of fright? Explain.

- Sir Arthur Conan Doyle perfected the art of using "red herrings." (A "red herring" can be defined as any diversion to distract attention from who the murderer really is.) Name the red herrings in *The Hound of the Baskervilles*. Did you fall for any of them?

- What key information was needed to solve the crime? How could Watson have obtained this information earlier and thereby beaten Holmes to the punch?

- If Sherlock Holmes walked into your house, what details about your personality would he be able to unveil?

Fish and Chips Are Elementary, Dear Watson!

Since Sherlock Holmes seems so quintessentially British to all of us Yanks, what better food to pair with this classic mystery than fish and chips? You can't get more British than that! I'm sure that on more than one occasion Holmes and Watson pondered a case over chips wrapped in newsprint—and most likely gleaned a clue from that very newsprint. While fish and chips are traditionally fried, I'm giving you a healthier baked version that is easier to prepare, with less mess. I've also included my favorite side dish for fish and chips—slaw. Serve with tartar sauce and lemon wedges on the side.

Fish and Chips

For the chips:

Cooking oil spray, for the baking sheet
8 medium baking potatoes, peeled
¼ cup olive oil
Salt and freshly ground black pepper to taste

For the fish:

Cooking oil spray, for the baking sheet
⅔ cup all-purpose flour

Salt and freshly ground black pepper to taste
2 large eggs
¼ cup water
1¼ cups crushed cornflakes
2 tablespoons grated Parmesan cheese
¼ teaspoon cayenne pepper
2½ pounds haddock fillets
Lemon wedges, for serving
Tartar sauce, for serving

To make the chips: Preheat the oven to 425°F. Coat a baking sheet with cooking oil spray. Cut the potatoes lengthwise into ½ inch strips. Combine the oil, salt, and pepper in a large bowl. Add the potatoes and toss to coat. Place the potatoes on the baking sheet. Bake, uncovered, for 25 to 30 minutes, or until golden brown and crisp.

Meanwhile, make the fish: Coat a baking sheet with cooking oil spray. Combine the flour, salt, and pepper in a shallow dish. In a second dish, beat the egg with the water. In yet another bowl combine the cornflakes, Parmesan cheese, and cayenne. Dredge the fish in the flour, then dip it in the egg mixture, then coat with the crumb mixture. Place the fish on the baking sheet. Place in the oven with the potatoes and bake for 10 to 15 minutes, or until the fish flakes easily with a fork. Serve with lemon wedges and tartar sauce.

Sherlock Slaw

1 medium cabbage, cored and
   shredded
1 medium onion, finely chopped
1 cup plus 1 teaspoon sugar
1 cup vinegar

1 teaspoon salt
1 teaspoon celery seed
1 teaspoon prepared mustard
¾ cup vegetable oil

In a large bowl, toss together the cabbage, onion, and 1 cup of the sugar. In a small saucepan, combine the vinegar, salt, celery seed, remaining 1 teaspoon sugar, the mustard, and oil. Bring to a boil over medium heat and cook for 3 minutes. Cool completely, then pour over the cabbage mixture and toss to coat. Refrigerate overnight before serving for best flavor.

Coast to Coast Ghosts

True Stories of Hauntings Across America

by Leslie Rule

*I*s this book fiction or nonfiction? You'll find it in the nonfiction section of your local bookstore, but will you really believe its claims? Regardless of what you might believe, this book is a lot of fun to read. Leslie Rule, the book's author, is the daughter of Ann Rule, the famous true crime writer. Leslie writes in the same easy-to-read, journalistic style as her mother, but she often inserts her opinion and personal experiences into each account. Rule also includes information as to where you can find the most haunted hotels, schools, and restaurants in the nation. If your group is up to it, why not brave a night at one of the listed haunted hotels . . . just make sure to prepare enough food for "unexpected guests"! (A note of caution: One weekend, my husband and I stayed at a bed and breakfast that has been in business for over one hundred years. It was creaky, drafty, dark, and absolutely scary. As we were drifting off to sleep the first night, it was pouring rain and, thinking out loud, my husband whispered, "I wonder if this place is haunted. . . ." I don't think I slept for the next forty-eight hours. This, of course, was before my husband learned that if I'm scared, he's going to have to sleep with all the lights on.)

Up for Discussion . . .

- After reading the introduction and learning about the author's somewhat psychic disposition, how did you feel about the credibility of the stories?

- How would the book be different if Leslie had chosen to leave herself and her experiences out of the picture? Do you think her involvement who did not better or worse? Why?

- How would this book be different if it were written by someone who did not believe in the paranormal?

- Do you believe in ghosts? Why or why not?

- If you do not believe in ghosts, how would you explain all of the sightings in this book?

- Do you have a ghost story or paranormal experience to share? Please feel free to share stories that you heard about a cousin of a friend of a friend—or any other person with whom you are distantly acquainted.

- What was your favorite ghost story in the book? Which did you find to be the most believable? Least believable?

- Would you ever stay in a supposedly haunted hotel? What would you do if you encountered a ghost?

- Discuss this quote: "Still, it is reasonable to assume that by about 2030, the equipment used by parapsychologists today will be obsolete." Do you think that their current equipment actually works? Why or why not?

- What do you think of the author's husband's account of their experiences at the Myrtle? Why do you think she chose to include his story? Do you think that this addition adds to the credibility of the book? Why or why not?

- For those of you who have read one of Ann Rule's books, compare and contrast Ann and Leslie's styles.

Goulash and Ghost Stories

What better way to keep warm during your graveyard ghost watch than with a hearty Goulash and warm spiced wine? If you don't plan on spending any time in a graveyard—and I don't blame you if you don't—this is still a great Halloween supper, complete with indoor s'mores, reminiscent of sitting around a campfire exchanging ghost stories!

Ghostly Graveyard Goulash

5 thick bacon slices, diced

1 cup beef stew meat cut into
   1-inch pieces

1 pound lamb stew meat, cut into
   1-inch pieces

1 pound pork stew meat, cut into
   1-inch pieces

2 tablespoons butter

2 onions, chopped

1 garlic clove, minced

1 cup all-purpose flour

1 teaspoon caraway seeds

3 tablespoons Hungarian paprika

1½ tablespoons red pepper flakes

1 cup red wine vinegar

1 (14.5-ounce) can diced tomatoes,
   with juice

5 cups beef stock

1 (12-ounce) bottle beer

½ tablespoon salt

3 cups water

2 red peppers, cored, seeded, and
   chopped

3 white potatoes, peeled and
   cubed

3 celery stalks, chopped

4 carrots, chopped

1 cup dry breadcrumbs

In a large stockpot over medium-high heat, fry the bacon for 5 to 10 minutes, or until well browned. Using a slotted spoon, remove the bacon from the pot and set aside on a paper towel–lined plate. In small batches, sauté the beef, lamb, and pork in the bacon drippings until browned. Remove with a slotted spoon and set the stew meat aside on a paper towel–lined plate.

Melt the butter in the same pot over medium heat. Add the onions and garlic and sauté for 5 minutes, or until softened. Stir in the flour, caraway seeds, paprika, and red pepper flakes. Continue to stir for 2 minutes, or until all the flour is incorporated. Whisk in the vinegar and tomatoes. The mixture should be very thick. Next, pour in the beef stock, beer, salt, water, red peppers, reserved bacon, and reserved beef, lamb, and pork. Bring to a boil, reduce the heat to low, cover, and simmer for 45 minutes. Stir in the potatoes, celery, and carrots and continue to simmer, covered, for 30 more minutes, or until all the vegetables are tender. Stir in the breadcrumbs until the goulash has thickened. Serve hot.

Warm Your Chilled Spine Spiced Wine

1 cup water
1 cup brown sugar
2 cups pineapple juice
1 cup orange juice
6 whole cloves

3 whole allspice berries
10 cinnamon sticks
½ teaspoon salt
Peel of 2 oranges
4 cups red wine

Combine the water, brown sugar, pineapple juice, and orange juice in a large non-reactive saucepan over medium heat. Add the cloves, allspice, 2 of the cinnamon sticks, and the salt. Cut the orange peel into strips and add to the mixture. Bring to a boil, reduce the heat, and simmer for 15 minutes. Pour in the wine. Heat to just boiling and remove from the heat. Serve hot with a cinnamon stick in each cup for garnish.

Indoor S'mores

3 tablespoons butter
6 cups mini marshmallows
¼ cup light corn syrup
1½ cups milk chocolate chips (or
    semisweet if you prefer dark
    chocolate)

3½ cups honey graham crackers
    broken into small pieces

These s'mores are easiest to serve in muffin papers. Line 2 baking sheets with muffin papers (you should be able to fit about 24 papers on 1 large baking sheet). Melt the butter in a large nonstick saucepan over medium heat. Add the marshmallows and corn syrup and stir constantly until melted. Add the chocolate chips and stir constantly until melted. Don't let it boil! Remove from the heat and cool for about 1 minute. Stir in the broken graham crackers, completely coating them with the chocolate marshmallow mix. Spoon into muffin papers and cool to room temperature, and allow to set 3 to 4 hours.

$\mathcal{D}$racula by Bram Stoker

$\mathcal{I}$ couldn't leave this Halloween classic out of the mix. Bram Stoker's *Dracula* is simply unmatched in the genre of gothic horror; in fact, according to bramstokercentre.org, it's actually the very book that inspired most modern gothic horror novelists. It's considered by many scholars to be the most bloody full-length book in English literature, and it has never gone out of print since its release. Originally published in 1897, *Dracula* has inspired countless movie, play, novel, and comic book spin-offs, and it would literally take months to read all of the psychological interpretations of the novel's characters and of Stoker himself. *Dracula* is a great selection for your group if you haven't read a classic in a while and you'd like to read a work in which the characters are unarguably supernatural. You may want to break out the garlic and your crucifix before you start, though!

$\mathcal{U}$p for $\mathcal{D}$iscussion . . .

- What personality traits do you think an author must possess in order to create characters and scenarios such as Stoker did in *Dracula*?

- Why do you think Stoker wrote the novel as a collection of journal entries, a ship's log, letters, and newspaper clippings rather than writing it in a more straightforward fashion? What effect does this format have on how the novel reads?

- List all of the vampires' supernatural powers. What are their limitations? Is there an unfair balance between the vampires' powers and limitations?

- What is the historical significance of *Dracula*'s many references to Christianity?

- Why did Stoker make Dracula a member of the aristocracy? What if Dracula were just a common man?

- Why weren't Dracula's victims street people? Why did he choose aristocratic women to feed off of?

- Why do you think Dracula seemed only to prey on women?

- What scenic elements add to the eeriness of the novel? Would it be as scary if it were set in modern times?

- What is the significance of Renfield's character?

- Why didn't Jonathan Harker become a vampire even though he was locked in Dracula's castle? Why was he spared?

- Name as many contemporary references to Dracula as you can, starting with the Count on *Sesame Street*. Why do Dracula-inspired characters remain so popular? Can you think of a comparable character that has stood the test of time?

- If you were a friend of Lucy's, would you have performed the ghastly ritual to send her spirit to heaven or would you have just let her wander?

- How would you protect yourself against a vampire?

Trust Me . . . It's Not the Paprika That's Giving You Nightmares

In the beginning of the book, Jonathan Harker is under the impression that his nightmares and evil premonitions are being caused by the paprika in his food. Obviously, he was mistaken! The following is my version of Chicken Paprikash—similar to what Jonathan was served on his travels through Transylvania, with a little extra garlic to keep you on the safe side. Serve this dish with a tossed green salad and crusty bread. I've topped it off with Red Velvet Cake—my mother's recipe that was published in 1970 in *Holiday Cookbook: Favorite Recipes of Home Economic Teachers*.

Garlic Chicken Paprikash

2 tablespoons butter
2 onions, chopped
4 garlic cloves, minced
4 pounds boneless, skinless
   chicken breasts, cut into 1-inch
   cubes
Salt and freshly ground black
   pepper
1 heaping tablespoon Hungarian
   paprika, plus some for garnish

1½ cups chicken broth
2 large tomatoes, diced
1 cup sour cream
Several dashes cayenne pepper
   sauce, according to taste
1 (16-ounce) package wide egg
   noodles, cooked according to
   package directions

Melt the butter in a large skillet over medium-high heat. Add the onions and sauté for about 3 minutes, or until softened. Reduce the heat to medium, add the garlic, and continue cooking for about 10 minutes, or until the onions are lightly browned. Add the chicken cubes and season with salt and pepper. Sprinkle the paprika over the chicken and onions and stir to coat well. Continue cooking the chicken for another 5 minutes, or until it's cooked through (if the pan gets too dry the paprika will burn—add a little water, 1 tablespoon at a time, if this happens). Pour in the chicken broth and scrape up the brown bits from the bottom of the pan. Add the tomatoes and simmer for about 10 minutes, or until the liquid is slightly reduced and the tomatoes are soft. Fold in the sour cream and cayenne pepper sauce. Serve over the egg noodles. Garnish with a pinch of paprika and have extra cayenne pepper sauce on the side for those who like to spice things up.

Red Velvet Cake

For the cake:

2½ cups all-purpose flour, sifted, plus some for dusting the pans
1 cup butter, plus some for greasing the pans
1½ cups sugar
2 large eggs
2 ounces red food coloring
1 teaspoon cocoa powder
1 teaspoon salt

1 cup buttermilk
1 teaspoon vanilla extract
1 teaspoon white vinegar
1 teaspoon baking soda

For the whipped cream frosting:

2 cups heavy whipping cream
¼ cup confectioners' sugar
½ teaspoon vanilla extract

To make the cake: Preheat the oven to 350°F. Grease and flour the bottoms of two 9-inch cake pans. In a large bowl, cream together the butter, sugar, and eggs using a handheld electric mixer. In a small bowl, combine the food coloring and cocoa powder. Add this to the butter mixture, and blend in well. Add the salt. Alternately add in the buttermilk and flour until well incorporated. Add the vanilla. In a small bowl combine the vinegar and baking soda and quickly fold into the batter. Beat at medium speed for 2 minutes. Pour the batter into the pans and bake for 30 to 35 minutes, or until a toothpick inserted in the center comes out clean. Cool completely before removing from the pans.

To make the frosting: In a large bowl, whip the cream with a handheld electric mixer set on high. Gradually add in the confectioners' sugar and whip until soft peaks form—do not overbeat or it will turn into butter! Fold in the vanilla and frost the cooled cake.

The Turn of the Screw by Henry James

*M*any critics don't know whether to classify this one as a ghost story or a psychological thriller—it all depends on whether you think the governess is sane or crazy. It is this very uncertainty, however, that makes *The Turn of the Screw* such a great book for groups to discuss—interpretations of the novel can really go either way, and James leaves it up to the reader to decide for herself. (I have my own opinion about the governess's sanity, but I won't try to sway you either way. . . .)

One potential advantage to choosing *The Turn of the Screw* is that it is a very short novel. So if you and your members are pressed for time yet you still want to read a novel with classic elements and substance, this is a good choice. Along the same lines, if you don't have the patience or time to read one of Henry James's other great novels (and I highly recommend reading *Daisy Miller,* if you get the chance), *The Turn of the Screw* will give you a taste of the renowned author without requiring that you make any long-term commitment.

Up for Discussion . . .

- Are the ghosts real or imagined? Support your answer with references from the novel.

- What are James's reasons for not giving the governess a name?

- What is the significance of the title?

- Where does the governess get the idea that the children are in cahoots with the ghosts? Do you think that her reasons for thinking this are valid?

- Why does Ms. Grose buy into the governess's ideas about the ghosts? Do you think that she believe the governess? Support your answer with references from the novel.

- Are the children evil? Explain your opinion to the group.

- Why did James make the children so angelically beautiful?

- What role does the children's uncle play in the novel? What are the governess's feelings toward him and what effect do those feelings have on her? Can you find any evidence that she might be infatuated with him?

- Why do you think an uncle would hire a governess to watch over the children and then demand that he not be told about any details of the children's lives?

- Why does Miles go out into the night and ask Flora to be his lookout?

- Would you describe the governess as being courageous or disturbed? Why? How would Mrs. Grose describe her?

- James tells the story from the governess's point of view and therefore is able to leave out large amounts of information. What does this withholding of information do to the story?

- Do you think that this is a ghost story or a psychological thriller? Why?

Just a Trifle Mad

I'm not going to reveal whether I think the governess is mad, but I will tell you that the English are mad about trifle! Below are two fall-inspired trifles that are great for your group's spooky Halloween gathering. If you were a guest at Bly, Mrs. Grose just may have prepared one of these delights for you. Don't look at the reflections in any of the windows, though—you might see someone lurking, wanting a taste of the trifle!

Pumpkin Trifle with Cranberry Compote

For the Pumpkin Butter Cake:

1¾ cups all-purpose flour
1¼ cups sugar
2½ teaspoons baking powder
1 teaspoon pumpkin pie
*   spice*
½ teaspoon salt
⅓ cup butter, softened, plus some
*   for greasing the pan*
1 cup milk
½ cup canned pumpkin puree

For the Cranberry Compote:

1 (16-ounce) can whole cranberry
*   sauce*
1 teaspoon orange extract

For the Pastry Crème:

2 (3-ounce) packages instant
*   vanilla pudding mix*
3 cups milk
1 (8-ounce) container frozen
*   whipped topping, thawed*

To make the Pumpkin Butter Cake: Preheat the oven to 375°F. Grease a 9-inch round cake pan and set aside. Place the softened butter and ⅔ cup of the milk in a large bowl and beat with a handheld electric mixer for about 2 minutes, until well blended. In a medium bowl, sift together the flour, sugar, baking powder, pumpkin pie spice, and salt. Slowly incorporate the dry ingredients into the butter and milk. Add the egg and remaining ⅓ cup milk and beat another 2 minutes. Fold in the pumpkin puree. Pour the batter into the cake pan and bake for 35 minutes, or until a toothpick inserted in the center comes out clean. Allow to cool in the pan for at least 30 minutes before inverting the cake onto a cutting board to cut into 1-inch cubes.

To make the Cranberry Compote: In a small nonstick saucepan, heat the cranberry sauce over medium-low heat until it melts and can be stirred. Stir in the orange extract. Remove from the heat and allow to cool to room temperature, stirring occasionally. Reserve 3 tablespoons of compote for garnish.

To make the Pastry Crème: In a large bowl, combine the pudding mix and milk and beat with a handheld electric mixer for 2 minutes. Fold in the thawed whipped topping.

To assemble the trifle: Place one-third of the cake cubes at the bottom of a large trifle bowl, or a large serving bowl. Drizzle over one-third of the Cranberry Compote and top with one-third of the Pastry Crème. Repeat layering, ending with Pastry Crème. Drizzle reserved Cranberry Compote on top to garnish. Refrigerate overnight to allow flavors to develop. Serve chilled.

Orange Trifle

1 package Pillsbury Date or Cranberry Quick Bread Mix, baked according to package directions and cooled

¼ to ½ cup orange-flavored liqueur (like Grand Marnier), or orange juice

1 (3.5-ounce) package vanilla pudding mix (not instant)

2 cups milk

1 tablespoon grated orange zest

1 cup frozen whipped topping, thawed

1 (12-ounce) jar (1½ cups) orange marmalade or peach preserves

Cut the bread into 1-inch squares. Place in a shallow baking dish and drizzle with the orange liqueur. Cover and let stand for about 2 hours. Meanwhile, combine the pudding mix, milk, and orange zest in a medium saucepan over medium heat. Bring to a boil, stirring constantly. Boil for 1 minute and remove from heat. Cover the surface with wax or parchment paper and cool 1 hour. Fold the whipped topping into the cooled pudding. Spread 1 cup of the pudding mixture in the bottom of a large glass bowl or trifle dish. And one-third of the bread squares, then spread one-third of the marmalade on top, followed by 1 cup of the pudding. Starting with the bread squares, repeat the layering two more times. Cover and chill at least 4 hours, or overnight, before serving.

NOVEMBER

Muckraking Madness

What are "muckrakers," you ask? In a nutshell, muckrakers are journalists who uncover inside information that the public is never meant to know about, and write about it, for the good of the people.

In America, where we embrace our first amendment rights, muckraking books are often hugely popular. Particularly around election time, a slew of books accusing incumbents of corruption are published with great success, unraveling the spin doctors' and speechwriters' work before our very eyes. But muckraking is not always done to sway political opinion—Rachel Carson's *Silent Spring* (one of the four books featured in this chapter) saved us all from being poisoned to death with DDT.

The books in this chapter are somewhat serious, but they are excellent for group discussion—after all, they were essentially written to encourage public dialogue (which was then intended to act as a springboard for change). These books can also be fun to read because they have that all-important "Oh . . . my . . . god—can you believe that?!?" quality that keeps the reader on her toes. Finally, with Thanksgiving right around the corner, these books hopefully will make you thankful for all that you have!

Fast Food Nation

The Dark Side of the All-American Meal

by Eric Scholsser

This is the book that, in 2001, brought muckraking back into the limelight. Portions of the fast food exposé first appeared in *Rolling Stone* magazine, a glossy with a liberal audience that is always open to reading about and reacting to muckraker style journalism. In our era of soaring obesity rates and corporate sponsorship of everything from concerts to ball games (a red flag for hidden corporate agendas . . .), the United States was ripe for *Fast Food Nation*. The book is filled with insider secrets about the fast food industry, many of which permanently changed the way I think about food and eating.

(A brief side note: I have to admit that, even after reading this book, I still get Big Mac attacks, and I love McDonalds french fries with a smoldering passion. I can't feel too guilty, though, because Schlosser *also* admits to liking many of the fast food items he had to eat for research purposes while writing the book. I wouldn't mind researching Dairy Queen if anyone wishes to give me a research grant!)

Up for Discussion . . .

- The book states that one in four of us has worked in a fast food restaurant at some point in our life. So, everyone who has worked in fast food, share your experiences! Were they similar to those described in the book? For those of you who have never worked in fast food, what kept you from choosing to work in this industry?

- What is your favorite fast food restaurant? What is your favorite item on their menu?

- For group members with children: since you've had kids, do you eat fast food more often, less often, or about the same as you did before? Why do you think this is the case?

- Discuss the three most shocking revelations about the fast food industry that you learned about from reading this book. Why did you find them so shocking?

- Did you have any previous negative misconceptions about the fast food industry that were cleared up by reading this?

- Discuss the significance and positive attributes of a family sitting down to a home-cooked meal every night. How can the benefits of sitting down to a home-coked meal be carried over to a family that chooses to eat at a fast food restaurant for dinner?

- How can a person eat fast food and still remain healthy and at a reasonable weight?

- How do large companies, such as Wal-Mart, compare to fast food companies such as McDonalds? How have all types of large companies changed the American fabric and landscape? The economy?

- What do you think about schools being sponsored by soda or fast food companies? What about non-food-related corporate sponsorship for schools? List other (potentially better) ways for schools to raise money.

- Do you plan to continue eating at fast food restaurants after reading this book? If your answer is yes, will you alter what you order at all? Do you plan to frequent fast food restaurants less often?

Home-Cooked Goodness

In *Fast Food Nation*, Schlosser expresses his wish that in the next century people will begin to view food as more than just fuel. He also argues that sitting down to a family dinner can be not only for eating, but also for sharing and enjoying one another's company. With that in mind, I've chosen an old fashioned Sunday supper for this menu—and I've stayed away from ground meat, for obvious reasons.

Deep-Dish Chicken Pot Pie

3 tablespoons olive oil

2 (2½ pound) broiler fryer free-range chickens, cut up

½ teaspoon freshly ground black pepper to taste

1 teaspoon dried marjoram

2 teaspoons salt, plus more to taste

4 cups water

2 bay leaves

1 tablespoon olive oil

2 large carrots, chopped

2 celery stalks, chopped

2 large onions, chopped

⅓ cup all-purpose flour, plus some for rolling out the puff pastry

1¾ cups milk (do not use skim or 1%)

1 (10-ounce) package frozen peas

½ pound white mushrooms, quartered

1 frozen puff pastry sheet, thawed according to package instructions

1 large egg, lightly beaten

Brown the chicken in olive oil in a 5-quart Dutch oven over high heat and season with the pepper, marjoram, and salt. Pour the water over the chicken and drop in the bay leaves. Cover and bring to a boil, then reduce the heat to low and simmer, covered, for about 35 minutes, or until the juices run clear.

Remove the pot from the heat and reserve 1 cup of the broth. Transfer the chicken to a cutting board and cool slightly. Remove the skin and bones from the chicken and chop the meat into bite-size pieces. Heat the oil in a large skillet over medium-high heat. Add the carrots, celery, and onions. Cook for about 4 minutes, or until the onions and celery are softened. Add the reserved broth to the skillet, bring to a boil, then reduce the heat to low, cover, and simmer for about 5 minutes, or until the carrots are soft but not mushy. Using a slotted spoon, remove the vegetables and place them in a bowl, reserving the broth in the skillet.

In a small bowl, whisk together the flour and milk until smooth. Pour into the reserved broth and whisk until smooth. Continue stirring over low heat until the sauce thickens. Stir in the chicken, cooked vegetables, frozen peas, and mushrooms. Season with salt and pepper. Pour the mixture into a 13 by 9-inch baking dish. Preheat the oven to 350°F.

On a lightly floured surface, roll out the thawed puff pastry to a 10 by 14-inch rectangle. Cut a small hole (about the size of a quarter) out of the center of the crust to allow the steam to vent. Lay the pastry on top of the chicken and vegetable mixture and flute the edges of the pastry to make a tight seal. Using a pastry brush, lightly brush beaten egg over the top of the pastry. Bake for 45 to 50 minutes, or until the crust is golden brown. Serve hot.

Dark Chocolate Cake—Vintage Junk Food

Before there were secret spice blends for chicken and other modern junk food delights, Americans loved the simplicity, flavor, and fat content of a good homemade chocolate cake.

For the cake:

½ cup vegetable oil, plus some for greasing the pans
1¾ cups all-purpose flour, plus some for dusting the pans
2 cups sugar
¾ cup Hershey's cocoa powder
1½ teaspoons baking powder
1½ teaspoons baking soda
1 teaspoon salt
2 large eggs

1 cup milk
2 teaspoons vanilla extract
1 cup boiling water

For the frosting:

½ cup butter
½ cup Hershey's cocoa powder
3⅔ cups powdered sugar
1½ teaspoons vanilla extract
Dash salt
⅓ cup water

To make the cake: Preheat the oven to 350°F. Grease and flour two 9-inch round baking pans or one 13 by 9-inch baking pan. Combine the sugar, flour, cocoa, baking powder, baking soda, and salt in a large bowl. Add the eggs, milk, oil, and vanilla and beat at medium speed with a handheld electric mixer for 2 minutes. Stir in the boiling water (don't worry, the batter should be thin). Pour the batter into the pans and bake for 30 to 35 minutes for the round pans, or 35 to 40 minutes for the 13 by 9-inch pan, or until a toothpick inserted in the center comes out clean. Cool in the pans before removing and frosting.

To make the frosting: Melt the butter in a medium saucepan over low heat. Add the cocoa and stir until smooth and well blended. Remove from the heat. Add the powdered sugar, vanilla, salt, and water and beat with a spoon or whisk until smooth and creamy. Additional water may be added if the frosting becomes too thick, but add it ½ teaspoon at a time. Frost the cooled cake.

Silent Spring by Rachel Carson

When the history of muckraking is taught in high schools across the nation, *Silent Spring* is often cited as the quintessential example of this type of journalism. Carson was inspired to research this book while working as chief of publications for the U.S. Fish and Wildlife Service; her investigation was catalyzed by a disturbing letter that she received from a woman who was horrified to find scores of dead birds two days after DDT was sprayed near her private bird sanctuary in Massachusetts. After receiving the letter, Carson began researching the effects that chemical pesticides had, not only on animals, but on humans, natural bodies of water, and soil as well. She published her findings, along with some alternative methods for the problems that DDT solved, in *Silent Spring*.

Silent Spring sold over 500,000 copies in its first year of publication (1962), but Carson was highly criticized by many government officials and executives in the chemical industry as being a "hysterical woman." One official at the Federal Pest Control Review Board said of Carson, "I thought she was a spinster. What's she so worried about genetics for?" Despite such criticism, *Silent Spring* changed history and led to the creation of the Environmental Protection Act.

Up for Discussion . . .

- Why does Carson start the book with a fictional story?

- Carson spends the first sixteen chapters describing the horrors of using toxic chemicals in the environment, and one chapter (Chapter 17) devoted to discussing alternatives to using the chemicals. Do you think that her argument would be more or less effective if she wrote *one* chapter about the toxic chemicals and *sixteen* chapters of alternatives? Why? What if the book was 50 percent about the dangers of the chemicals and 50 percent about the alternatives?

- What about Carson's style made *Silent Spring* so effective as to instigate historic policy changes (e.g., DDT and other insecticides were banned in the years following its release)?

- Which of Carson's emotional appeals spoke to you the most? Sympathy for the earth? Plants? Animals and birds? Humans?

- Do Carson's alternative measures of pest control seem credible to you as a "nonexpert?"

- Does this book make you rethink your use of pesticides and herbicides in your own lawn and garden?

- How does Carson portray the chemical users? As ignorant government officials? As villains? How does this portrayal of the chemical users help or hurt her argument?

Hold the Pesticides, Please

Is it any wonder that the country has gone organic-crazy? After reading *Silent Spring* your group may want to join the craze. Below is a simple, delicious menu that incorporates organic products. (If you aren't that concerned about organic versus nonorganic, and you also want to save some money, feel free to substitute nonorganic products for the organic ones—just make sure to disclose that information before serving your guests; you don't want to be the victim of muckraking!)

Happy Jumping Salmon with Organic Yogurt Sauce

Serve this salmon with the steamed organic vegetable of your choice.

For the Salmon:

8 (8-ounce) salmon fillets (If you want to stick with the book's theme, I recommend using wild salmon fillets.)
Olive oil
Salt and freshly ground black pepper to taste

For the Yogurt Sauce:

2 cups organic plain yogurt
3 garlic cloves, minced
½ cup chopped fresh dill
1 tablespoon fresh lemon juice

To make the salmon: Preheat the broiler. Line a broiler pan with foil and place the salmon fillets skin side down on the pan. Brush each fillet with oil and season with salt and pepper. Broil the salmon for 8 to 10 minutes, until cooked through. Season with salt and pepper.

To make the yogurt sauce: In a small bowl, combine the yogurt, garlic, and dill, then stir in the lemon juice, salt, and pepper. Serve the salmon with the yogurt sauce on top.

For the Beauty of the Earth Whole Wheat Herb Bread

¼ cup butter, melted and cooled, plus some for greasing the pan
1 cup unbleached all-purpose flour
1 cup whole wheat flour
1 teaspoon baking powder
½ teaspoon baking soda
½ teaspoon salt
2 large eggs, beaten (Again, use organic eggs if you can to stay true to the theme!)

1 cup organic plain yogurt
½ cup honey
1 teaspoon dried dill
½ teaspoon dried oregano
½ teaspoon dried thyme
½ teaspoon dried basil
½ teaspoon dried tarragon

Preheat the oven to 350°F. Grease an 8 by 4-inch loaf pan and set aside. Sift the all-purpose flour, whole wheat flour, baking powder, baking soda, and salt together into a large bowl. In a separate medium bowl using a handheld electric mixer set to medium speed, beat the butter, eggs, yogurt, and honey until frothy; add the dill, oregano, thyme, basil, and tarragon and continue beating. Make a well in the center of the flour mixture. Pour the egg and butter mixture into the well and stir with a wooden spoon until thoroughly blended. Pour into the loaf pan and bake for 40 to 50 minutes, or until a toothpick inserted in the center comes out clean. Allow to cool in the pan for 30 minutes before slicing. Slice and serve with butter.

Nickel and Dimed

On (Not) Getting By in America
by Barbara Ehrenreich

Reading *Nickel and Dimed* helped me to view our society's many minimum-wage-earning workers with new eyes. In fact, the book not only opened my eyes, but it inspired me to change my behavior: Since reading Ehrenreich's book, I leave a bigger tip for the housekeeper when I check out of a hotel; I am more understanding and patient (not a trait that comes naturally to me) when I'm at a busy restaurant and the service is slow; and I always re-hang and remove the items from a dressing room when I'm finished trying them on (another trait that does not come naturally to me, just ask my mother).

Nickel and Dimed addresses, in a compelling style, the plight of people who, in our nation of excess, are barely breaking even, though working from dusk 'til dawn. In Sarasota, Florida, where I live, the service industry is enormous, namely because our population is comprised mainly of the elderly, the retired, and tourists. The average cost of a house in my town is well over $200,000, yet the average person, who most likely works in a service type job, cannot afford a house anywhere near that price, let alone pay the exorbitant maintenance fees charged so that everyone's mailbox can be the same shade of off-white. After reading this book, my understanding of and empathy for these workers increased ten-fold. So, I challenge you: Read this book and see the world with new eyes.

Up for Discussion . . .

- This book is about the working poor—have your group come to a consensus on a definition for "working poor."

- Some believe that the solution to the problems of the working poor is simply for them to work harder, or to get a better job and make more money. After reading *Nickel and Dimed*, what does your group think about this attitude?

- Are the services that are described in this book truly necessary, and what would happen to your lifestyle if workers quit performing them?

- Could you survive on minimum wage? What luxuries would you have to give up in order to survive? How could you creatively supplement your income?

- The author was single and struggling to survive; how do individuals with families to support make ends meet on minimum wage?

- What role did intimidation and power have in keeping workers "in their place"? How would you have reacted to this if you were in the workers' role?

- How do you think the author's experience would have been different if she were a recent immigrant or a non-Caucasian?

- What is a "living wage," and should everyone be entitled to it?

- If a majority of middle class jobs are outsourced to foreign countries, what impact will that have on our society?

- What impact has welfare reform had on forcing people into the class of working poor? Do you think that the lives of people in this situation improve?

- Would you be willing, as an employer, to pay higher prices for goods so that your employees could earn a living wage?

- What is *your* solution to the problems of the working poor? Discuss.

- Has this book changed the way you view the working poor? Has it changed your beliefs, and do you think it might change your behavior?

Dinner on a Dime

In the spirit of the book, this menu is intended to help your group experience what it's like to not always be able to afford a fancy meal, and to give you a chance to empathize with the hard-working people described in the book. Beans are an inexpensive and quality source of fiber and protein, and spaghetti is always a cheap dish to feed a crowd. Serve the pasta with a loaf of bread from your supermarket's bakery and a tossed salad.

Pasta on a Tight Budget

¼ cup extra-virgin olive oil
1 large onion, finely chopped
2 small green peppers, cored, seeded, and finely chopped
6 celery stalks, finely chopped
5 garlic cloves, minced
1 (16-ounce) can small white beans, rinsed and drained
1 (16-ounce) can cannellini beans, rinsed and drained

3 cups chicken stock
3 to 4 teaspoons hot pepper flakes, according to taste
2 (12-ounce) cans water-packed albacore tuna, drained and broken up into chunks
Salt and freshly ground black pepper to taste
1½ pounds spaghetti, cooked according to package directions

Heat the oil in a large skillet over moderately low heat. Add the onion and cook until softened, about 5 to 7 minutes. Add the green peppers, celery, and garlic and cook for another 3 minutes. Stir in the white beans, cannellini beans, and chicken stock. Raise the heat, bring to a boil, then lower the heat and simmer for 5 minutes, mashing the beans slightly with the back of a spoon. Add the hot pepper flakes and tuna, season with salt and pepper, and simmer until heated through. Toss the spaghetti and sauce together in a large serving bowl, and serve.

Pound Cake Sundaes

1 store-bought pound cake
½ gallon of your favorite ice cream

Chocolate syrup

Slice the pound cake into 8 slices. Pop each slice in the toaster on the low-medium setting. When the pound cake is lightly toasted, place on dessert plates or in shallow bowls, top with a scoop of ice cream, and drizzle with chocolate syrup. Serve immediately.

The Jungle by Upton Sinclair

"To the workingmen of America" reads the dedication of Upton Sinclair's masterful piece of muckraking. When you read *The Jungle*, you will sense Sinclair's total passion and determination to help every man and woman who worked in the horrific conditions of the turn-of-the-century Chicago meatpacking industry that he describes. *The Jungle* is very graphic, so if you feel disturbed at any point, just start skimming until you get back to the storyline; the book will still have a profound effect on you.

The Jungle is the only book in this chapter that uses fictional characters to inspire readers to demand social change—and demand they did! The book's release in 1906 instigated the passage of pure food laws, setting the stage for workplace reform. I worked in a butcher shop during my sophomore year in college, while all of my girlfriends worked at the mall (I have no idea why I didn't choose to just work at Gap), and I can assure you that government regulations kept me sanitizing, wrapping, and dating packages of fresh meat nine hours at a time on Saturdays and Sundays. I cannot even begin to imagine being faced with the horrors Sinclair describes in the Chicago stockyards. Brace yourself—he didn't title it *The Jungle* for nothing!

Up for Discussion . . .

- Describe the individual family members as you meet them at the Lithuanian wedding in the beginning of the book. What were the families' hopes as they traveled to America?

- Describe the family members' impressions as they tour the factory for the first time.

- What causes Jurgis's hopeful, trusting outlook to begin to change? When does he discover that "I'll just work harder" will not make things better?

- What services and information about "the system" would have helped this immigrant family?

- Contrast Ona and Marija—why was one a survivor?

- Throughout the book, why does "fairness have nothing to do with it?"

- What laws and regulatory agencies today prevent things from happening the way they are described in the book?

- Do you think that any of the unjust or unsafe things that happen in the book can and/or do occur today?

- Tell the group how you would rewrite the book's ending if you were given the opportunity.

- In what ways does Sinclair make his pleas for reform? Why is his style so effective? Do you think it was the book's graphic nature or its storyline that incited people to demand change? Did Sinclair have to make the book so graphic for it to be effective? Cite examples from the book.

- Sinclair says of this book, "I wrote with tears and anguish, pouring into the pages all the pain that life had meant to me." Discuss how these feelings show through in each of the characters.

- If you were going to write a fictional novel that pushed the public to demand positive change, what would your cause be?

Hold the Meat!

After reading *The Jungle*, you may not be able to stomach any meat or meat products. Vegetarian Lasagna is just as hearty as any meal with meat, and it is also as filling as any comfort food (one might need to be comforted after reading a work as disturbing as *The Jungle* . . .). The Garlic Parmesan Pull Apart Ring is great for dinner parties because it's fun to share, and it's so addictive you may want to make two!

Vegetarian Lasagna

2 pounds ricotta cheese
4 large eggs
1 cup grated Parmesan cheese
⅓ cup chopped fresh parsley
2 teaspoons dried basil
Freshly ground black pepper to
    taste
½ cup olive oil
1½ cups chopped onion
1 cup sliced carrots
1¼ cups chopped green pepper

1 (16-ounce) package chopped
    frozen broccoli, thawed and
    drained
3 cups chunky-style jarred
    spaghetti sauce
2 (12-ounce) packages lasagna
    noodles, cooked according to
    package directions
3 cups shredded mozzarella
    cheese

In a large bowl, combine the ricotta cheese, eggs, Parmesan cheese, parsley, basil, and pepper. Stir to blend, and set aside. Heat the oil in a large saucepan over high heat. Add the onion and sauté for about 5 minutes, or until transparent, stirring occasionally. Add the carrot slices and sauté about 2 minutes, then stir in the green pepper and broccoli. Stir and reduce the heat to medium. Cook until tender, about 5 minutes. Allow the vegetables to cool slightly. Add the vegetables to the ricotta mixture and mix well. Preheat the oven to 350°F.

Ladle 1 cup of the spaghetti sauce into a 9 by 13-inch baking dish and spread evenly over the bottom. Place 2 strips of lasagna noodles lengthwise in the dish, then spread about 4 cups of the filling over the noodles. Sprinkle 1 cup of the mozzarella cheese over the filling, then repeat layers, finishing with 1 cup mozzarella. Bake for 1 hour, or until the cheese is golden brown. Remove from the oven and let stand for 15 to 20 minutes before serving.

Garlic Parmesan Pull Apart Ring

**5 tablespoons butter, melted, plus
  some for greasing the pan**
3 tablespoons minced onion
**3 tablespoons chopped fresh
  parsley**
1½ teaspoons garlic powder

¼ teaspoon salt
2 large eggs
**2 (1-pound) loaves frozen bread
  dough, thawed**
¾ cup grated Parmesan cheese

Preheat the oven to 350°F. Grease a 10-inch Bundt pan or tube pan. In a medium bowl, mix together the onion, parsley, garlic powder, salt, butter, and eggs until well blended. Break the bread dough off in 1-inch pieces and form into balls. Dip each ball into the egg mixture. Place the coated dough balls into the prepared pan. Once you have a layer of balls covering the bottom of the pan, sprinkle with Parmesan cheese. Repeat, sprinkling each layer with Parmesan cheese until all the dough is in the pan. Cover loosely and let rise until doubled in size, about 45 minutes. Bake for 30 minutes, or until golden brown. Remove the pan from the oven and allow to cool for about 10 minutes in the pan. Invert onto a serving plate and serve.

DECEMBER

 All Is Calm?

Let's face it: The lyric "all is calm" in the song "Silent Night" does not seem to pertain to the modern holiday season. My husband, who works in retail, puts in sixty to seventy hours a week during this "peaceful" time of year, and when I'm not at work, reading, writing, or testing recipes, I am shopping for, wrapping, and mailing countless gifts that most likely will be forgotten or re-gifted by their recipients come next holiday season.

I imagine that you have similar tales of holiday madness, whether you're planning menus, hanging miles of Christmas lights outside in the snow, or attending work parties that force you to socialize with the very people you want to take a vacation from. If you and your group members are feeling a little frazzled, why not read one of these stories, set at Christmastime and filled with mayhem, murder, or ghosts? Hopefully, they will help you to put your life in perspective and realize that, even though your in-laws are bound to make some rude comments that push you to your limits, at least you're not being haunted by ghosts in your sleep! You might just come away from one of these books exclaiming, "God bless us, every one!"

A Christmas Carol by Charles Dickens

Ebenezer Scrooge didn't exactly have a tranquil Christmas Eve. He was forced—by a ghost, no less—to rethink his entire life and all of his actions, much like having Dr. Phil knock on your door at midnight to give you some tough love. (I don't think I'd be up to opening presents on Christmas morn after such a grueling experience. . . .) But, since calmness isn't what we're going for in this chapter, this is a perfect selection. Charles Dickens's *A Christmas Carol* is so popular that it had been made into over twenty-five different movies starring none other than Mr. Magoo, The Jetsons, The Muppets, Mickey Mouse, and even Vanessa Williams. My favorite version is the one released in 1951, staring Alastair Sim, the British actor, as Scrooge—it's very dark and almost scary, until the end, when Scrooge's face is so animated that it brightens even the dull black-and-whiteness of the film. None of the film interpretations, however, can compare to the book. Regardless of the craziness going on in your life this holiday season, if you read *A Christmas Carol* in the evening next to the glow of your Christmas tree, you won't be able to contain your Christmas spirit.

Up for Discussion . . .

- Is it possible to scare someone into being a nicer person? Why or why not? If so, is the transformation permanent?

- If you were to look objectively at your past, present, and future, which do you think would change your attitudes and behaviors the most? Would it be a mistake you made in you past, a poor judgment you made recently, or events that you think are yet to come? What event or events made you chose as you did?

- Why do you think Charles Dickens wrote this Christmas book?

- Who, in our contemporary world, needs a visit from the ghosts of his or her past, present, and future?

- Who was your favorite character in the story? Your least favorite?

- How do you think life changed for the Cratchit family after that Christmas?

- How do you think Scrooge's business changed?

- How would Scrooge's life have been different if he had married? Do you think he would have evolved into such a miserly man? Why or why not?

- How would Scrooge's life have been different had he been a father? Do you think he would have been so cold and heartless to Bob Cratchit and Cratchit's family? Why or why not?

- What do you think Scrooge regrets the most from his past?

- How did Scrooge's childhood relationship with his father shape him as an adult?

- How would Scrooge's life have been different had his sister not died and if the two had maintained a close relationship over the years?

- What about the holiday season gives you the "Bah Humbugs"?

- Which is your favorite movie version of *A Christmas Carol*? Why?

- What is your favorite Christmas movie? Song? Activity? Food?

The Cakes of Christmas Past

I can just imagine being at Feziwig's Christmas celebration with cakes proudly displayed and served to his staff by his jolly wife. These cakes are fun to make together as a group, and they're a good alternative to cookie making (cooking at Christmastime with your favorite reading compadres is a great way to get into the Christmas spirit!). They are best served with hot coffee and good friends.

Fan's Merry Christmas Cake

If you don't like candied citrus peel, simply substitute 1 cup of another dried fruit like dried cranberries or chopped dried apricots. This is a modern version of the classic fruitcake, so it doesn't have to sit for days, just overnight.

½ cup butter, plus some for greasing the pan	1 cup packed brown sugar
	½ cup light molasses
2½ cups thinly sliced almonds or pecans	½ cup strong black coffee
	8 eggs, separated, at room temperature
2½ cups finely chopped raisins	
1 cup dried currants	1 teaspoon ground cinnamon
½ cup candied lemon peel	½ teaspoon baking soda
½ cup candied citron peel	½ teaspoon freshly grated nutmeg
4½ cups all-purpose flour	¼ teaspoon ground cloves

Preheat the oven to 350°F. Generously grease a 10-inch tube pan; line the bottom of the pan with parchment paper, then grease the paper. Combine the almonds, raisins, currants, lemon peel, and citron peel in a medium bowl. Dust lightly with ½ cup of the flour and set aside.

In a large bowl, cream the butter with the brown sugar. Mix in the molasses and coffee, followed by the egg yolks. Sift in the remaining 4 cups flour, the cinnamon, baking soda, nutmeg, and cloves and beat gently until blended. Fold in the nut-fruit mixture. In a separate bowl, beat the egg whites until stiff and gently fold them into the batter. Pour the batter into the pan and bake until lightly browned and firm to the touch, about 1 hour.

Remove from the oven and cool in the pan for 15 minutes, then loosen the cake from the pan with spatula or knife (run the blade between the pan and cake around the sides and then around the center cone). Using 2 plates, turn the cake out of the pan onto 1 plate, and then turn right side up onto the other plate. When completely cooled, cover with aluminum foil and allow the cake to mellow overnight. Cut into thin slices and serve.

Marley's Bah Humbug Seedy Loaf

1 pound butter, softened, plus
some for greasing the pans
3 ¾ cups all-purpose flour, sifted
¼ cup cornstarch
2 teaspoons baking powder
1 teaspoon salt
1 teaspoon freshly grated nutmeg
3 cups sugar
8 large eggs

1 cup milk
2 tablespoons fresh lemon juice
1 tablespoon vanilla extract
1 teaspoon finely grated lemon
zest
½ cup finely chopped golden
raisins
2 teaspoons caraway seeds
(optional)

Preheat the oven to 350°F. Grease two 8 by 4-inch loaf pans. Line the pans with parchment paper, leaving a little extra over the edges of the pans to allow for easy removal. In a large bowl, sift together the flour, cornstarch, baking powder, salt, and nutmeg and set aside. In a second large bowl, cream the butter thoroughly. Gradually add the sugar, beating until light and fluffy. Add the eggs, one at a time, beating well after each addition. In a third bowl, combine the milk, lemon juice, vanilla, and lemon zest, then alternately add the flour mixture and milk mixture to the butter mixture; stir until just well blended. Fold in the raisins and caraway seeds, if using. Pour the batter into the pans and bake until the loaves are firm to the touch, or until a toothpick inserted in the center comes out clean, 65 to 70 minutes. Let the loaves cool in the pans for about 10 minutes, then carefully remove from the pans and transfer to a wire rack to cool completely. Cut into thin slices and serve.

Fezziwig's Jolly Gingerbread Cake

½ cup butter, plus 1 tablespoon
for greasing the pan
2 cups all-purpose flour,
sifted
1½ teaspoons baking soda
1 teaspoon ground cinnamon
1 teaspoon ground ginger
½ teaspoon ground cloves

½ teaspoon salt
½ cup packed brown sugar
2 eggs, beaten to the consistency
of whipped cream
¾ cup light molasses
1 cup boiling water
Freshly whipped cream, for
serving

Preheat the oven to 350°F. Grease a 13 by 9-inch baking pan with the table-spoon butter. In a medium bowl, sift together the flour, baking soda, cinnamon, ginger, cloves, and salt, and set aside. In a large bowl, cream the ½ cup butter until lemon colored. Gradually add the brown sugar, beating until light and fluffy, then gradually add the eggs, stirring thoroughly. Add a quarter of the flour-spice mixture to the butter-egg mixture and blend well, then add the molasses and beat until smooth. Next, beat in the remaining flour-spice mixture, then the boiling water, and stir until well blended. Pour into the baking pan and bake until firm to the touch, or until a toothpick inserted in the center comes out clean, 40 to 45 minutes. Remove from the oven and cool in the pan for at least 10 minutes. Serve warm with whipped cream.

Money, Money, Money

A Novel of the 87th Precinct

by Ed McBain

*B*ig city, big crime. If you like the big city scene, you'll love Ed McBain. This is a great book for the frazzled, as it is very fast paced and packed with suspense. (Since you're already going to be lacking in the sleep department from wrapping gifts into the wee hours of the morning, you'll need something to get that adrenaline pumping!) The 87th Precinct series is so entertaining that it would make a great prime-time TV show. This novel is set during the Christmas holiday, when the "big city," as McBain calls it, is buzzing with holiday cheer despite the murder and mayhem going on.

Up for Discussion . . .

- Have you ever seen a counterfeit bill? When and where?

- Do you think that the money laundering/drug trafficking link to terrorism, as described in the book, is accurate? Why or why not?

- If you were given the chance to deliver a package for $50,000 cash, yet you didn't know what the package contained, would you do it? What if there was a guarantee that you wouldn't get caught? How much money would it take to get you to deliver this package? List the first three things that you would buy with the money.

- Can you think of a worse way to die than being eaten by a pack of lions? What type of message does killing someone in this way send to other criminals?

- What relevance does the side plot of Detective Steve Carella's family drama have to the rest of the story?

- Would it be possible to run a cover business like Wadsworth and Dodds did and not get caught? How? What keeps them from getting caught? If you had to run a cover business, what type would you choose? Why?

- If you knew you had a counterfeit $100 bill and you could use it without getting caught, would you use it? If so, would you use it to pay the electric bill? Donate it to a political party that you aren't associated with? Spend it on something frivolous?

- Which detective would you rather have solving a crime that you were a victim of, Fat Ollie or Steve Carella? Why? What if you were the perp? Why?

Fat Ollie's Have Yourself a Big Hoagie Christmas

When you're out on your beat catching perps and locking up scumbags, you're going to get hungry. And if you are out on the town with Fat Ollie, you're going to be eating—*a lot*. Here are some hot hoagie sandwiches much like the ones Fat Ollie got fat on. Don't worry, eating them just this once won't hurt your figure!

Hearty Meatball Hoagie

1½ pounds lean ground beef
⅓ cup Italian seasoned
    breadcrumbs
½ small onion, chopped
1 teaspoon salt
1 tablespoon freshly ground black
    pepper

1 teaspoon garlic powder
½ cup shredded mozzarella cheese
½ cup jarred marinara sauce
3 hoagie rolls, split lengthwise but
    kept intact as these are closed-
    face sandwiches

Preheat the oven to 350°F. In a medium bowl, mix together the ground beef, breadcrumbs, onion, salt, pepper, garlic powder, and half of the mozzarella cheese. Form the mixture into a log and place it in an 8 by 8-inch baking dish. Bake for 50 minutes, or until the center is no longer pink. Let stand for 5 minutes, then cut into ½-inch slices. Place a few slices onto each hoagie roll, cover with marinara sauce, and sprinkle with the remaining mozzarella cheese. Wrap each sandwich in aluminum foil and return to the oven for 15 minutes, or until the bread is lightly toasted and cheese is melted. Let stand for 15 minutes before serving. Cut each sandwich into 3 pieces and serve on a platter.

Hot Turkey and Provolone Hoagies

1 tablespoon butter
6 large white mushrooms, sliced
1 small onion, chopped
4 hoagie rolls, split lengthwise
¾ pound sliced deli turkey meat

¾ pound sliced provolone cheese
 (or Swiss if you prefer)
¼ cup sliced black olives
4 tomato slices
4 iceberg lettuce leaves

Preheat the oven to 400°F. Melt the butter in a small skillet over medium heat. Add the mushrooms and onion and sauté until tender; set aside. Place the bottom halves of the bread on a parchment-lined cookie sheet. Top each with 1 or 2 slices of turkey, some of the mushrooms and onions, and 1 or 2 slices of cheese. Bake for about 5 minutes, or until the cheese is melted. Toast the tops of the rolls in the oven for 2 to 3 minutes. Remove from the oven and top each sandwich with olives, tomato, and lettuce. Place the top halfs of the rolls on each sandwich, cut each sandwich into 3 pieces, and serve on a platter.

Hercule Poirot's Christmas by Agatha Christie

*A*gatha Christie isn't the number one bestselling mystery author for nothing—she is one of the most consistently excellent authors I have ever had the pleasure of reading, and every time I read one of her books I am stunned by her brilliance and creativity. According to the World Almanac, she is the most published author of all time (in all genres), with over two billion of her books in print.

Hercule Poirot's Christmas is one of my favorite Christie books. If you think your family is crazy, you'll love the Lees—the greedy, dishonest, and dysfunctional lot around whom this story revolves. Oh yes, this is the kind of family Poirot finds himself dealing with during the Christmas holiday. Thus, it isn't surprising to Poirot, nor to the reader, that Simeon Lee is murdered during his hatefully orchestrated holiday family reunion. Since Christie is never short on surprise twists and endings, you'll come away from this novel feeling more satisfied than after eating your Christmas goose!

Up for Discussion . . .

- Was Simeon Lee asking for trouble when he arranged this holiday get-together? How? Do you think that he expected to be killed? Why or why not?

- Of all Simeon Lee's legitimate children, who did you think was most capable of murder? Why? What about his children's spouses? Considering the sequence of events prior to the murder, who had the strongest motive?

- Who do you think Christie used as the red herring? Who did you suspect was the murderer? Reconstruct how you thought the murder was committed and why (before you learned the truth).

- What did you think was the true identity of Stephan Farr?

- How did Poirot's style of detecting differ from that of the police? Why do you think his style was more effective?

- Why do you think characters chose to reveal information to Poirot, even if it painted a less than favorable picture of them?

- Can you recount a family holiday that went completely wrong? Feel free to refer to your in-laws!

- What are the pros and cons of having a quiet, intimate Christmas? What are the pros and cons of spending Christmas at a family re-union?

- As a reader, did you think it was fair for Christie to introduce so many surprises to you at the end? Why or why not? Was it possible to predict who the murderer was? Why or why not?

- If you were a family therapist attending the Lee Christmas reunion—before Simeon Lee's murder—what would you say to each character to ensure a harmonious holiday? How would you get them to act like a functional family? Is it even possible?

- If you were Lydia Lee, would you have been able to put up with Simeon Lee's control over every aspect of your life? Discuss.

- If you were Lydia, what would you say to Simeon (pre-murder)?

- Which one of the Lee boys would you marry if you *had* to marry one of them? Why did you chose as you did?

Simeon Lee's "I'd Rather Be in Africa" Christmas Dinner

Simeon Lee obviously was fond of his days in Africa, given the affection he showed toward his uncut diamonds. Unfortunately, he did not show that same affection with his family members, and they, in turn, were a little too in love with his diamonds and money. What a blessed family Christmas! To remind us of Simeon's fondness for Africa, here is a delicious pot roast with exotic African flavors. Although pot roast is usually an all-American favorite, this variation has a distinctly African taste and a comforting appeal—much more so than spending the holiday with the Lee family!

African Diamonds Pot Roast

2 tablespoons vegetable oil
1 (3 to 4-pound) boneless beef rump roast, all visible fat trimmed
Salt and freshly ground black pepper to taste
1 cup thinly sliced onion
1¼ cups water
1 teaspoon dried thyme leaves, crushed

½ teaspoon cayenne pepper
½ cup creamy peanut butter, melted until smooth in the microwave
⅓ cup fresh lemon juice
¼ cup tomato paste
3 tablespoons all-purpose flour
2 cups couscous, cooked according to package directions

Preheat the oven to 325°F. Heat the oil over medium heat in a large Dutch oven. Season the entire roast generously with salt and pepper. Add the meat to the pot and brown on all sides. Add the onion and cook an additional 4 to 5 minutes, or until the onions are transparent. Add 1 cup of the water, the thyme, cayenne, peanut butter, lemon juice, and tomato paste and stir until well combined. Cover and place in the oven. Cook for 2½ to 3 hours, or until the meat is completely cooked and tender. Transfer the meat to a cutting board, cover loosely with foil, and let rest for 10 minutes.

Skim the fat from the top of the remaining liquid in the Dutch oven. Place the Dutch oven on the stovetop over medium heat. In a small bowl combine the flour and remaining ¼ cup water, whisking out any lumps. Slowly add to the hot liquid, stirring constantly until thickened. Slice the meat across the grain and serve with the sauce and couscous on the side.

Death of a Snob by M. C. Beaton

At 148 pages, *Death of a Snob* is such a quick read that you'll have plenty of time for your annual viewings of *It's a Wonderful Life* and *A Christmas Story* on TV. It's fast-paced, light, and a lot of fun. The story takes place in Scotland (you'll get to enjoy some interesting dialect) at a "health farm"—the equivalent of an American spa—where the owner has invited some friends and regular guests to share a private Christmas with her. The characters are all contemporary and believable, which should keep your discussion gossipy and lighthearted—even though the central theme of the book is murder. I especially like the inappropriately-dressed health farm owner—if she worked in my office, we would have a heyday gossiping about her too-short, too-tight outfits!

Up for Discussion . . .

- What role does Christmas play in the novel?

- Have you ever gone away to an exotic locale for Christmas? If so, where? If not, where would you like to escape to for the holiday?

- Of the health farm guests, who would you most likely hang out with in real life? Why? Which of the health farm guests would you steer clear from? Why?

- Why do the townspeople hate Jane so much?

- Why would a person establish a health farm in an area where everyone hates them and the idea of their business?

- Would you rather go to a health farm in Eileencraig or in the Bahamas? Why? What geographical and climatic conditions would assist you in reaching your health goals?

- What were the various characters' motives for murdering Heather? What would your motive have been?

- In many mystery novels, the local police rarely give any concrete assistance to the detective. Why is that trend significant to the mystery novel genre as a whole?

- Do you think Inspector Blair and his team could have solved the murder by themselves? Why or why not?

- What advantages did Hamish have over Blair?

- Was Geordie's truck really possessed? Why or why not?

- What makes the people of Eileencraig so strange? Can you think of an American city that may be similar?

- Heather obviously goes a bit overboard with her openly negative opinions of romance novels and their readers. Why does she do this?

- Before the real murderer was revealed, who did you think killed Heather?

Easy Holiday Supper for Eight Murder Suspects/Guests

It can be difficult to simultaneously solve a murder *and* prepare a Christmas dinner, especially when all of your dinner guests are suspects. Harriet, the author of well-respected "cookery books," may very well have had this elegant yet simple menu up her sleeve for Christmas dinner at the health farm. I wanted to steer clear of turkey and ham because, most likely, you'll have had enough of those by the end of December, and I wanted to include cranberries in this menu because there is no better holiday food combination than cranberries and anything! Also, the hot Wassail Punch will keep you warm. If you want to add a "bit of cheer" to it, add brandy to the pot, 1 to 1½ cups (depending on how cheerful you wish to get), right before serving.

Heather's "Stuff It" Cranberry Chicken

Serve this holiday specialty with baked russet potatoes (with butter and sour cream on the side) and the steamed vegetable of your choice.

¾ cup light cream cheese
3 garlic cloves, minced
1 bunch fresh sage leaves, chopped
1 tablespoon dried thyme
Salt and freshly ground black pepper to taste

8 (6 to 8-ounce) bone-in chicken breasts
1 tablespoon olive oil
2 medium onions, finely chopped
3 ½ cups chicken broth
1 can whole cranberry sauce

Preheat the oven to 450°F. Line two 9 by 13-inch pans with foil and set aside. In a small bowl, combine the cream cheese, garlic, 1 tablespoon of the sage, the thyme, salt, and pepper. Place the chicken breasts in the foil-lined pans. Using the tip of a sharp knife, cut small (2 inches in length) pockets into each chicken breast. Stuff each pocket with a spoonful of the cream cheese mixture. Season each chicken breast with salt and pepper. Place in the oven and bake for 25 to 30 minutes, or until the juices from the chicken run clear.

Meanwhile, heat the oil in a medium saucepan over medium-high heat. Add the onions and sauté for about 10 minutes, or until lightly browned. Add the remaining sage and season with salt and pepper. Stir in the chicken broth. Bring to a boil, then reduce the heat and simmer, uncovered, until slightly reduced, about 7 minutes. Stir in the cranberry sauce. Increase the heat to medium and continue cooking for 5 to 7 minutes, allowing the cranberries to melt into the chicken broth mixture. The sauce will thicken slightly when it cools. Serve the chicken with the cranberry sauce on top, with any remaining sauce on the side.

Wassail Punch

1½ cups sugar
8 whole cloves
3 cups water
3 cinnamon sticks

1½ cups orange juice
1 cup fresh lemon juice
1 gallon apple cider

Combine the sugar, cloves, water, and cinnamon sticks in a large stockpot over high heat. Bring to a boil, and continue to boil for 10 minutes. Remove from the heat, cover, and cool for 1 hour. Stir in the orange juice, lemon juice, and apple cider. Return to the heat, bring to a boil, and boil for 10 to 15 minutes, or until slightly reduced. Remove the cloves and cinnamon sticks before serving. Serve hot.

BONUS CHAPTER 1

The Classics

I've always been a little intimidated by what some people refer to as "classic litera-ture." When I was in college, a professor assigned Tolstoy's *War and Peace,* and I balked at the thought of reading the 1,400-page novel. I brilliantly opted to watch the movie version instead, and a few weeks later, I proudly handed in my term paper on the "book." When I received my paper back, though, in place of a grade, the profes-sor had simply written, "Didn't you just *love* Audrey Hepburn? SEE ME!" at the top. Not only did this professor tell me that I had to read all 1,400 pages of *War and Peace,* but he also made me take an exam covering its every intimate detail. When I finally cracked open the monstrous novel, I was surprised to find that it wasn't nearly as eso-teric or tedious as I had imagined. Since then, I've found this to be true for many clas-sic novels.

People define classic books in so many different ways that it was challenging to decide which selections to include in this chapter. Some people believe that a classic is a book that is "an excellent model of its time," but there are hundreds of books pub-lished each year that fit this definition. Others argue that only the critics can decide what is (and isn't) a classic. A third, more literal, way to define a classic book is "one that is among the art and literature of the ancient Greeks and Romans." Finally, a book can also be labeled classic if it is "traditional," as in, "such and such book is a *classic* love story," or "that book is a *classic* mystery novel."

In this chapter, you will find four outstanding books that fit one (or usually more) of the definitions above. I give you my word that none will cause exasperated eye rolling or feelings of dread!

The Odyssey by Homer

The Odyssey is the sequel to another famous Greek epic, *The Iliad*, and it is written in poem form, much like the structure in which it was recited orally a few thousand years ago. This classic has been loved by millions of readers (and listeners!) for so many centuries because it's filled with all of the elements of a great epic story: love, passion, adventure, suspense, magic and myth, and, of course, a happy ending. It may be difficult for you to get into the rhythm of the epic at first, but stick with it—you'll eventually get the hang of it.

The movie *O Brother, Where Art Thou?* (Buena Vista, 2000) claims that it is patterned after Odysseus's travels. If your group is up for movie night (and who isn't when George Clooney is involved?), watch the movie and try to draw parallels between the two.

Up for Discussion . . .

- Reading this ancient epic poem obviously was different from reading a modern novel. Did the structure throw you off? Did you find it difficult or easy to read? How did it compare to reading Shakespeare?

- In the beginning of the epic, we find Odysseus trapped on Kalypso's island. He claims that he was detained there, yet he was Kalypso's lover. He also says that his loyalty was to his home and to Penelope—do you accept that statement? Why or why not?

- Kalypso offers Odysseus immortality if he will stay with her. What can be said about Odysseus for rejecting that offer? Would you give up your home and family for eternal life?

- What role does Athena play in this epic? Who is the epic's central female character, Athena or Penelope? Explain.

- Discuss Odysseus's role as hero. Is he always heroic? Does he always do the right thing? Explain how a flawed person can become a hero.

- If you were Penelope, how could you creatively stall the suitors?

- Using references from the poem, trace Telemakos's coming of age.

- What would Telemakos have become if Odysseus had not returned home?

- Who do you think Penelope would have married had Odysseus not returned home? How much longer could she have warded off the suitors?

- Could you wait twenty years for your husband to return home if you didn't have any information—even questionable, secondhand information—of his whereabouts?

- Discuss Greek hospitality. Are you as hospitable as the Greeks? What would our society be like if we incorporated their unconditional hospitality into our daily lives?

Classically Greek

Before Odysseus leaves Kalypso's island, he dines with the goddess for the last time. She eats the food of the gods—ambrosia—and he eats the food of the humans—most likely something Greek! My favorite Greek dish, a Greek salad with basil-seasoned chicken, which I've included below, is extremely simple. Followed by ambrosia for dessert, this menu makes for a delicious and filling meal.

Welcome Home Greek Salad

2 (10-ounce) bags romaine lettuce, chopped

1 large green pepper, cored, seeded, and diced

1 large red onion, diced

1 large seedless cucumber, diced

2 large tomatoes, diced

2 tablespoons extra-virgin olive oil

2½ pounds boneless, skinless chicken breasts, cut into 1-inch strips

Salt and freshly ground black pepper to taste

2 tablespoons dried basil

1 cup pitted kalamata olives, for garnish

1 cup jarred banana peppers, drained, for garnish

2 cups drained and crumbled brined feta cheese

Greek Dressing (recipe follows)

Pita bread, warmed in the oven (wrap it in foil and bake in a 300°F oven for about 10 minutes) and cut into triangles

In a large bowl, combine the lettuce, green pepper, red onion, cucumber, and tomatoes. Toss well. Heat the oil in a large skillet over medium heat. When pan is hot add the chicken strips and season with salt and pepper. Sprinkle the basil over the chicken and stir to coat. Sauté the chicken strips until cooked through, 5 to 7 minutes. Arrange the tossed salad on 8 plates and top each with cooked chicken strips. Garnish with the olives and banana peppers. Top each plate with ¼ cup crumbled feta cheese. Serve with Greek Dressing on the side and place the pita triangles in a basket to pass around.

Greek Dressing

½ cup red wine vinegar

2 garlic cloves, minced

1 teaspoon dried oregano

½ teaspoon dried basil

¼ teaspoon freshly ground black pepper

¼ teaspoon salt

⅛ teaspoon onion powder

1 teaspoon Dijon mustard

¾ cup extra-virgin olive oil

In a medium bowl, mix together the vinegar, garlic powder, oregano, basil, pepper, salt, onion powder, and mustard. Slowly whisk in the oil. Serve with the Welcome Home Greek Salad.

Kalypso's Ambrosia

1 (11-ounce) can mandarin oranges, drained
1 (8-ounce) can crushed unsweetened pineapple, drained
3 ½ cups frozen whipped topping, thawed

2 cups shredded sweetened coconut
2 cups mini marshmallows (the colored ones look pretty!)
½ cup milk
1 cup maraschino cherries, for garnish

In a large bowl, combine the oranges, pineapple, whipped topping, coconut, marshmallows, and milk. Mix well and chill for 1 hour. Garnish with the cherries, and serve.

Middle Passage by Charles Johnson

*M*iddle Passage is not only an excellent model of its time, but it is also critically acclaimed. Published in 1990, the novel was that year's winner of the National Book Award. It was also, incidentally, a bestseller.

Middle Passage presents a realistic perspective on the horrors of the slave trade and how it affected everyone involved. In my opinion, it has everything that a classic (meaning traditional) book should have: adventure, romance, history, and philosophy. It will make you keenly aware of human injustice, and it will give you a new appreciation for one of the greatest blessings we have as Americans: reasonably clean water.

Up for Discussion . . .

- Summarize the message Charles Johnson wanted to convey through this novel.

- Would Rutherford have reacted differently on the ship if he had been one of the mistreated plantation slaves? Explain.

- What do you think of the book's format (i.e., its use of journal entries)? How would the story have been different if it was told by an unknown narrator?

- What do you think of the novel's graphic realism?

- What would have happened if Rutherford married Isadora instead of boarding the ship? What course would his life have taken? Would Isadora have been able to change him?

- If the sailors had not attempted mutiny, how would the Africans have attempted to take over the ship?

- Rutherford talks about not having an identity before he went on the ship, but instead being a tapestry of "pieces of fragments of all the people who [had] touched [him], places [he] had seen and houses [he] broke into." After he returned home, how do you think he would define his identity?

- Do you really think that people like Papa were involved in the slave trade through investments but didn't know it?

- If you weren't killed in the mutiny, how would you have survived on the Republic?

Papa's New Orleans Shrimp Feast

The first thing I would do after returning from a hellish journey like the one described in *Middle Passage* would be to take a shower. Next, I would take a nap, and then I would drink a bottle of clean, fresh water. Finally, of course, I would eat a decent meal. Here is a great New Orleans–style feast—perfect with ice cold beer!

The following two shrimp recipes should be served with hot white rice and Creole Succotash (see page 223). Plan on ½ to ¾ cup of cooked rice per person.

Cajun Shrimp

2 tablespoons unsalted butter
2 ¼ cups chopped onions
1½ cups chopped green peppers
¾ cup chopped celery
3 cups chopped tomatoes
1 cup prepared canned tomato sauce
3 tablespoons minced jalapeño chile
2 bay leaves
2 garlic cloves, minced

1 to 2 tablespoons cayenne pepper, according to taste
¾ teaspoon salt
1 teaspoon freshly ground black pepper
2 ¼ cups canned seafood stock or broth
1½ tablespoons dark brown sugar
1½ pounds large shrimp, peeled and deveined

Melt the butter in a 4-quart saucepan over medium-high heat. Add the onions, peppers, and celery and sauté about 2 minutes, stirring frequently, until the vegetables start to soften. Reduce the heat to medium and add the tomatoes, tomato sauce, jalapeños, bay leaves, garlic, cayenne, salt, and black pepper.

Cook for about 3 minutes, stirring frequently, until the tomatoes start to soften. Reduce the heat to low, add the seafood stock and brown sugar, and simmer for about 20 minutes, stirring occasionally. Increase the heat and bring to a boil. Remove from the heat and add the shrimp. Cover and let stand for 7 to 10 minutes, or until the shrimp are firm and opaque. Serve over hot white rice.

Shrimp Creole

1/2 cup butter
1 cup chopped onions
1 cup diced green peppers
1 cup chopped celery
1 large garlic clove, minced
3 tablespoons chopped fresh parsley
1/2 teaspoon salt
1 teaspoon dried thyme
1/2 teaspoon freshly ground black pepper

1/8 to 1/4 teaspoon cayenne pepper, according to taste
Tabasco sauce to taste
2 tablespoons all-purpose flour
2 cups chopped fresh tomatoes
1 cup canned seafood stock or broth
2 pounds large shrimp, peeled and deveined

Melt the butter in a large skillet over medium heat. Add the onions, green peppers, celery, and garlic and sauté for about 3 minutes, or until the vegetables start to soften. Reduce the heat to low, then add the parsley, salt, thyme, black pepper, cayenne, and Tabasco sauce. Stir in the flour and cook for 2 minutes, stirring constantly. Stir in the tomatoes and seafood stock. Cook for about 3 minutes, or until thickened. Stir in the shrimp and cover and simmer for 3 minutes, or until the shrimp are firm and opaque. Serve over hot white rice.

Creole Succotash

½ cup olive oil
1 large onion, chopped
3 parsley springs chopped
2 pounds okra, cut into pieces
1 medium green pepper, cored, seeded, and diced
1 (16-ounce) can chopped tomatoes

1 (10-ounce) box frozen lima beans
½ pound ham, diced
2 (10-ounce) cans of corn, drained
Salt and freshly ground black pepper to taste

Heat the oil in a large saucepan over medium heat. Add the onion, parsley, okra, and green pepper. Sauté for about 3 minutes or until the vegetables start to soften. Add the tomatoes, lima beans, and ham. Cover and cook for 20 minutes, or until the tomatoes are soft and the mixture is slightly thickened. Add the corn, salt, and pepper and cook for an additional 10 to 15 minutes, or until heated through.

Jane Eyre by Charlotte Brontë

The first time I read *Jane Eyre,* I was in college, struggling to keep up with all the reading that is required of a literature major. It was the same semester that I had to tackle *War and Peace* (see page 215) and *The Canterbury Tales.* As luck would have it, a few days before I had to finish reading the book for class, my college town got snowed in. I had been dreading reading the book—when I'd asked a classmate what she thought of it, she'd groaned that it was about a miserable young woman with a miserable existence. But, with nothing else to do on that miserable day, I cracked open this supposedly miserable book and was more than pleasantly surprised. *Jane Eyre* is filled with mystery and passion; it is a triumphant story about a determined, honest young woman who succeeds despite cruel and unusual circumstances. I define it as a classic because (a) it is popularly considered to be one, and (b) it was an excellent model of its time.

A great follow-up to this novel is Jean Rhys's *Wide Sargasso Sea* (reprinted in 1999), which was written as a prequel to *Jane Eyre* and tells the story of Bertha and Rochester. I highly recommend it for groups that would like to dig deeper into this story line.

Up for Discussion . . .

- Modern critics cite problems with the dates and sequence of events in *Jane Eyre.* Did anyone find errors or inconsistencies?

- Brontë was certainly ahead of her time as far as feminism is concerned. Discuss Jane's feminist traits, in comparison to (what the group thinks) was the norm for women in 1847 England. Does the group think that most nineteenth century women craved financial, intellectual, and social equality in their marriage, as Jane did? Why wouldn't she settle for less?

- Describe the virtues of Helen Burns. How does she contribute to Jane's happiness at Lowood? How does Maria Temple contribute to

Jane's happiness at Lowood? How do Jane's experiences at Lowood change her?

- How did Jane's windfall inheritance change her character?

- Take a look at all of the "evil" characters: Mrs. Reed, John, Eliza and Georgiana Reed, and Mr. Brockelhurst. Did they break Jane or make her stronger? Both? Discuss.

- How would you have fared in the Red Room? What effect do you think it had on Jane? What do you think the Red Room symbolizes?

- Rochester: Would you marry him? Why or why not?

- Why was Rochester a preferable husband for Jane over St. John Rivers? Who would you prefer to have as a husband?

- Bertha Mason Rochester: tragic or evil character? Why?

- Compare and contrast Rosamond Oliver and Jane.

- Everyone put themselves in Jane's shoes. Would you have made the same decisions as Jane did? How would the story have ended if you were in her place, making the decisions? Would you have taken the entire inheritance and moved to Paris to live the high life?

Thornfield Manor Tea Sandwiches

Step into the drawing room for a late afternoon tea at Thornfield Manor, where you will discover that your favorite characters have been turned into tea sandwiches. Plan on making four to five tea sandwiches for each person. Sandwiches can be secured with toothpicks if you wish. Serve the sandwiches with Raspberry Leaf or Lemon Verbena tea. Pour a little whole milk at the bottom of each teacup and then add the freshly brewed tea.

The Rochester (slightly torched)

16 to 20 slices whole grain bread, crusts removed, cut into quarters
¼ cup goat cheese

½ pound roast beef, thinly sliced
¼ cup hot mango chutney
¼ cup chopped fresh flat-leaf parsley

Spread a thin layer of goat cheese over 1 one bread square. Add a layer of roast beef, followed with a small dollop of mango chutney, and sprinkle on the parsley. Top with another bread square. Repeat with the rest of the bread and filling.

The Bertha (a bit nutty)

16 to 20 slices whole grain bread, crusts removed, cut into quarters
½ cup (4 ounces) cream cheese, softened

1 teaspoon pure maple syrup
2 tablespoons chopped walnuts
½ pound roast turkey, thinly sliced
¼ cup whole fresh basil leaves

In a small bowl combine the cream cheese, maple syrup, and walnuts. Stir until well blended. Spread some of the cream cheese mixture over 1 bread square. Add a layer of turkey breast followed with 1 fresh basil leaf. Top with another bread square. Repeat with the rest of the bread and filling.

The Grace Poole (somewhat fishy)

16 to 20 slices whole grain bread, crusts removed, cut into quarters
½ cup sour cream
2 tablespoons chopped fresh dill (or 1 tablespoon dried)
1 tablespoon minced shallots

1 tablespoon fresh lemon juice
¼ teaspoon salt
¼ teaspoon freshly ground black pepper
½ pound smoked salmon, thinly sliced

In a small bowl, combine the sour cream, dill, shallots, lemon juice, salt, and pepper. Stir until well blended. Chill for at least 30 minutes before using. Spread some of the sour cream mixture over 1 bread square and top with some smoked salmon. Repeat with the rest of the bread and filling.

The Jane (plain, strong, and good)

16 to 20 slices whole grain bread, crusts removed, cut into quarters
¼ cup grainy mustard

½ pound ham, thinly sliced
¼ pound sharp cheddar cheese, thinly sliced

Spread grainy mustard over 1 bread square, then add a layer of ham, followed with a slice of sharp cheddar cheese. Top with another bread square. Repeat with the rest of the bread and filling.

The Last of the Mohicans

by James Fenimore Cooper

This novel is commonly referred to as an all-American classic. Written in 1826, *The Last of the Mohicans* is actually part of a series of novels called *The Leatherstocking Tales*, the series that made James Fenimore Cooper the first and most popular American novelist of the nineteenth century. A bit of trivia for you: Cooperstown, New York, home of the Baseball Hall of Fame, is named for Cooper's father, Judge William Cooper.

If you've already seen the 1992 movie *The Last of the Mohicans* starring Daniel Day Lewis, you might be a bit confused while you're reading the book because the screenplay bears only a faint resemblance to the novel. After you get your bearings, though, you'll discover that the book is far richer than the movie. In the book, Cooper addresses several weighty issues, such as racism, interracial relationships, and the declining relevance of organized religion in the frontier setting.

Up for Discussion . . .

- Modern critics point out several inconsistencies and discrepancies in the plot and subplots of this novel. Did you notice any?

- Discuss the various disguises used by Hawkeye and the other characters. Did they seem too far-fetched for the modern reader?

- *The Last of the Mohicans* is said to contain elements of both an adventure story and a sentimental novel. How do these elements work together in this book? Can you name other books, movies, or television shows that combine similar elements?

- What role does the frontier setting play in the novel? How would the novel have worked if Cooper had chosen to set the story during a later date, when the frontier had been mostly settled?

- Compare the father-son relationship of Chingachgook and Uncas to the father-daughter relationships of Munro and his daughters.

- In what ways is Cooper guilty of invoking racial stereotypes in his portrayal of Indians (i.e., he views the Indians as being either *very* good or *very* bad characters)?

- Discuss David Gamut. Did Cooper include his character simply for comic relief, or as a vehicle to express his thoughts on religion?

- Discuss the interracial relationships in the book. Why do none of the romantic ones last?

- Name as many subplots in *The Last of the Mohicans* as you can. What is the relevance of each one? If you were editing this novel, which subplots would you cut and which would you feel are relevant enough to stay?

- This novel is considered to be the best action and adventure story of its time. Compare and contrast this novel to a contemporary action and adventure movie. What differences can you cite regarding violence? Romance? What do those differences say about the changes in American society?

Peaceful Native American Puddings

The following puddings would have been an exorbitant luxury for anyone living in North America at the time when *The Last of the Mohicans* is set. For the characters in the novel, food was most likely bland because of a lack of spices and sugar and was viewed more as sustenance than entertainment. These recipes are reminiscent of traditional Native American puddings, yet the flavors are a bit more modern. Serve with a freshly brewed pot of coffee or tea.

Popcorn Pudding

Native Americans used corn for just about everything. They introduced the settlers to popcorn, and the settlers used it in place of flour to create traditional recipes,
such as this pudding.

**2 cups plain popcorn (you can use
the microwave variety as long
as it's plain)
3 cups milk
4 tablespoons butter, melted, plus
some for greasing the pan**

**3 large eggs, beaten
½ cup brown sugar
1 teaspoon vanilla extract
½ teaspoon salt**

Grind all but a small handful of the popcorn in a food processor. Heat the milk in
a small saucepan over medium heat until scalded (hot but not boiling). Pour the hot
milk over the ground popcorn, stir in the butter, and let sit for 1 hour. Preheat the
oven to 300°F. Grease a 8 by 8-inch baking dish. In a medium bowl, beat the eggs
with the brown sugar until light, then add the vanilla and salt. Beat in the corn mixture and turn into the baking dish. Sprinkle the reserved popcorn on the top. Bake
for 45 to 60 minutes, or until the custard is set and the pudding browned on top.

Pumpkin Pudding with Fire Water Sauce

Nothing says cozy like the smell of pumpkin in the kitchen! This recipe makes 36 muffins.

For the Pumpkin Pudding:

½ cup butter, plus some for greasing the muffin tins
1 quart milk
1 cup light molasses
2 cups stone-ground cornmeal
6 large eggs, beaten
Grated zest of 2 lemons
1 tablespoon ground cinnamon
1 tablespoon freshly grated nutmeg

⅛ teaspoon salt
2 cups golden raisins
2 cups canned pumpkin puree

For the Fire Water Sauce:

½ cup butter
½ cup rum
2 tablespoons brown sugar
2 tablespoons orange juice

To make the Pumpkin Pudding: Preheat the oven to 300°F. Grease three 12-hole muffin tins and set aside. Combine the milk, molasses, and butter in a large saucepan over medium heat. Heat until hot but not boiling. Place the cornmeal in a large non-reactive bowl and pour the warm liquid over it. Cover and let sit for 1 hour. In a medium bowl, combine the eggs, lemon zest, cinnamon, nutmeg, salt, raisins, and pumpkin puree. Add the pumpkin mixture to the cornmeal mixture. Spoon the batter into the muffin tins and bake for 45 minutes to 1 hour, or until a toothpick inserted in the center of a muffin comes out clean. Allow to cool in the pan for 30 minutes. Before inverting onto a serving platter, loosen by running a spatula around the edge of each muffin.

Meanwhile, make the Fire Water Sauce: Melt the butter in a small saucepan over medium heat and add the remaining ingredients. Serve warm over the Pumpkin Pudding.

BONUS CHAPTER 2

Beach-Worthy Biographies

I am a celebrity junkie. I've been known to purchase stacks of *People*, *Us Weekly*, and *InStyle* magazines at a time, and I regularly fill the waiting room in my office with tabloids so patients can actually enjoy waiting, and sometimes even squeal with delight when they see a new *In Touch* magazine displayed. At least I know I'm not alone in my guilty pleasure: Since the dawn of VH1's *Behind the Music*, E!'s *E! True Hollywood Story*, and Lifetime's *Intimate Portrait*, America has become obsessed with celebrity gossip.

If your reading group feels like taking a break from the heavier titles and dipping its toes into the refreshing pool of celebrity biographies, the tumultuous tabloid-esque biographies that I've included in this chapter—all great beach reads—will be just what the doctor ordered. While basking in the summer sun, it's much more gratifying to reflect on how the rich and famous are not always as perfect as they seem than to ponder how your thighs look in your new bathing suit. The discussion for these selections is very light, so if your group is sick of using words like "metaphorical" and "quintessential," now's the time to take a breather and get yourself a drink. The menus for the books in this chapter are simple to make and serve, from a tea party on your back porch to drinks and appetizers by the pool. Get ready ladies, it's time to gossip!

The Royals by Kitty Kelley

*I*f you're looking for a juicy scandal, you'll love Ms. Kelley's royal tell-all. I won't vouch for its journalistic integrity, but I can tell you that it's a blast to read. The first time I read *The Royals*, I was so shocked by its content that I read several passages aloud to my husband, followed by an incredulous, "can you *believe* that?" He, of course, could not.

Kitty Kelley is notorious for writing yummy exposés that are filled with shocking stories. *The Royals* was published in 1997 and includes juicy tidbits on the lives of Queen Elizabeth II, the Queen Mum, Princess Margaret, Prince Phillip, Prince Charles, the late Princess Diana, Camilla Parker-Bowles, Fergie, and Prince Andrew, not to mention all of their forbearers in the House of Windsor who seemed to get into just as much trouble, if not more! According to *Entertainment Weekly*, this was the fourth best selling book of 1997.

Up for Discussion . . .

- What are the two most shocking rumors you read about in *The Royals*? What made these two rumors stand out in your mind?

- Name three stories from the book that you don't believe are true. Why are you skeptical? In each case, what motives did the disclosing party have (if any) to make up the story?

- Name your two favorite members of the royal family. Why are they your favorites?

- Name the member of the royal family that you most closely identify with. Why did you chose as you did?

- Who is your least favorite member of the Royal family? Why?

- Compare (and contrast) British royalty to popular American movie stars. How are they treated by/in the media. Do we as the public have the same expectations for royalty as we do for movie stars? Is this fair?

- How do you think Americans would feel about supporting a royal family with our tax dollars? Do you think the monarchy will survive the next generation of British taxpayers?

- Why do you think the older royal women tolerated martial indiscretions and the younger women (like Princess Di) just wouldn't?

- Finish this sentence: If I were Princess Di I would have . . .

- Finish this sentence: If I were in the Windsor family I would . . .

- Would you allow yourself to be scrutinized and controlled in order to marry into the royal family?

- How would you handle the courtiers?

- What do you think the most fun part of being royalty would be?

- If you were given a coronation, what would your gown look like?

- If you had to oversee the construction and design of the royal yacht, what special features would you give it?

Scandelicious Treats

Time for a spot of tea out on the porch. Here we have the Queen Mum's World War II Victory Cake and Edward, Duke of Windsor's Abdicakes with Tropical Exile Cream for abdicating the throne to marry his "common" and twice divorced American sweetheart. Talk about romantic! To accompany these sweet treats, brew up a fresh pot of orange pekoe tea.

Queen Mum's Victory Cake

This cake was quite popular during World War II, as it is eggless, butterless, and milkless and therefore did not waste precious rations. But . . . did the royal family stay within their rations? You be the judge.

⅓ cup vegetable shortening (although it's not authentic, butter-flavored Crisco works well here), plus some for greasing the pan

2 cups all-purpose flour, plus some for dusting the pan

1 cup brown sugar

1¼ cups water

2 cups raisins

½ teaspoon freshly ground nutmeg

2 teaspoons ground cinnamon

½ teaspoon ground cloves

1 teaspoon salt

1 teaspoon baking soda, dissolved in 2 tablespoons water

1 teaspoon baking powder

Preheat the oven to 325°F. Grease and flour an 8 by 8-inch cake pan and set aside. Combine the brown sugar, water, shortening, raisins, nutmeg, cinnamon, and cloves in a medium saucepan over medium heat. Bring to a boil, lower the heat, and simmer for 3 minutes. Remove from the heat and cool. Stir in the salt and dissolved baking soda. In a separate bowl, sift together the flour and baking powder. Slowly mix the dry ingredients into the wet. Pour the batter into the pan and bake for 40 to 50 minutes, or until a toothpick inserted in the center of the cake comes out clean. Allow to cool for 30 minutes before inverting onto a serving plate. This cake is delicious served warm.

Abdicakes with Tropical Exile Cream

The Duke and Duchess of Windsor's specialty.

Abdicakes

1 cup butter
1½ cups sugar
3 large eggs
4 cups all-purpose flour
2 teaspoons baking powder
1 teaspoon baking soda
½ teaspoon salt
¼ cup buttermilk
1 teaspoon almond extract

For the Tropical Exile Cream:

1 cup cream cheese
1 cup heavy whipping cream
¼ cup confectioners' sugar
¼ cup canned crushed
   unsweetened pineapple
¼ cup sweetened coconut flakes

To make the Abdicakes: In a large bowl, cream together the butter and sugar with a handheld electric mixer at medium speed. When the mixture is fluffy, beat in the eggs, one at a time. In a separate bowl, combine the flour, baking powder, baking soda, and salt. Add to the butter mixture alternately with the buttermilk until completely combined. Stir in the almond extract. Cover the bowl with plastic and refrigerate for at least 1 hour (you can make the dough a day ahead of time and chill overnight if you wish).

Preheat the oven to 350°F. Roll out the dough to a ¼-inch thickness and cut out pieces with a 2-inch heart-shaped cookie cutter (because it's all in the name of love!). Place on baking sheets lined with parchment paper and bake for 12 to 15 minutes, or until the edges are lightly browned. Remove to a wire cooling rack and allow to cool completely.

Meanwhile, make the Tropical Exile Cream: In a large bowl, beat together the cream cheese, whipping cream, and confectioners' sugar until stiff peaks form. Fold in the pineapple and coconut. Serve immediately in a chilled bowl with the Abdicakes.

Orange Pekoe Tea

8 thin orange slices
8 whole cloves

8 small pieces candied ginger
Large pot of orange pekoe tea

Place an orange slice, clove, and a small piece of candied ginger in each teacup and pour in hot tea. Serve immediately.

An Affair to Remember

The Remarkable Love Story of Katharine Hepburn and Spencer Tracy
by Christopher Anderson

Although its title sounds like the famous movie, this book is actually about the real-life love affair between Katharine Hepburn and Spencer Tracy. Throughout the couple's entire twenty-six-year relationship, Spencer was married to someone else. How is this romantic, you may ask? Well, I'm not sure it is. Nevertheless, theirs is quite an interesting story, and what's especially intriguing is that their affair was not made public by the media until after Tracy's death in 1967.

Read the book, then get your group together for a screening of one of the many movies Hepburn and Tracy made together. In my opinion, the film that best displays their amazing chemistry is *Adam's Rib*. (It can be difficult to find this one at your local Blockbuster, but many public libraries have a large selection of old movies. Also, keep an eye out for it in your cable listings—I was able to see almost every movie Hepburn and Tracy made together in about a week's time by taping them on the classic movie channels.)

Up for Discussion . . .

- Do you think this love affair is romantic? Why or why not?

- Could you be someone's mistress for twenty-six years? What type of man would your lover have to be to make you sacrifice as much as a mistress obviously must?

- How do you think Hepburn was able to stay with Tracy all those years, while he was married to someone else?

- How would the media treat Hepburn and Tracy's relationship today?

- How were they able to keep their affair a secret for so long? (They even avoided media speculation!)

- If you were Louise Tracy, would you put up with Spencer's behavior? If you would, how would you do it?

- Spencer's depression and alcoholism would be more treatable today than fifty or sixty years ago, when the story takes place. How well do you think our modern treatments would work on him? Which of his inner demons would he need to conquer in order to recover?

- What part of Spencer's personality do you think attracted Katharine? What part of Katharine's personality attracted Spencer?

- What do you think of the couple's on-screen chemistry? How would it have been different had they not had an off-screen affair?

Dips and Doubles

Here are some perfect snacks for a summertime gathering out on the deck. Katharine Hepburn certainly would have approved of this simple, elegant menu, and Spencer Tracy would have been satisfied by the extra-tall drinks. Serve these dips with assorted crackers, pita wedges, and fresh veggies.

Avocado Dip

2 ripe avocados, pitted and peeled
2 tablespoons fresh lemon juice
2 tablespoons anchovy paste
¼ cup very finely chopped red onions

½ teaspoon crushed red pepper flakes
1 garlic clove, minced
¼ cup sherry

Place all the ingredients in a blender and blend until smooth. Transfer to serving bowl. Chill at least 1 hour before serving.

Red Bean Dip

2 teaspoons olive oil
1 red onion, chopped
2 garlic cloves, chopped
2 plum tomatoes, chopped
2 tablespoons golden raisins
6 dried apricots, chopped
2 tablespoons orange juice
1½ cups rinsed and drained
  canned red kidney beans

½ teaspoon ground cumin
¼ teaspoon ground cinnamon
¼ teaspoon ground cloves
¼ teaspoon curry powder
¼ teaspoon chili powder
¼ teaspoon salt

Heat the oil in a medium nonstick skillet over medium heat. Add the red onion and garlic and sauté until just softened, about 2 to 3 minutes. Reduce the heat, cover, and cook for 2 to 3 minutes, or until the onions are transparent. Stir in the tomatoes, raisins, apricots, and orange juice. Cover and cook for 2 to 3 minutes, or until the tomatoes are soft. Stir in the beans, cumin, cinnamon, cloves, curry, chili, and salt. Remove from the heat to cool slightly. Transfer the mixture to a blender and blend until smooth. Transfer to a serving bowl and chill for at least 1 hour before serving.

Eggplant Dip

2 large eggplants, pierced in
  several places with a fork
¼ cup fresh lemon juice
¼ cup nonfat sour cream
¼ cup smooth peanut butter

1 tablespoon extra-virgin olive oil
1 garlic clove, minced
2 teaspoons ground cumin
1½ teaspoons salt
1 teaspoon cayenne pepper sauce

Preheat the broiler. Place the eggplants on a foil-lined broiler pan and broil for 30 minutes, turning every 5 minutes. Remove from the broiler and cool completely. Cut off the stem ends and remove the skins. Cut the pulp into large chunks and place in a food processor along with the remaining ingredients. Process to a puree. Transfer to serving bowl and chill at least 1 hour before serving.

Sweetness

SERVES 1

Juice of ½ lemon
1 tablespoon pure maple syrup
2 shots dark rum
2 splashes grenadine

Cracked ice
1 pineapple wedge
1 orange slice
1 maraschino cherry

Shake the lemon juice, maple syrup, rum, and grenadine in a martini shaker with cracked ice. Pour into a tall glass filled with ice. Garnish with the cherry, and serve immediately.

Zombie

SERVES 1 . . . AND REQUIRES A DESIGNATED DRIVER!

2 shots white rum
2 shots dark rum
1 splash apricot brandy
1 shot unsweetened pineapple juice
1 shot papaya nectar

Cracked ice
Juice of 1 lime
1 pineapple wedge
1 maraschino cherry
Pinch confectioners' sugar

Shake the white and dark rums, brandy, pineapple juice, and papaya nectar in a martini shaker filled with cracked ice. Pour, unstrained, into a large glass. Garnish with the pineapple wedge and cherry, sprinkle the confectioners' sugar on top, and serve immediately.

Sassy (But Sober . . .) Fizzer

SERVES 1

Cracked ice
3 shots cranberry juice

1 tablespoon fresh lemon juice
Chilled ginger ale

Fill a tall glass with cracked ice. Add the cranberry juice and lemon juice, and top off with ginger ale. Stir, and serve immediately.

Lucille

The Life of Lucille Ball
by Kathleen Brady

*W*ho doesn't love Lucy? I love her because when I was little, I performed (poorly) on the stage of the Lucille Ball Little Theatre in Jamestown, New York. Since Lucille Ball continues to be Jamestown's most famous former resident (she was born and raised there) and her first acting experience was on stage at the Little Theatre of Jamestown, the theater was renamed after her when she died in 1990. It was driven into our young Hollywood-wannabe minds that if Lucy made it, so could we! Unfortunately, my awkwardly long arms, thick glasses, and sheer lack of talent didn't offer much help in the way of becoming the next comic goddess.

My Hollywood aspirations aside, Lucille Ball is one of the most beloved television stars of all time—but what went on behind the scenes? This well-researched book, published in 1994, presents a more balanced picture of Lucille Ball's entire career than her other biographies, and it digs deeper than the many television documentaries about her life—so even if you've seen them all, you will still learn something new from the book.

Have a member of your group record an episode of *I Love Lucy* (its reruns air constantly) and watch it together before or after you've discussed the book.

Up for Discussion . . .

- Lucille Ball is best known for a role that she created on television. The assumption is often made that she is the same person as Lucy Ricardo. Compare and contrast her true self as presented in this book to her character in *I Love Lucy*.

- How did her family situation and upbringing in western New York shape her personality and ambitions?

- Reading a biography of someone extremely well-known is always eye-opening, as you often learn that things are not as they appear to be. Case in point: Lucille Ball was not a natural redhead! What other facts about her true life surprised you?

- While Lucille demonstrated many of her famous mannerisms (e.g., exaggerated facial expressions) long before she became a star, it took the actress several failed attempts before she became a successful entertainer. How did she overcome many of the criticisms that led to her less-than-successful early attempts?

- Compare and contrast Lucille's and Desi's childhoods and cultures. How do these differences help to explain their tumultuous marriage?

- Describe Lucille's friendships with her peers in Hollywood. How, as an adult, was she able to find the familial support she felt that she lacked growing up?

- What were some of the challenges that arose in the production of *I Love Lucy*? How many of those were a product of Lucille and Desi's relationship? Cite examples from the book.

- How did the final breakup of their marriage affect the careers of Lucy and Desi?

- How would Lucille's life have been different if she had worked predominantly in film?

- If Lucille and Desi hadn't had the television show, weren't famous, and were simply an average American couple, do you think their marriage would have worked? Why or why not?

Tumultuous Cocktails with Lucy and Desi

Add a little *cha cha cha* to your discussion with some cocktails and quesadillas, Desi style. The margaritas have just the right touch of orange to make them Lucy-i-fied! However, they have quite a kick, so go easy on them so you don't resemble Lucy in her famous "Vita-meta-vegiman" spot!

Margaritas with a Touch of Orange

Salt
2 limes, quartered
Ice cubes
2 cups sweet-and-sour mix

1 cup triple sec
1½ cups gold tequila
⅓ cup Grand Marnier

Salt the rims of 8 glasses by pouring salt onto a small plate, rubbing the rims of the glasses with lime, and then pressing them into the salt. Fill the glasses with ice. In a blender, combine the sweet-and-sour mix, triple sec, tequila, and Grand Marnier. Blend until smooth. Pour into the prepared glasses, squeeze a lime quarter into each glass, and serve immediately.

Desi's Chicken Quesadillas

2 tablespoons olive oil
3 pounds boneless, skinless chicken breasts, cut into small cubes
1 large onion, chopped
1 small green pepper, cored, seeded, and chopped
1 small red pepper, cored, seeded, and chopped
1 small yellow pepper, cored, seeded, and chopped
Salt and freshly ground black pepper to taste

2 teaspoons garlic powder
1 tablespoon ground cumin
2 cups shredded Mexican cheese (you can find this blend of Colby and Monteray Jack cheeses in your supermarket's dairy section)
16 small flour tortillas
Sour cream, for serving
Guacamole (recipe follows)

Warm the oil in a large skillet over medium-high heat. Add the chicken, onion, green pepper, red pepper, and yellow pepper. Sauté until tender, about 5 to 7 minutes. Add the salt, pepper, garlic powder, and cumin. Cook, covered, for 7 to 10 minutes, or until the chicken is completely cooked.

Preheat the oven to 300°F. Place 2 tortillas on a separate large nonstick skillet over medium heat. Heat for about 1 minute on each side, using a spatula to mash the air bubbles out. Once you've flipped the first tortilla over, add a layer of cheese, followed by a layer of the chicken mixture, then another layer of cheese. Top with the second tortilla shell. Remove from the skillet and cut into 4 slices. Continue with the rest of the tortillas. Place the quesadillas in the oven as you make them to keep them warm. Serve with sour cream and freshly made Guacamole.

Guacamole

6 avocados, peeled and pitted
Juice of 2 limes
2 teaspoons salt
1 cup finely diced onion
⅓ cup chopped fresh cilantro

4 Roma tomatoes, diced
1 garlic clove, minced
¼ teaspoon cayenne pepper
   (optional)

Mash together the avocados, lime juice, and salt in a medium bowl. Mix in the onion, cilantro, tomatoes, garlic, and cayenne. Refrigerate for 1 hour before serving.

Gold Digger

The Outrageous Life and Times of Peggy Hopkins Joyce
by Constance Rosenblum

The title of this book alone makes it irresistible, but what you will find between the covers (pun intended) is even better. *Gold Digger* is the story of the many loves and many spending sprees of Peggy Hopkins Joyce. Peggy was the inspiration for Marilyn Monroe's famous "material girl" character, Lorelei, in *Gentleman Prefer Blondes*—the song "Diamonds Are a Girl's Best Friend" sums Peggy up quite well. Peggy was married six times, and at one point she managed to spend $1 million of one of her husbands' money in one week! Peggy had a short-lived film career, but she was basically famous for being famous. Her escapades were followed meticulously in the early tabloidish society pages, back when the nation was enthralled with glamour (have we really changed so much?). *Gold Digger* reads like a tabloid, but it is written by Constance Rosenblum, the well-respected editor of the City section of the *New York Times*.

Up for Discussion . . .

- Explain what Rosenblum means when she refers to a "culture of personality."

- How was Peggy able to manipulate men?

- In an age that viewed divorces as scandalous, what factors contributed to Peggy's beliefs about marriage and divorce?

- How did fashion and beauty contribute to Peggy's celebrity?

- In the brilliant social circle of Washington, D.C., how was Peggy able to become a much-sought-after socialite?

- A person of little talent and substance, Peggy leveraged her assets to become a star. Were their any male stars of her generation that did the same thing?

- What female or male celebrities today could you compare to Peggy? Do you think their lives will play out similarly to the way hers did?

- What role did the media play in creating Peggy's celebrity? Explain her love/hate relationship with the media.

- Looking back on the whole of Peggy's life, do you feel that she was a success, a failure, or something in between? Why?

- What factors contributed to Peggy's decline? Was the fun that she had early in her life worth the events of her later life?

- Is the celebrity life the life for you? Why or why not?

- If you were Peggy's closest confidant, how would you have advised her at various key points throughout her life?

- If you were Peggy, what decisions would you have made differently?

Elegant Appetizers and 1920s Cocktails

If you're going to attempt to pick up a string of wealthy suitors, you don't want it to look like you eat too much, so you'll just pick at some elegant finger foods. And what will make you more sparkling than a glass of champagne? In the 1920s, when French style was the rage and alcohol was prohibited, champagne could only be enjoyed by those who could travel out of the country to enjoy it, or those who had the means to smuggle it into the United States. Nowadays, we seem to enjoy champagne only on New Year's Eve or at weddings. Ice-cold champagne is a great summertime beverage that's refreshing and chic, especially with a few frozen strawberry slices placed in the bottom of the glass.

Smashing Smørrebrød

8 slices pumpernickel bread, cut in
   half
¼ cup whipped cream cheese
½ pound smoked salmon, thinly
   sliced
6 large eggs

⅔ cup small curd cottage cheese
1 tablespoon minced chives
2 tablespoons butter
32 steamed asparagus tips
Freshly ground black pepper to
   taste

Spread cream cheese over each piece of bread. Follow by a layer of smoked salmon. In a medium bowl, whisk together the eggs, cottage cheese, and chives. Melt the butter in a large nonstick skillet over medium heat and pour in the egg mixture. Cook, stirring as needed, until firm, about 2 minutes. Spoon a thin layer of eggs on top of the salmon and garnish with 2 asparagus tips. Sprinkle with pepper and serve.

Lamb Pita Triangles

½ pound lean ground lamb
6 green onions, white and green
   parts, minced
¼ cup minced fresh parsley
1 tablespoon tomato paste
3 garlic cloves, minced
Finely grated zest of 1 lemon

¼ cup minced fresh cilantro
2 tablespoons Dijon mustard
1 tablespoon minced fresh mint
Salt and freshly ground black
   pepper to taste
2 pita breads, split open (to make
   4 pita circles)

Combine all the ingredients except the pitas in a large bowl and mix well. Refrigerate for at least 2 hours for the flavors to mingle. Preheat the oven to 450°F. Cut the pitas into triangles and spread some of the lamb mixture over each triangle. Place on an ungreased cookie sheet and bake for about 10 minutes, or until golden brown. Serve hot.

Greek Potstickers

Extra-virgin olive oil, for greasing
the cookie sheet and brushing
the potstickers
1 pound ground turkey, cooked in
a skillet and drained on paper
towels
1 cup cooked white rice
½ cup crumbled feta cheese
2 garlic cloves, minced
½ cup minced fresh parsley
10 pitted kalamata olives

2 green onions, white and green
parts, minced
½ teaspoon dried oregano
Salt and freshly ground black
pepper to taste
2 (20-count) packages potsticker
wrappers (most likely these will
be in the produce section of
your grocery store, near the
tofu)

Preheat the oven to 375°F. Brush a cookie sheet with oil and set aside. Combine all of the ingredients except the oil and potsticker wrappers in a food processor and process until well combined. Place a generous teaspoonful of the mixture in the center of each potsticker wrapper and fold in half. Slightly dampen the outer edges with cold water and press with the tines of a fork to seal. Place on the cookie sheet. Brush the tops of each potsticker with oil and bake for 15 minutes, or until the potstickers are a light golden brown. Serve hot.

Olive Cheddar Puffs

¼ cup butter, softened
1 cup grated cheddar cheese
½ cup all-purpose flour, sifted
¼ teaspoon salt

¼ teaspoon paprika
24 medium green stuffed olives,
drained well

In a medium bowl, combine the butter and cheese. Add the flour, salt, and paprika and blend well. Line a baking sheet with parchment paper. Cover each olive with about 1 full teaspoon of the dough, form into a ball with the olive in the center, and place on the baking sheet. Refrigerate for at least 2 hours. Preheat the oven to 400°F and bake for 10 minutes, or until golden brown. Serve hot.

BONUS CHAPTER 3

The Mane Event

A girl could argue that there's nothing more fun than attending an event that requires buying an adorable, fancy hat. (Of course, when you buy the fancy hat, you're going to *have* to buy shoes to match!) By these standards, the Kentucky Derby is as fun as they come. One of the oldest and most prestigious sporting events in the United States, the Derby began in 1875 as a deliberate attempt to copy the Epsom Derby in England, at which stylish clothes and parties were as much a part of the event as the race itself. The Kentucky Derby is only two minutes long, but the elaborate celebrations last for the entire day, if not the entire week—now that's my kind of sporting event! With over 100,000 live Derby spectators, and millions more who tune in on their televisions and radios, it's clear that America loves this horse race.

America also loves reading about horses—according to amazon.com, over 90,000 horse-related fiction and nonfiction books are currently in print. In this chapter, I've included Equestrian-themed classics and bestsellers that are sure to please. If you place your bet on any one of these four titles, odds are your group will have cause to celebrate. Wearing hats to the discussion is strongly encouraged!

Black Beauty by Anna Sewell

Published in 1877, Sewell wrote this story to publicize man's ill treatment of horses and to try to generate empathy and understanding from horse owners. At the time, horse owners made up a huge percentage of the population, comparable to the percentage of Americans who own cars today. Sewell wanted to illustrate that horses are not machines, but living beings, worthy of respect and dignified treatment.

Narrated by Black Beauty, a wise, regal horse, the book teaches a timeless lesson: animals will serve humans well if they are treated with kindness and respect. (It's a great one to share with children or teenagers.) Sewell does a superb job balancing the poignant with the inspirational, the good characters with the bad. In addition, the book has the most beautiful ending you can imagine.

Up for Discussion . . .

- In the first chapter, Black Beauty describes his first home, which was filled with love and tenderness. How do you think his joyful beginning shaped him throughout his life?

- In the second chapter, we learn that a boy and his horse, Rob Roy (who is Black Beauty's brother), were both killed during a hunt. Black Beauty says of this, "but 'twas all for one little hare." What are the other characters' (both human and horse) feelings about that hunt and its consequences? What are your thoughts about such a hunt?

- Discuss Black Beauty's "breaking in." How does it compare to some of the other horses' experiences?

- What are the consequences (for both horse and master) of breaking in a horse the wrong way or breaking in a horse with harsh words or cruelty? What are the rewards (for both horse and master) of breaking in with kindness?

- How does Black Beauty's "breaking in" compare to a child's first day of kindergarten, or a young adult's first day of work? What could a teacher or employer learn from Black Beauty's first master?

- Even though Black Beauty has a wonderful life at Birtwick Park, he still says that he wishes most for liberty—for the freedom to hang out in the meadow all day long and run around when he pleases. If you were given "liberty"—i.e., freedom to do whatever you wanted all day long—what would you choose to do? How would your life be different if you didn't have to do what you didn't want to do? Would you choose that type of life over your current life?

- In what ways would Black Beauty's life be less rich had he been free to do what he pleased all day?

- On several occasions, the horses talk about the evils of "fashion"— that they are made to have their tails bobbed and later tortured by bugs, or they are made to have their necks jacked up when pulling the ladies in their carts. Sir Oliver, one of the horses at Birtwick Park, is especially troubled by this and says, "Why don't [these people] cut their own children's ears into points to make them look sharp, or cut the ends off their noses to make them look plucky? What right do they have to torment and disfigure God's creatures?" Discuss some examples in *Black Beauty* in which humans turned fashion into cruelty, and the effect this had on their animals.

- What are some destructive things people do to themselves in the name of fashion? Why do we feel compelled to do these things to ourselves and our animals?

- In one scene, Black Beauty refuses to go over a bridge because he knows that it isn't safe. He obviously is unable to tell his master this, but by refusing to go forward, he saves everyone's life. His master says that God gives men reason to find things out for themselves, but gives animals knowledge without reason to save men's lives (in other words, sharper instinct). Can you share a story in which an animal saved a human's life by its sheer instinct? What special powers of perception, if any, do your family pets have?

- When Joe fails to properly care for Black Beauty, Tom Green claims it was only because of ignorance. Joe erupts and says that ignorance is the worst thing in the world next to wickedness. What does he mean by that? Do you agree with that statement? Why or why not?

- Black Beauty always tries to live as best he can, regardless of his circumstances, some of which are less than ideal. How does this attitude separate Black Beauty from some of the other horses?

- Has there been a period in your life in which you had to try to live as best you could, despite the circumstances? What positives did you focus on to keep going?

A Simple Breakfast at the Stables

I greatly admire Joe's simple though rich life. He says no more than needs to be said, but he makes certain that every word counts. I can imagine Joe eating a simple breakfast in the stables as the sun is slowly rising behind him, and I bet that he would share his food with his beloved charges. Serve these scones with a freshly brewed pot of your favorite tea—Orange Spice or Earl Grey goes great with them. Don't forget the butter and jam!

Chocolate-Almond Scones

2 cups all-purpose flour, plus some
   for rolling out the dough
¼ cup sugar
1 tablespoon baking powder
¼ teaspoon ground cinnamon
6 tablespoons butter, chilled and
   cut into small pieces
¼ cup chopped almonds

1 large egg, beaten
½ cup plus 1 tablespoon
   buttermilk
1 teaspoon vanilla extract
1 ounce semisweet chocolate,
   melted and cooled
¼ cup sliced almonds

Preheat the oven to 400°F. In a large bowl, combine the flour, sugar, baking powder, and cinnamon. Using a pastry blender or 2 knives, cut in the butter until it resembles coarse crumbs. Stir in the chopped almonds. In a small bowl, combine the egg, ½ cup of the buttermilk, and the vanilla. Add the wet ingredients to the dry. Add the melted chocolate and stir until just moistened. Turn the dough out onto a lightly floured surface and knead the dough 10 to 12 times, or until nearly smooth. With floured hands, pat into an 8-inch circle and using a sharp knife, cut into 8 wedges. Place the wedges on an ungreased baking sheet, brush each with the remaining tablespoon buttermilk, and sprinkle with the sliced almonds. Bake for 15 to 18 minutes, or until the bottoms are lightly browed. Remove from the oven and cool on wire racks.

Blackberry Scones

Nonstick cooking spray for the pan
1½ cups rolled oats
1½ cups all-purpose flour, plus some for rolling out the dough
⅓ cup sugar
1 tablespoon baking powder
½ teaspoon baking soda
½ teaspoon salt
½ cup butter, chilled and cut into small pieces
¾ cup buttermilk
3 tablespoons seedless blackberry all-fruit spread
1 large egg, beaten

Preheat the oven to 375°F. Lightly spray a baking sheet with nonstick cooking spray. In a food processor, combine the oats, flour, sugar, baking powder, baking soda, and salt. Whirl until the oats are finely ground, about 1 minute. Transfer to a large bowl and cut in the butter with a pastry blender or 2 knives. Add the buttermilk to form a dough. Turn the dough out onto a lightly floured surface. With floured hands, pat the dough into a 10 by 8-inch rectangle about ½ inch thick. Using a sharp knife, cut into 2½-inch squares. With the tip of a knife, gently cut an X in the surface of each round. Fill each cut with blackberry spread and gently press into place with your fingers. Brush each round with beaten egg and bake until golden, about 12 minutes. Remove from the oven and cool on wire racks.

The Horse Whisperer by Nicholas Evans

*W*hen you read *The Horse Whisperer*, it will become immediately apparent why Robert Redford snatched the movie rights. This book is absolutely captivating—I skipped a week's worth of lunch-hour gossip sessions with my coworkers so that I could read it. And it's written like a cinematographer's dream, filled with amazing imagery of beautiful Midwestern landscapes.

The Horse Whisperer tells the story of Annie Graves, a jaded and career-driven woman on a quest to help her daughter and horse recover from a horrific accident. When Annie brings them both from New York to Montana to work with the mysterious Horse Whisperer, she gets a little more than she bargained for. This novel is packed with romance, so if your group is in the mood to read something steamy—but still primarily about horses—this is a great choice!

Up for Discussion . . .

- In the first chapter, several foreboding images and events foreshadow something about to go very wrong. Name as many of these images as you can.

- How does each image or event act as a negative foreshadow? Start with the truck drivers' run-in with the local police. Why does Evans use this technique to open the novel?

- How does Evans use foreshadowing throughout the entire novel?

- How would Grace's recovery have played out had they stayed in New York? Do you think that she would have had the chance to fully recover in New York?

- How would Pilgrim's recovery have played out had Annie kept him in the same stables in New York and not moved him to Montana? What was so different about Montana that helped Grace and Pilgrim to heal?

- What type of person would Annie have become later in life, if it weren't for her experiences in Montana?

- What role does Annie's career play in Grace's life prior to the accident? How does that role (and Annie's career) change throughout the novel? How does Grace feel about Annie's career? How does Annie's career affect their relationship?

- List instances in which Annie's ambition and drive was helpful to Grace's recovery.

- What role does Robert (Grace's father) play immediately following the accident? How does his role evolve throughout the novel?

- In what ways would Grace's Montana experience have been different had Robert accompanied her instead of Annie? What if both parents had gone with her?

- How does Tom Booker heal horses?

- Why does Annie feel that Grace cannot heal unless Pilgrim does? Do you agree or disagree? Why?

- Did Annie and Robert's relationship stand a chance? Did it stand more—or less—of a chance directly following the accident? While Annie and Grace were in Montana? After they returned? How could they start to repair it?

- Describe Darlene's feelings toward Tom. What does Tom think about Darlene's feelings toward him? Do you think that Hank is aware of these feelings? If you were Hank, what would you say to Darlene about her behavior toward Tom? What do you think Darlene really wants?

- What did Tom see in Annie? Do you share his feelings? How would Tom and Annie's relationship have played out if Annie had stayed in Montana? If Tom had moved to New York?

- How would Grace have reacted had Tom and Annie stayed together?

- What did you think of the ending? If you were the author, how would you have ended the novel?

Big Ranch Hoe Down

Hey now . . . don't be sneaking off with your lover during the Hoe Down—you're bound to get caught by your snooping, jealous sister-in-law/hostess! Here is some spectacular chili that will keep everyone concentrating on the food, instead of their adulterous fantasies!

Hot Lovin' Chili

2 tablespoons vegetable oil

2 onions, chopped

3 garlic cloves, minced

1 pound ground beef

¾ pound beef sirloin, cubed

1 (14.5-ounce) can diced tomatoes with juice

1 (12-ounce) bottle dark beer

1 cup strong brewed coffee

2 (6-ounce) cans tomato paste

1 (14-ounce) can beef broth

¼ cup packed brown sugar

3 tablespoons chili powder

1 tablespoon ground cumin

1 tablespoon unsweetened cocoa powder

2 teaspoons dried oregano

1 to 3 teaspoons cayenne pepper, according to taste

2 teaspoons dried cilantro

1 teaspoon salt

2 (15-ounce) cans kidney beans, drained and rinsed well

2 to 4 fresh hot chile, according to taste, seeded and chopped

2 (15-ounce) cans black beans, drained and rinsed well

Shredded cheddar cheese, for serving

Sour cream, for serving

Tortilla chips, for serving

Heat the oil in a large saucepan over medium heat. Add the onions, garlic, ground beef, and beef sirloin and cook for 8 to 10 minutes, or until the meat is well browned and the onions are transparent. Stir in the diced tomatoes, beer, coffee, tomato paste, and beef broth until well incorporated. Stir in the brown sugar, chili powder, cumin, cocoa powder, oregano, cayenne, cilantro, and salt. Stir in the kidney beans and chiles. Reduce the heat to low and simmer for 1½ hours. Stir in the black beans, and simmer for an additional 30 minutes. The chili should be thick. Serve hot with cheddar cheese sprinkled on top and a dollop of sour cream. Serve the tortilla chips on the side for those who like to dip.

Cool as Tom Booker Cucumber Salad

4 large cucumbers, sliced
1 small Vidalia onion, thinly sliced
1 cup white vinegar

½ cup water
¾ cup sugar
1 tablespoon dried dill

Toss together the cucumbers and onion in a large bowl. Combine the vinegar, water, and sugar in a small saucepan over medium-high heat. Bring to a boil, stirring to dissolve the sugar, and pour over the cucumbers and onion. Stir in the dill, cover, and refrigerate until chilled. (The salad can also be eaten at room temperature, but be sure to allow the cucumbers to marinate for at least 1 hour.)

Seabiscuit

An American Legend
by Laura Hillenbrand

*W*ho doesn't love a story about the underdog (or in this case, underhorse) becoming a champion against all odds? In the 1930s, America was packed with underdogs, and the people needed a little horse named Seabiscuit to show them that things could always take a turn for the better. You will likely come away from this book wondering how the characters (in this case, real people) were able to conquer the incredible and seemingly insurmountable challenges placed before them. This book not only tells an inspirational story, but it also gives us a glimpse into that dark chapter of American history, the Great Depression.

Up for Discussion . . .

- Hillenbrand describes racing a thoroughbred horse as "a task much like perching on the grille of a car while it speeds down a twisting, potholed freeway in traffic." Now I get it! Can you come up with an equally effective comparison after reading of the jockeys' exploits?

- What athletic skills must a jockey possess? What kind of personality do you think is ideal for a jockey?

- How would you compare jockeys with any of the following: an Olympic-style wrestler, a surfer, or a hockey player?

- Because of the dangerous nature of horse racing and its inextricable connection with wagering, jockeys continually face the dilemma of: "perform as if I won't get another chance to win," or "perform so that I do have another chance (and thereby minimize my fear and pain)." Either way a price is paid. How did the 1940 Santa Anita One Hundred Grander (the unattained goal first attempted in 1936) pose the dilemma for every principal character connected to Seabiscuit?

- In order to win the Detroit Governor's Handicap in August 1936 (amazingly, Seabiscuit's fiftieth race), Seabiscuit had to emerge from a seemingly impenetrable four-horse scrum on the final turn. Hillenbrand describes it as follows: "Pollard, in the lingo of jockeys, asked Seabiscuit the question. Seabiscuit, for the first time in is life, answered." Discuss the meaning of this quote. Have you been asked "the question"? How did you answer?

- Much of the Seabiscuit legend can be understood in terms of what Hillenbrand describes as "the burgeoning industry of escapism" and the "dawning of the modern age of celebrity" in 1937. What social and political events were taking place at that time to cause these cultural currents? How did expanded ownership and use of radios contribute? Could this captivating American legend have taken place without these social forces and technological advances?

- How would we react to Seabiscuit's success today? Why?

- Early in the book, Hillenbrand discusses the notion of equine pride and how it relates to thoroughbred horse racing. She makes several references the Seabiscuit's competitiveness, easily the defining characteristic of his personality (recall the awesomely written race scenes of Santa Anita, Arlington, Hollywood Park, Suffolk Downs, and so on). Describe Seabiscuit in terms of his racing. What aspects of his racing persona make him a champion?

- After War Admiral's defeat by Seabuscuit at the long-awaited Pimlico Special Run in March 1939, George Woolf makes the following statement: "Horses, mister, can have crushed hearts just like humans." What does this tell you about the Iceman, his sense of the developing legend, and his understanding of thoroughbreds?

- Seabiscuit is said to have amassed more inches of press coverage during 1938 than any other public figure. Rate Seabiscuit as an American legend when compared to his peers in the 1930s. What does this suggest about the horse and his times? What impact did the ownership of Charles Howard, the training of Tom Smith, and his association with the Iceman and the Cougar have on Seabiscuit's image?

- Dubbed the "Great Traveler," Seabiscuit logged nearly 50,000 railroad miles traveling to and from racetracks during his career. How might the regimen of heavy travel have affected Seabiscuit's health? To what extent was cross-country travel a contributing factor to his celebrity?

Dinner on the Train

In the 1930s, stews were very popular because they could be easily stretched, and they were hot and comforting. If we were on the train with Seabiscuit traveling through Kentucky on a chilly day, Kentucky Burgoo would be just the thing to eat. I couldn't resist adding a recipe for "Seabiscuits" to this menu because nothing goes better with stew than a fluffy homemade biscuit. In Kentucky, Butterscotch pie traditionally would be served, but straight butterscotch is a little sweet for most people's taste, so I've added chocolate to the recipe to cut the sweet and to make chocolate lovers happy. So, step into the dining car and let's celebrate one of Seabiscuit's triumphs!

Kentucky Burgoo

5 cups water
1 (28-ounce) can diced tomatoes with juice
1½ pounds beef chuck roast, cut into 1-inch cubes
1 tablespoon instant chicken boullion granules
1½ pounds chicken thighs or drumsticks, skinned
4 medium white potatoes, peeled and cubed

1 (10-ounce) package frozen succotash
1 (10-ounce) package frozen cut okra
3 carrots, sliced
1 large onion, chopped
1 tablespoon curry powder
1 teaspoon sugar

Combine the water, tomatoes, chuck roast, and chicken boullion granules in a large Dutch oven over medium heat. Bring to a boil, cover, reduce the heat to low, and simmer for 30 minutes. Add the chicken pieces, turn up the heat, and bring to a boil. Cover, reduce the heat to low, and simmer for an additional 40 minutes, or until the chicken is cooked through. Remove the chicken pieces and set aside. Increase the heat to medium and add the potatoes, succotash, okra, carrots, onion, curry powder, and sugar. Bring to a boil, cover, and reduce the heat to low once again. Simmer for about 25 minutes, or until the Burgoo is nicely thickened. When the chicken is cool enough, remove the meat from the bones. Discard the bones and add the meat to the pot. Cook an additional 5 minutes, or until heated through.

Seabiscuits

**4 cups all-purpose flour, plus some
  for rolling out the dough
2 tablespoons baking powder
2 teaspoons salt**

**2 teaspoons sugar
½ teaspoon baking soda
2 cups sour cream
½ cup vegetable shortening**

Preheat the oven to 425°F. In a large bowl, combine the flour, baking powder, salt, sugar, and baking soda. Cut in the sour cream and shortening with a pastry blender until the mixture resembles coarse crumbs. Turn the dough onto a lightly floured board and knead 6 to 8 times to mix thoroughly. If dough is a bit dry add water, 1 teaspoon at a time, while kneading. With a lightly floured rolling pin, roll the dough to ½-inch thickness. With a floured 2½-inch round cookie cutter, cut out biscuits and place them on an ungreased baking sheet. Press the trimmings together and roll and cut as above until all the dough is used. Bake 10 to 15 minutes, or until the biscuits are golden.

Chocolate Butterscotch Pie

**¾ cup packed brown sugar
⅓ cup all-purpose flour
½ teaspoon salt
2½ cups milk
6 tablespoons chocolate syrup
2 large egg yolks, beaten**

**2 tablespoons butter
½ teaspoon vanilla extract
1 (9-inch) frozen pie shell, baked
  according to package directions
1 (8-ounce) container frozen
  whipped topping, thawed**

Combine the brown sugar, flour, and salt in a large saucepan (don't put it on the stove yet). Stir in the milk, chocolate syrup, and egg yolks. Place the saucepan over medium heat and cook, stirring frequently, until thickened, about 7 minutes. Remove from the heat and stir in the butter and vanilla. Pour into the prepared pie shell, cool, and place in the refrigerator to chill overnight. Serve with the whipped topping on top.

Horse Heaven by Jane Smiley

*M*y first horse racing experience took place at Keeneland Racetrack in Lexington, Kentucky, with my older sister Moriah. Ever since that first race, I've been totally hooked! Not on the gambling, of course—I've never bet more than $2, which keeps me from winning or losing more than $20 in an afternoon. What I'm hooked on is the atmosphere. The brightly colored silks and the shiny coats of the horses create quite a spectacle, and you can actually feel the horses' hooves hitting the track as they pass—it makes my heart skip a beat!

Horse Heaven is a wonderful novel for anyone who enjoys going to the races, or for anyone who has ever wanted to experience how thrilling horse racing can be. Written by Pulitzer Prize–winning author Jane Smiley, *Horse Heaven* is a *New York Times* Notable Book and bestseller. The book spans two years on the racing circuit, during which Smiley introduces the reader to a lengthy cast of characters, both human and equine. Smiley writes with a dry sense of humor that keeps the novel from getting too heavy. If your group is looking for a fictional exposé of sorts, *Horse Heaven* is a good choice.

Up for Discussion . . .

- There are several characters in this book who make their living in the horse industry, while their significant other is not very interested in the business. How do the pressures of breeding and training thoroughbreds strain or strengthen their relationships? Does a career in the horse industry seem more or less stressful than other careers with which you are familiar?

- Compare your image of thoroughbred racing before and after reading this book. Does the book's portrayal of the industry make it seem more or less competitive than you had originally thought? More or less glamorous?

- Describe the relationship between the owners and the trainers—the book contains several examples of power struggles between the two.

How do you think this compares to the owner/coach relationship in a professional sports team? How about to a restaurant owner/ manager relationship?

- While Smiley tells most of the story from the third person, she occasionally switches to the voice of one of the horses. What does this switch add to the novel? What does it say about her perception of thoroughbred horses?

- In the beginning of Chapter 6, the reader is introduced to Deirdre Donohue. We learn that Deirdre has been labeled "too loud, too opinionated, not pretty, without charm, [and] badly dressed." What barriers or struggles for women in the racing industry are described in the book? Are these unique to the horse industry? If they are unique, why? If not, how are they similar to those encountered in other businesses?

- Farley Jones had a posting on his office door of the "6 Commandments" from the *Tibetan Book of Thoroughbred Training*. Two of the commandments, "Do not find fault in anyone" and "Do not take anything to heart," are appropriate for most professional relationships. Name some similarities and differences in how people work together around horses and how they work together around inanimate objects, like computers. Does the fact that thoroughbreds sell for hundreds of thousands of dollars change people's attitudes or work habits? How?

- Thoroughbred racing is often portrayed as a sport for the rich. How do the characters feel about and describe wealthy horse owners?

- If you were as well off financially as these owners, do you think you would make the same spending decisions? How would your decisions be different? Would you become involved with thoroughbred racing for the prestige? The sport? The love of horses?

- In Chapter 21, an unnamed character states: "There's no place like the racetrack, son. Everyone of every sort is there. No one is excluded at the racetrack." Keeping this quote in mind, discuss the diversity of the novel's characters in terms of gender, race, socioeconomic standing, interests, values, family history, and goals. (Refer to the the Cast of Characters in the front of your book if you need to refresh your memory.) Do all industries accommodate such diversity? What would horse racing be like if the only people involved were wealthy? What if they were all poor, undereducated folk?

Supper at the Races

What follows is a traditional Kentucky Derby meal that is served in both homes and restaurants on the day of the big event. Now that you've had a look behind the scenes of horse racing, you might as well enjoy a proper racing supper!

Mint Julep

These really pack a punch. I've added an alternative below for those of you (myself included) who have trouble sipping bourbon!

SERVES 1

6 mint leaves
1 teaspoon superfine sugar
Cracked ice

2 to 3 ounces bourbon
Mint sprigs, for garnish
½ ounce whiskey

Place the mint leaves in the bottom of a tall glass. Sprinkle the sugar over the leaves and mash with a spoon. Place the glass in the freezer for 15 to 20 minutes to frost. Fill the glass three quarters full with cracked ice. Pour in the bourbon and stir. Top off with more cracked ice and pour the whiskey on top. Garnish with mint sprigs, and serve.

Champagne Julep

6 mint leaves	**Cracked ice**
1 teaspoon superfine sugar	**Chilled champagne**
1 teaspoon cold water	**Mint sprigs, for garnish**

Place the mint leaves in the bottom of a tall glass. Sprinkle the sugar over the leaves, then add the water and mash with a spoon. Place the glass in the freezer for 15 to 20 minutes to frost. Fill the glass to the top with cracked ice. Pour the champagne on top. Garnish with mint sprigs, and serve.

Kentucky Hot Brown

This is extremely filling, so if you are serving light eaters, you can simply half the recipe to make eight half-sandwiches.

1 cup butter	**16 slices bread, toasted**
¾ cup all-purpose flour	**2 tomatoes, thinly sliced**
6 cups milk	**2 pounds thinly sliced cooked**
1 cup freshly grated Parmesan	**turkey**
cheese	**12 slices bacon, cooked and**
2 large eggs, beaten	**crumbled**
Salt and freshly ground black	
pepper to taste	

Melt ½ cup of the butter in a large skillet over medium heat. Stir in enough flour to absorb all of the butter. Slowly whisk in the milk until the mixture is smooth. Then stir in 6 tablespoons of the Parmesan cheese. Stir in the eggs to thicken the sauce— *do not allow mixture to boil!* Remove the skillet from the heat and season with salt and pepper. Preheat the broiler.

For each Hot Brown, place 2 slices of toast on a heatproof plate or dish. Cover the toast with a couple of tomato slices. Place a liberal amount of turkey on top of the tomatoes, and pour a generous amount of sauce over the turkey. Sprinkle some of the remaining Parmesan cheese over the top. Place the dish under the broiler until the sauce is speckled brown and bubbling. Remove from broiler, sprinkle the crumbled bacon on top, and serve.

Kentucky Derby Pie

2 large eggs
½ cup all-purpose flour
½ cup granulated sugar
½ cup packed brown sugar
1 cup butter, melted and cooled

1 cup semisweet chocolate chips
1 cup chopped walnuts
1 (9-inch) frozen pie shell, thawed
Whipped cream or ice cream, for
serving

Preheat the oven to 325°F. In a large bowl, beat the eggs until foamy. Add the flour, granulated sugar, and brown sugar and beat until well blended. Stir in the butter and then the chocolate chips and walnuts. Pour the batter into the pie shell. Bake for about 1 hour, or until a toothpick inserted in the center comes out clean. (Note: You may see some melted chocolate on it—that's OK.) Serve warm topped with whipped cream or ice cream.

BONUS CHAPTER 4

 How Does Your Garden Grow?

During the dreary days of winter, nothing cheers me more than reading about colorful flowers growing in the sunshine. I'm convinced that the seed and plant catalogs that appear in my mailbox in February and March are more therapeutic than any antidepressant could ever be. And though I'm not much of a green thumb, when my husband and I built our first home in Lancaster, New York, I went a little garden crazy. I bought books, tools, plants, rose bushes, seeds, gadgets—you name it—so that I could have the yard that all my new neighbors would envy. I had daydreams of people passing by . . .

"That's the Gardners' house."

"Yes, they do have amazing gardens."

"No, that's really their last name—the Gardners."

"Well, isn't that apropos!"

What I ended up with was horticultural chaos. I had plants that were like Napoleon, taking over every bit of space they could possibly find, strangling out what was once there. To make matters worse, one day while I was weeding the perennial garden, I saw a mouse. Well, that was the end of tending to those flowers—they were on their own! I wasn't sticking my hand in the dirt if mice were going to be running amuck. My husband had some creative ideas for "eliminating" them, but alas, they were still furry creatures—I couldn't bear to see them murdered. So every mouse on the block moved into my perennial garden. They lived in the toad house, ate the fallen birdseed, and mocked me all the while. The gardens got so out of hand that I only felt relief when we sold the house and moved to Florida, where I now container garden.

If you need a little glimpse of sunshine in the gloomy days of late winter and early spring, the books discussed in this chapter will get your group talking and dreaming about gardens of all shapes and sizes. I've paired each book with recipes loaded with produce that, in lieu of growing yourself, you can buy from your local supermarket.

One Man's Garden by Henry Mitchell

*H*enry Mitchell had a love affair with his garden. Mind you, it isn't a mushy love affair, filled with perfection and fairy tale–like conditions. It was more of a typical marriage, filled with hard work, conflict, resolution, and the blissful acceptance that the other party is not only far from perfect, but will also never change some of those pesky characteristics, and yet the love is still strong. I think it's quite lovely, in fact. I wish I had the patience to tend a garden with as much affection as Mitchell did, but it's just as nice reading about the author's experiences—and with no ant bites, bee stings, or ruined French manicures!

For twenty years, Henry Mitchell wrote the popular weekly column "The Essential Earthman" for *The Washington Post*; *One Man's Garden* is a collection of his favorite columns and was published before his death in 1993. (Before *One Man's Garden*, Mitchell published a collection of his columns named, appropriately, *The Essential Earthman*.) The columns in *One Man's Garden* are written in an engaging and conversational style, and they're also packed with gardening tips, including how to begin planning your summer gardens in the late winter and early spring.

Up for Discussion . . .

- If you have a garden, do you have a passion for yours like Mitchell does for his? If not, what is your passion?

- If you had the patience and/or time, what would you like to plant outside your house this spring? Why?

- If you garden, what is the most interesting thing you've ever planted? What made you want to plant it? What happened?

- If you don't garden, what is the most interesting thing (idea, project, etc.) you've ever "planted" in your own life?

- What is your favorite flower? Why?

- Recall some of the gardening adventures that Mitchell describes in his book. Which did you find most interesting? Which of Mitchell's gardening projects do you wish you could recreate in your own space? For example, would you like to try your hand at raising water lilies or irises?

- Mitchell goes to great lengths on occasion to save a plant or to keep it alive during the winter. What are some things to which you show the same devotion?

- If you had to garden for a living, what would you grow?

- Despite Mitchell's passion for gardening, he states that not all people are cut out for it, that people "should not be cajoled into a world they have no sympathy for." Do you agree? Why? Why not? Have you ever felt cajoled into such a world? When and why?

- What characteristics do you have that would make you cut out for gardening? What characteristics do you lack?

- Mitchell says that planting a garden will never go as planned. What does that teach us about life? What is one thing in your life that you cannot change, that you can or must learn to embrace? What does Mitchell learn from his failures and changed gardening plans?

- In one section, Mitchell discovers that some seeds he has been looking forward to planting are missing, and he thinks his wife accidentally threw them away. If your spouse or significant other accidentally threw away something important of yours, would he admit to it? Would you fess up if you threw something important of his away? Share some real life examples (don't worry, you're among friends!).

- If you had to choose between planting your favorite flower that blooms for only three days a year, or any old flowers that bloom for months, which would you choose? Why?

- Have you ever tried to start plants or flowers from seed indoors, in the dead of winter, which you planned to plant outside as soon as spring emerged? Any luck? Would you do it again?

A Classy Garden Dinner

When I chose this menu I simply shut my eyes and thought of Henry Mitchell, sitting out on his garden terrace during the springtime in Washington, D.C. A refreshing strawberry and kiwi salad and vegetarian couscous surrounded by cherry blossoms—I can't think of a better way to celebrate the impending spring!

Garden Couscous

2 medium eggplants, stems and
   root ends removed, thinly sliced
Salt and freshly ground black
   pepper to taste
2 pounds tiny new potatoes (cut
   in half if they aren't bite size)
1 cup chicken broth
½ cup dry white wine
¼ cup balsamic vinegar
1 large onion, chopped
4 shallots, minced
3 tablespoons peeled and grated
   fresh ginger
¼ cup minced fresh basil
1 tablespoon ground cumin
2 tablespoons ground coriander

2 teaspoons ground cinnamon
1 teaspoon powdered saffron
1 (13-ounce) jar roasted red
   peppers packed in oil, drained
   and thinly sliced
1 yellow pepper, cored, seeded,
   and thinly sliced
2 (16-ounce) cans chickpeas,
   drained and rinsed
1 (16-ounce) can diced tomatoes,
   drained
½ cup dried currants
3 cups uncooked couscous,
   prepared according to package
   directions

Preheat the oven to 425°F. Line a baking sheet with parchment paper. Place the eggplant slices in a single layer, season with salt and pepper, and bake until tender, about 15 minutes. Remove from the oven and cool. While the eggplant is baking, bring a large pot of salted water to a boil, add the potatoes, reduce the heat, and simmer until the potatoes are tender, about 10 minutes. Drain and set aside.

Bring the chicken broth, wine, and vinegar to a simmer in a large skillet over medium-high heat. Add the onion, peppers, shallots, ginger, basil, cumin, coriander, cinnamon, and saffron. Reduce the heat to medium and simmer until the liquid has been almost completely absorbed, about 10 minutes. Stir in the roasted red peppers and chickpeas. Add the tomatoes and continue cooking, stirring, until reduced to a thick sauce, about 5 minutes. Stir in the currants, eggplant slices, and potatoes. Season with salt and pepper. Reduce the heat to low, cover, and simmer an additional 10 minutes. Check the liquid level, adding water, 2 tablespoons at a time, if necessary to prevent burning. Place the couscous on a serving platter. Make a hole in the center and spoon the vegetables into the center.

Strawberry and Kiwi Salad

⅓ cup heavy cream
¼ cup balsamic vinegar
2 tablespoons sugar
½ teaspoon salt
5 kiwis, peeled and chopped

1 quart strawberries, hulled and sliced
1 large handful basil leaves, chopped
2 cups baby field greens

In a medium bowl, whisk together the heavy cream and vinegar, then add the sugar and salt. Add the kiwis and strawberries, tossing to coat. To serve, divide the field greens among 8 small salad plates. Spoon the fruit over the field greens and sprinkle basil over the fruit just before serving.

A Patch of Eden

America's Inner-City Gardeners
by H. Patricia Hynes

This beautiful, inspiring book is a testament to the healing and restorative power of all things green. The people who lead the inner-city gardening movement have an incredible passion for their communities and for the people who live in them. They devote their lives to healing broken lives and broken spirits.

Hynes, who is an environmental engineer and professor at Boston University, became inspired to write this book after she viewed a slide show about inner-city gardening projects in 1992. She then began interviewing the leaders and participants (who are primarily women and residents in the areas that they garden) of the Greening of Harlem Coalition, San Francisco Horticulture and Garden Projects, several independent Philadelphia community gardens, and Chicago's Cabrini Greens and Inner-City Horticultural Foundation. Her research from those interviews is the basis for this book, which was published in 1996.

Warning: this book will compel you to help make your community more beautiful. Please use the resource guide in the back to find out more about how you can get involved!

Up for Discussion . . .

- How does living with and around nature keep us balanced? Why is it important to maintain natural elements in the typical inner-city landscape?

- In the first chapter we learn that it takes two generations to break the cycle of knowledge. For example: Two generations ago, many of the residents of Harlem kept kitchen gardens and some even kept large-scale gardens, but those skills were not passed down, so gardening was forgotten. What do you wish had been passed down to you that wasn't? What would you like to ensure that two generations from you learn?

- If it takes two generations to break the cycle of knowledge, what relevance does that have to poverty? Violence and abuse? Addiction? Why are these cycles so difficult to break?

- How does this book change the way you feel about community? Do you have a community? What can you do to make life better there?

- An entire chapter is dedicated to why women make great leaders in the inner-city gardening projects. What qualities do you think help to make a great leader? In what circumstances are women better leaders than men? In what circumstances are men better leaders than women?

- What activities can help people to feel like they are part of a true community? What types of behavior can help people to feel this way?

- How do you feel about the community that you live in? Do you feel like you belong? If not, how could you change that?

- Has farming "lost its dignity to the briefcase"? If you answered yes, discuss the implications of this loss.

- How can gardening heal a person?

- One of my favorite quotes in this book is: "You can be weeding your (garden) and it's like weeding your life." Discuss. What would you like to weed out of your life?

- Sometimes weeds can be pretty, like a field full of dandelions in bloom. No one planted those weeds and, most likely, no one knew they wanted them. What parts of life can be beautiful even though they weren't planned for or wanted?

- Here is another great quote: "You can't rush nature, and you can't rush life." How is this true for the inmates who are being rehabilitated? How is this true for you? How is this lesson important for parents as they rear their children in this day of instant messaging, constant entertainment, and information overload?

- In one of the gardening rehabilitation programs featured in *A Patch of Eden,* the participants are encouraged not only to take home fresh fruits and vegetables, but also fresh flowers. How can fresh flowers be as important as fresh vegetables?

- We spend more tax money on incarceration than we do on education. Why? What if it were the reverse? Discuss.

Very Veggie Community Pizza Party

After a long day of volunteering in the community gardens, what could be more fun than relaxing and refueling with one of America's favorite foods—pizza! And as long as we're gardening, why not make use of the harvest of fresh veggies and herbs? These pizzas are quick and easy to assemble. Serve with soda or ice cold beer.

All of these pizzas can be made with any store-bought prebaked pizza shells, such as Boboli. If you'd like to make appetizer-sized pizzas, use refrigerator biscuits (just stretch them out a bit and bake on parchment paper–lined baking sheets).

Tomato, Basil, and Chèvre Pizza

1 (14-ounce) prebaked pizza shell
2 tablespoons extra-virgin olive oil
½ cup shredded basil leaves
½ to ¾ cup canned tomato puree
2 tomatoes, diced
6 ounces chèvre (a type of goat cheese), crumbled (You can find it in the cheese section of your local supermarket.)

3 tablespoons freshly grated Parmesan cheese
¼ teaspoon crushed red pepper flakes
Salt and freshly ground black pepper to taste

Preheat the oven to 425°F. Place the pizza shell on a baking sheet. Brush the pizza shell with 1 tablespoon of the oil. Scatter the basil on top. Spread the tomato puree on top, followed by a layer of diced tomatoes. Sprinkle on the chèvre, then the

Parmesan cheese and red pepper flakes. Top with salt and pepper and drizzle the remaining 1 tablespoon oil on top. Bake for 10 to 15 minutes, or until the cheese is melted and the pizza shell is heated through.

Tomato, Fennel, and Olive Pizza

1 (14-ounce) prebaked pizza shell
2 tablespoons extra-virgin olive oil
½ to ¾ cup canned tomato puree
1 cup fennel sliced as thin as you can get it
¾ cup freshly grated mozzarella cheese

1 cup black Greek olives, pitted and chopped
3 tablespoons freshly grated Parmesan cheese
1 teaspoon dried oregano
Salt and freshly ground black pepper to taste

Preheat the oven to 425°F. Place the pizza shell on a baking sheet. Brush the pizza shell with 1 tablespoon of the oil. Spread the tomato puree over the pizza shell and scatter the fennel on top. Sprinkle the mozzarella cheese over the fennel, then top with the olives. Next, layer on the Parmesan cheese, oregano, salt, and pepper. Drizzle the remaining 1 tablespoon oil on top. Bake for 10 to 15 minutes, or until the cheese is melted and the pizza shell is heated through.

Roasted Red Pepper and Walnut Pizza

1 (14-ounce) prebaked pizza shell
3 tablespoons extra-virgin olive oil
2 large garlic cloves, minced
1 jar roasted red peppers packed in oil, drained and sliced
½ teaspoon crushed red pepper flakes

¾ cup freshly grated mozzarella cheese
3 tablespoons freshly grated Parmesan cheese
½ cup walnut halves
¼ cup chopped fresh parsley

Preheat the oven to 425°F. Place the pizza shell on a baking sheet. Combine the oil and garlic in a small skillet over medium heat. Sauté for about 2 minutes, or until the garlic is light brown. Brush over the pizza shell, reserving 1 tablespoon to drizzle over the top. Layer the red pepper slices over the pizza shell, then sprinkle on the red pepper flakes. Top with the mozzarella cheese, followed by the Parmesan cheese. Evenly distribute the walnut halves and top with the parsley. Drizzle the reserved oil and garlic on top. Bake for 10 to 15 minutes, or until the cheese is melted and the pizza shell is heated through.

Mushroom and Spinach Pizza

1 (14-ounce) prebaked pizza shell
2 tablespoons extra-virgin olive oil
1/4 cup minced onion
2 large garlic cloves, minced
1 cup diced white mushrooms
1 cup diced shiitake mushrooms
1/4 cup dry white wine

1/2 (10-ounce) package fresh baby spinach leaves, stemmed and shredded
3/4 cup freshly grated Parmesan cheese
Salt and freshly ground black pepper to taste

Preheat the oven to 425°F. Place the pizza shell on a baking sheet. Combine 1 tablespoon of the oil, the onion, and garlic in a large skillet over medium heat. Sauté for 3 to 4 minutes. Add the mushrooms and sauté until slightly softened, about 3 to 5 minutes. Add the wine and bring to a boil, reduce the heat to low, and simmer for about 5 minutes, or until the liquid is almost completely absorbed. Add the spinach leaves and cook until just barely wilted. Drain completely. Brush the pizza shell with the remaining 1 tablespoon oil, top with the mushroom and spinach mixture, and sprinkle Parmesan cheese on top. Season with salt and pepper. Bake for 10 to 15 minutes, or until the cheese is lightly browned and the pizza shell is heated through.

The Secret Garden by Frances Hodgson Burnett

This was my favorite book growing up—I can't even count the number of times I've read it. I loved the idea of having a place all to myself, a place that remained a mystery to everyone else but me. When I read this again as an adult, it resonated just as much—the idea of having a secret, quiet place all to myself is perhaps even more appealing to me now when faced with the pressures of adulthood. I can also better identify with the adult characters, which makes for a richer read. *The Secret Garden*'s tone can best be described by a quote from the author just before she died: "With the best that was in me I have tried to write more happiness into the world." Frances Hodgson Burnett also wrote *The Little Princess,* another favorite of little girls everywhere and the basis for the classic movie starring Shirley Temple.

It's best to read *The Secret Garden* on a rainy spring day. You'll feel just like Mary Lennox sitting in her room at Misselthwaite Manor on the always-rainy Yorkshire moors.

Up for Discussion . . .

- While several characters in the book refer to a secret garden, the same physical space represents different things to different characters. What is the secret garden to Mary? To Colin? To Mr. Craven? To Ben Weatherstaff?

- The friendship between Mary, Colin, and Dickon was, for each child, an important relationship. How did their friendship help Mary? How did it help Colin?

- What is the magic that is referred to so often in the book?

- Colin's life before the secret garden centered on his perceived illness. Discuss the origin of his condition, which we learn when we first meet him. Who encouraged the situation? What was his father's perception of his illness? How do people today inflict this same sort of condition on themselves? Have you ever known a hypochondriac? Worked with one?

- Each member of the Sowersby family plays a role in bringing the Craven family closer together. Discuss how the actions of Martha, Dickon, and Mrs. Sowersby are so important to Mary, Colin, and Mr. Craven.

- What is the significance of the moors? How are they different from the landscape at the Craven property?

- At the beginning of Chapter 27, Burnett writes about the major discoveries of the past century. She writes: "One of the new things people began to find out in the last century was that thoughts—just mere thoughts—are as powerful as electric batteries—as good for one as sunlight is, or as bad for one as poison." How does this apply to Mary and Colin? Are they the only ones whose well-being was influenced by their state of mind?

- How can the above quote be applied to modern society? Cite an idea that has been as good for people as sunlight, and another that has been as deadly as poison.

- Mrs. Craven's family and staff all have different memories of her. How was she memorialized before Mary's discovery of the secret garden? How do you think her memory will be honored going forward?

- Where do you imagine the characters would be ten years beyond the completion of the story? Where would they have been if it weren't for the garden?

- Describe in detail what you would like your own secret garden to look like. Would you keep it a secret? Who would you let in?

Tea Party in the Secret Garden

If Mary Lennox were to entertain in her garden, she most certainly would have a proper tea party. Serve these goodies on your prettiest dessert plates, and break out the good tablecloth, too. Serve with a freshly brewed pot of your favorite herbal tea.

Berry Trifle

1 package butter cake mix, prepared according to package directions and cooled

2 (3-ounce) packages instant vanilla pudding mix

3 cups milk

1 (8-ounce) container frozen whipped topping, thawed

3 cups assorted fresh berries (Raspberries, blackberries, strawberries, blueberries—any combination will do. If you want to use frozen berries, make sure they are thawed and drained well.)

2 shots spiced rum (optional)

Cut the cake into 1-inch cubes. In a large bowl, combine the pudding mix and milk and beat with a handheld electric mixer for 2 minutes. Fold in the whipped topping. Place one third of the cake cubes in the bottom of a trifle bowl (if you don't have a trifle bowl, just use any decorative bowl—no one will know the difference). Top with 1 cup of the berries and one third of the pudding mixture. Layer with another third of the cake cubes and another third of the berries. Add the rum at this point, if desired, then another third of the pudding mixture. For the last layer, start with the remaining third of the cake cubes, then the remaining third of the pudding mixture, and the remaining berries. Refrigerate overnight and serve chilled.

Lemon Bisque

1 package lemon Jell-O
⅓ cup honey
3 tablespoons fresh lemon juice
Grated zest of 1 lemon

⅛ teaspoon salt
1¼ cups boiling water
1 can evaporated milk, chilled
2 cups crushed vanilla wafers

Place the Jell-O, honey, lemon juice, lemon zest, and salt in a large bowl. Add the boiling water. Let stand until slightly congealed, about 10 to 15 minutes. In a medium bowl, beat the evaporated milk for about 2 minutes using a handheld electric mixer, then stir in the gelatin mixture. Spread half of the crushed vanilla wafers over a 13 by 9-inch baking pan. Add the gelatin mixture and sprinkle with the remaining vanilla wafers. Chill overnight in the refrigerator before serving.

Key Lime Cookies

½ cup butter, plus some for
    greasing the cookie sheets
1 cup sugar
1 large egg
1 egg yolk
¼ cup key lime juice

1½ teaspoons grated lime zest
1½ cups all-purpose flour
1 teaspoon baking powder
½ teaspoon salt
½ cup confectioners' sugar, for
    dusting

Preheat the oven to 350°F. In a large bowl, cream the butter, sugar, egg, and egg yolk until smooth. Stir in the key lime juice and lime zest. In a medium bowl, sift together the flour, baking powder, and salt and add to the butter mixture. Refrigerate the dough for at least 30 minutes.

Grease two large cookie sheets. Roll the dough into ½-inch balls and place them on the cookie sheets. Bake 8 to 10 minutes, or until lightly browned. Transfer the cookies to a wire rack and lightly dust with confectioners' sugar. Allow cookies to cool before serving.

A Country Year

Living the Questions

by Sue Hubbell

While we often attempt to make a small plot of nature, such as a yard, fit into our surroundings and lifestyle, Sue Hubbell takes the opposite route and decides to completely immerse herself in her natural surroundings (creepy crawly creatures and all!). In *A Country Year*, Hubbell, a former college librarian, writes about her solitary life on a hundred-acre farm in the Ozarks, where she makes a living tending to two hundred beehives. A painful divorce led her to her move to the countryside, and the book is the story of how she finds her way after the separation by living off the land, observing wildlife, and running her own business.

This is another collection of essays, some of which have appeared in Hubbell's column, "Hers," that runs in *The New York Times*; others have appeared in *Country Journal* and the *St. Louis Post-Dispatch*. This book will give you an in-depth glimpse into country life and an intriguing look at the practice of beekeeping.

Up for Discussion . . .

- Suppose you were given the money and packing assistance to pick up and move to your dream setting. To where would you move to? What attracts you to that area?

- The book is divided into seasons because this structure best represents the phases of Hubbell's life as a beekeeper. If you were to write a book about a year of your life, how would you structure it or break it into chapters?

- Prior to the opening text of the book, a quote by Rainer Maria Rilke appears: "Be patient toward all that is unsolved in your heart and try to love the questions themselves. . . . Do not . . . seek the answers, which cannot be given you because you would not be able to live them." Clearly, this quote is the inspiration for the subtitle, *Living the Questions.* Give some examples of how Hubbell attempts to "live the questions." What are some examples in your everyday life where it would be better to "live the questions" than to seek the answers?

- In the first section of the book, "Spring," Hubbell talks about her divorce from her childhood sweetheart. This emotionally charged event obviously shaped her attitudes and lifestyle choice. Has a major life event ever drastically steered your choices, attitudes, or lifestyle? Discuss with the group.

- Throughout the book, Hubbell describes encounters with creatures that I would not consider to be friendly, such as bats, copperhead snakes, and hornets. Instead of reacting as I would, though (i.e., shrieking at the top of her lungs), she sees the benefit in each one's existence. List some things in your life that forced you to look past first impressions to see their true value.

- What are some things about Hubbell's life that you envy? What are some things about her life that you would rather leave to her?

- If you had to raise one species of animal or creature for a living, what would it be, and why? What type of animal or creature would you refuse to raise, even if you were given a million dollars? Snakes? Rats?

- At the end of the book, Hubbell reflects over the past year and measures how far she has progressed. How do you measure your progression at the end of a year?

A Country Supper

What better way to end a day in the mountains than with a hearty vegetable stew and freshly baked bread? If you don't like to make bread, or don't have the time (or couldn't be bothered), simply purchase a freshly baked loaf at your supermarket's bakery. Try to choose one that you've never tried before, or at least one that appears more homemade than Wonder Bread.

Sweet Potato Bread

This recipe will make two loaves. Share one with your group and keep one for yourself; it makes yummy toast the next morning.

1¼ cups water
1 medium sweet potato, peeled
    and cubed
1 cup buttermilk
2 tablespoons butter, plus some
    for greasing the bowl

2 tablespoons honey
2 teaspoons salt
6 to 6½ cups all-purpose flour
2 packages active dry yeast
1 large egg

Place the water and sweet potato in a medium saucepan over medium-high heat. Bring to a boil, cover, reduce the heat to low, and simmer for 10 to 12 minutes, or until the sweet potatoes are very tender. *Do not drain*. Mash the sweet potatoes in the water and measure. The mixture should equal 1½ cups; if it doesn't, add enough water to equal that amount. Return the sweet potatoes to the saucepan. Mix in the buttermilk, butter, honey, and salt. The mixture should be warm (120°F to 130°F); if it isn't, warm or cool accordingly.

In a large mixing bowl, combine 2 cups of the flour and the yeast. Add the sweet potato mixture and the egg. Beat with a handheld electric mixer for about 3 minutes, scraping the sides of the bowl constantly. Stir in the remaining 4 to 4½ cups of flour, as needed—start with 1 cup at a time for the first 3 cups, then add ½ cup at a time thereafter.

Divide the dough in half and turn half of the dough onto a lightly floured surface. Knead in any additional flour to make a moderately stiff dough. Place the kneaded dough onto a greased surface (I like to use a large bowl greased with shortening) and turn the dough over once so that both sides are greased. Cover lightly and let rise in a warm place for about 45 minutes. Repeat with the second half of the dough. When the first dough half is about doubled in size, punch down and turn out onto a lightly floured surface and form the dough into a nicely shaped oval. Repeat with the second dough half. Line 2 baking sheets with parchment paper. Place each dough ball onto the baking sheets, loosely cover, and let rise in a warm place for another 30 minutes, or until almost doubled in size. Preheat the oven to 375°F. Bake the loaves for about 40 minutes, or until the bread sounds hollow when tapped. Cool the loaves on wire racks.

Country Veggie Stew

3 tablespoons extra-virgin olive oil

2 large red onions, coarsely chopped

2 fennel bulbs, chopped

5 garlic cloves, minced

1 large green pepper, cored, seeded, and chopped

1 (13-ounce) jar roasted red peppers in oil, drained and chopped

3 medium eggplants, chopped

2 cans diced tomatoes, with juice

4 small zucchini or yellow summer squash, coarsely chopped

1 package presliced white mushrooms

1 cup dry white wine

4 cups chicken stock or canned broth

1 tablespoon dried basil

1 tablespoon dried oregano

2 teaspoons dried thyme

Salt and freshly ground black pepper to taste

Heat the oil over medium heat in a large stockpot. Add the red onions, fennel, and garlic. Cook for 5 to 7 minutes, stirring frequently, or until the vegetables are soft. Add the green pepper and cook for an additional 2 minutes. Add the roasted red peppers and eggplant and cook for 2 minutes. Add the diced tomatoes, zucchini, mushrooms, wine, chicken stock, basil, oregano, and thyme. Season with salt and pepper. Bring to a boil, reduce the heat to low, and simmer for 30 minutes, or until thickened.

Quick Reference Guide

The Adventures of Huckleberry Finn
Author—Mark Twain
ISBN—0142437174
Pub Date—12/02
Publisher—Penguin Classics
Pages—368
Fiction, List Price Under $10, Deals with Controversial Subject Matters, Dinner

An Affair to Remember: The Remarkable Love Story of Katharine Hepburn and Spencer Tracy
Author—Christopher Anderson
ISBN—0380731584
Pub Date—5/98
Publisher—William Morrow & Company
Pages—513
Nonfiction, List Price Under $10, Romance, Drinks and Appetizers

American Pie: Slices of Life (and Pie) from America's Back Roads
Author—Pascale Le Draoulec
ISBN—0060957328
Pub Date—3/03
Publisher—HarperCollins
Pages—368
Nonfiction, Desserts

Angela's Ashes: A Memoir
Author—Frank McCourt
ISBN—068484267X
Pub Date—5/99
Publisher—Simon & Schuster
Pages—368
Nonfiction, Soup and Bread Supper

Anne of Green Gables
Author—L. M. Montgomery
ISBN—0140367411
Pub Date—1/96
Publisher—Puffin
Pages—384
Fiction, List Price Under $10, Dinner with Dessert

Autobiography of a Fat Bride
Author—Laurie Notaro
ISBN—037576092X
Pub Date—7/03
Publisher—Random House
Pages—272
*Nonfiction, Collection of Essays, Light
Read, Dinner*

**The Autobiography of Eleanor
Roosevelt**
Author—Eleanor Roosevelt
ISBN—030680476X
Pub Date—4/92
Publisher—Da Capo Press
Pages—504
Nonfiction, Desserts

Black Beauty
Author—Anna Sewell
ISBN—0140366849
Pub Date—11/94
Publisher—Puffin
Pages—272
*Fiction, List Price Under $10,
Breakfast/Brunch*

Busman's Honeymoon (A Lord Peter
Wimsey Mystery)
Author—Dorothy L. Sayers
ISBN—0061043516
Pub Date—3/95
Publisher—HarperCollins
Pages—416
*Fiction, List Price Under $10, Mystery,
Vegetarian Dinner with Dessert*

The Catcher in the Rye
Author—J. D. Salinger
ISBN—0316769487
Pub Date—5/91

Publisher—Little, Brown
Pages—214
*Fiction, List Price Under $10, Deals with
Controversial Subject Matters, Quick Read
(Under 250 pages), Dinner*

Chocolat
Author—Joanne Harris
ISBN—0140282033
Pub Date—12/99
Publisher—Penguin
Pages—320
Fiction, Dessert

A Christmas Carol
Author—Charles Dickens
ISBN—0451522834
Pub Date—11/88
Publisher—Signet Classics
Pages—218
*Fiction, List Price Under $10, Quick Read
(Under 250 pages), Desserts*

**Ciao, America!: An Italian Discovers
the U.S.**
Author—Beppe Severgnini
ISBN—0767912365
Pub Date—5/03
Publisher—Broadway Books
Pages—256
*Nonfiction, Collection of Essays, Sandwich
Supper*

The City of Joy
Author—Dominique Lapierre
ISBN—0446355569
Pub Date—9/86
Publisher—Warner Books
Pages—528
*Nonfiction, List Price Under $10, Dinner
with Ethnic Flair*

Coast to Coast Ghosts: True Stories of Hauntings Across America
Author—Leslie Rule
ISBN—0740718665
Pub Date—8/01
Publisher—Andrews McMeel
Pages—272
Nonfiction, Dinner and Dessert

The Color Purple
Author—Alice Walker
ISBN—0156028352
Pub Date—3/03
Publisher—Harvest Books
Pages—300
Fiction, Deals with Controversial Subject Matters, Desserts

Confessions of a Shopaholic
Author—Sophie Kinsella
ISBN—0385335482
Pub Date—2/01
Publisher—Dell
Pages—310
Fiction, Light Read, Romance, Dinner with Ethnic Flair

A Country Year: Living the Questions
Author—Sue Hubbell
ISBN—0395967015
Pub Date—4/99
Publisher—Random House
Pages—221
Nonfiction, Collection of Essays, Vegetarian Meal

Death of a Snob
Author—M. C. Beaton
ISBN—0804109125
Pub Date—5/92
Publisher—Ballantine

Pages—148
Fiction, List Price Under $10, Quick Read (Under 250 pages), Mystery, Dinner

Diary of a Mad Bride
Author—Laura Wolf
ISBN—0385335830
Pub Date—1/02
Publisher—Dell
Pages—294
Fiction, Light Read, Dinner and Dessert with Ethnic Flair

Dracula
Author—Bram Stoker
ISBN—014143984X
Pub Date—4/03
Publisher—Penguin Classics
Pages—512
Fiction, You'll Need Your Thinking Cap, Dinner with Dessert

Emma
Author—Jane Austen
ISBN—0141439580
Pub Date—5/03
Publisher—Penguin Classics
Pages—512
Fiction, List Price Under $10, Romance, Tea-Time Snacks

Fast Food Nation: The Dark Side of the All-American Meal
Author—Eric Schlosser
ISBN—0060938455
Pub Date—1/02
Publisher—HarperCollins
Pages—400
Nonfiction, Deals with Controversial Subject Matters, Dinner and Dessert

Founding Brothers: The Revolutionary Generation
Author—Joseph J. Ellis
ISBN—0375705244
Pub Date—2/02
Publisher—Knopf
Pages—304
Nonfiction, Dinner

Gesundheit!: Bringing Good Health to You, the Medical System, and Society Through Physician Service, Complementary Therapies, Humor, and Joy
Author—Patch Adams, M.D., with Maureen Mylander
ISBN—089281781X
Pub Date—5/98
Publisher—Inner Traditions
Pages—224
Nonfiction, Quick Read (Under 250 pages), Dinner

Gold Digger: The Outrageous Life and Times of Peggy Hopkins Joyce
Author—Constance Rosenblum
ISBN—0805050892
Pub Date—3/00
Publisher—Henry Holt
Pages—288
Nonfiction, Appetizers

Gone with the Wind
Author—Margaret Mitchell
ISBN—0446365386
Pub Date—7/93
Publisher—Warner Books
Pages—1024
Fiction, List Price Under $10, Romance, Brunch

Harry Potter and the Sorcerer's Stone
Author—J. K. Rowling
ISBN—0590353403
Pub Date—8/98
Publisher—Scholastic
Pages—309
Fiction, Deals with Controversial Subject Matters, Dinner

Headhunters
Author—Jules Bass
ISBN—0515131334
Pub Date—6/01
Publisher—Jove
Pages—336
Fiction, List Price Under $10, Light Read, Romance, Drinks and Appetizers

Hercule Poirot's Christmas
Author—Agatha Christie
ISBN—0425177416
Pub Date—11/00
Publisher—Berkley
Pages—272
Fiction, List Price Under $10, Mystery, Dinner

Horse Heaven
Author—Jane Smiley
ISBN—0804119430
Pub Date—8/03
Publisher—Random House
Pages—614
Fiction, Dinner with Dessert

The Horse Whisperer
Author—Nicholas Evans
ISBN—0440222656
Pub Date—11/96
Publisher—Bantam Doubleday Dell
Pages—451

Fiction, List Price Under $10, Romance, Dinner

The Hound of the Baskervilles
Author—Sir Arthur Conan Doyle
ISBN—014043786X
Pub Date—10/01
Publisher—Penguin Classics
Pages—240
Fiction, List Price Under $10, Quick Read (Under 250 pages), Mystery, Dinner

Jane Eyre
Author—Charlotte Brontë
ISBN—0142437204
Pub Date—2/03
Publisher—Penguin Classics
Pages—576
Fiction, List Price Under $10, You'll Need Your Thinking Cap, Tea Sandwiches

The Jungle
Author—Upton Sinclair
ISBN—1593080085
Pub Date—5/03
Publisher—Barnes & Noble Books
Pages—448
Fiction, List Price Under $10, You'll Need Your Thinking Cap, Vegetarian Dinner

The Last of the Mohicans
Author—James Fenimore Cooper
ISBN—0140390243
Pub Date—7/86
Publisher—Penguin Classics
Pages—384
Fiction, List Price Under $10, Desserts

The Love Letter
Author—Cathleen Schine
ISBN—0452279488

Pub Date—12/97
Publisher—Plume
Pages—257
Fiction, Light Read, Romance, Breakfast

Lucille: The Life of Lucille Ball
Author—Kathleen Brady
ISBN—0823089134
Pub Date—5/01
Publisher—Watson-Guptill Publications
Pages—424
Nonfiction, Drinks and Appetizers

Lucy Sullivan Is Getting Married
Author—Marian Keyes
ISBN—0060090375
Pub Date—5/02
Publisher—HarperCollins
Pages—624
Fiction, Romance, Desserts

The Mammy
Author—Brendan O'Carroll
ISBN—0452281032
Pub Date—4/99
Publisher—Plume
Pages—172
Fiction, Light Read, Quick Read (Under 250 pages), Desserts

Middle Passage
Author—Charles Johnson
ISBN—0684855887
Pub Date—6/98
Publisher—Simon & Schuster
Pages—209
Fiction, Quick Read (Under 250 pages), Deals with Controversial Subject Matters, Dinner

Money, Money, Money: A Novel of the 87th Precinct
Author—Ed McBain
ISBN—0743410327
Pub Date—9/02
Publisher—Simon & Schuster
Pages—352
Fiction, List Price Under $10, Mystery, Sandwich Supper

The Moorchild
Author—Eloise McGraw
ISBN—068982033X
Pub Date—3/98
Publisher—Simon & Schuster
Pages—256
Fiction, List Price Under $10, Dinner

Mount Vernon Love Story: A Novel of George and Martha Washington
Author—Mary Higgins Clark
ISBN—0743448944
Pub Date—6/03
Publisher—Simon & Schuster
Pages—254
Fiction, List Price Under $10, Romance, Dinner with Dessert

Nickel and Dimed: On (Not) Getting By in America
Author—Barbara Ehrenreich
ISBN—0805063897
Pub Date—4/02
Publisher—Henry Holt
Pages—240
Nonfiction, Quick Read (Under 250 pages), Deals with Controversial Subject Matters, Dinner and Dessert

The Odyssey
Author—Homer
ISBN—1593080093

Pub Date—5/03
Publisher—Barnes & Noble Books
Pages—384
Fiction, List Price Under $10, You'll need Your Thinking Cap, Dinner and Dessert

One Man's Garden
Author—Henry Mitchell
ISBN—03959577699
Pub Date—4/99
Publisher—Houghton Mifflin
Pages—262
Nonfiction, Collection of Essays, Vegetarian Meal

A Patch of Eden: America's Inner-City Gardeners
Author—H. Patricia Hynes
ISBN—0930031806
Pub Date—5/96
Publisher—Chelsea Green
Pages—208
Nonfiction, Dinner

The Princess Bride
Author—William Goldman
ISBN—0345348036
Pub Date—6/87
Publisher—Ballantine Books
Pages—283
Fiction, List Price Under $10, Romance, Breakfast/Brunch

Quentins
Author—Maeve Binchy
ISBN—0451209907
Pub Date—8/03
Publisher—Signet
Pages—488
Fiction, List Price Under $10, Dinner with Dessert

The Royals
Author—Kitty Kelley
ISBN—0446605786
Pub Date—10/98
Publisher—Warner Books
Pages—751
Nonfiction, Light Read, Desserts

Seabiscuit: An American Legend
Author—Laura Hillenbrand
ISBN—0449005615
Pub Date—3/02
Publisher—Random House
Pages—399
Nonfiction, Dinner with Dessert

The Secret Garden
Author—Frances Hodgson Burnett
ISBN—0140366660
Pub Date—11/94
Publisher—Puffin
Pages—304
Fiction, List Price Under $10, Desserts

Silent Spring
Author—Rachel Carson
ISBN—0618249060
Pub Date—9/02
Publisher—Houghton Mifflin
Pages—400
Nonfiction, You'll Need Your Thinking Cap, Deals with Controversial Subject Matters, Organic Dinner

The Story of a Shipwrecked Sailor
Author—Gabriel García Márquez
ISBN—067972205X
Pub Date—2/89
Publisher—Random House
Pages—106
Nonfiction, Small Taste of a Notable Author, Quick Read (Under 250 pages), Dinner with Dessert

To Kill a Mockingbird
Author—Harper Lee
ISBN—0060935464
Pub Date—3/02
Publisher—HarperCollins
Pages—336
Fiction, Deals with Controversial Subject Matters, Desserts

The Tortilla Curtain
Author—T. C. Boyle
ISBN—014023828X
Pub Date—9/96
Publisher—Penguin Books
Pages—368
Fiction, Deals with Controversial Subject Matters, Dinner with Ethnic Flair

Travels with Charley: In Search of America
Author—John Steinbeck
ISBN—01420000701
Pub Date—2/02
Publisher—Penguin Books
Pages—224
Nonfiction, Small Taste of a Notable Author, Quick Read (Under 250 pages), Dinner with Dessert

Treasure Island
Author—Robert Louis Stevenson
ISBN—0140437681
Pub Date—12/99
Publisher—Penguin Classics
Pages—240
Fiction, List Price Under $10, Quick Read (Under 250 pages), Dinner

A Tree Grows in Brooklyn
Author—Betty Smith
ISBN—006092988X
Pub Date—7/98
Publisher—HarperCollins
Pages—496
Fiction, Soup Supper

The Turn of the Screw (also included in this edition is James's *The Aspern Papers*)
Author—Henry James
ISBN—0141439904
Pub Date—9/03
Publisher—Penguin Classics
Pages—272 (including *The Aspern Papers*)
Fiction, List Price Under $10, Quick Read (Under 250 pages), Small Taste of a Notable Author, Desserts

Up from Slavery
Author—Booker T. Washington
ISBN—0451527542
Pub Date—1/00
Publisher—Signet Classics
Pages—256
Nonfiction, List Price Under $10, Dinner

Valley of the Dolls
Author—Jacqueline Susann
ISBN—0802135196
Pub Date—9/97
Publisher—Grove/Atlantic
Pages—442
Fiction, Drinks and Appetizers

The Wind in the Willows
Author—Kenneth Grahame
ISBN—0684179571
Pub Date—1/91
Publisher—Simon & Schuster
Pages—244
Fiction, Quick Read (Under 250 pages), Dinner

Index

About the Author

Sarah Gardner is the founder and publisher of *The Literary Gathering*, a bimonthly newsletter that celebrates and integrates the two popular pastimes of book clubs and cooking. Founded in 2002, the hip, witty, and occasionally irreverent newsletter has an ever-growing subscriber base and has garnered attention from the likes of *Bon Appétit* and a number of national newspapers, from *The Reno Gazette-Journal* and *The Buffalo News,* to *The Oakland Press,* and the *Sarasota Herald Tribune.*

Gardner lives in Sarasota, Florida, with her husband, Jim, and her son, James.